The FRUIT EXPERT

Dr. D.G. Hessayon

1st Impression   **300,000**

Other books in the EXPERT Series:
THE FLOWER EXPERT
THE TREE & SHRUB EXPERT
THE ROSE EXPERT
THE LAWN EXPERT
THE GARDEN EXPERT
THE VEGETABLE EXPERT
THE HOUSE PLANT EXPERT
THE INDOOR PLANT SPOTTER
THE HOME EXPERT

Acknowledgements

The author wishes to acknowledge the painstaking work of Gill Jackson, Linda Fensom and Constance Barry. Grateful acknowledgement is also made for the help or photographs received from Angelina Gibbs, Joan Hessayon, Jacqueline Norris, Jane Llewelyn, The House of Heyes, Crown Copyright : Brogdale EHS, Harry Smith Horticultural Photographic Collection, Pat Brindley, Michael Warren and A–Z Collection.

John Woodbridge provided both artistry and design work. Mike Standage prepared most of the paintings for this book. Other artists who contributed were Norman Barber, Bob Bampton, Richard Bell and David Thelwell.

pbi PUBLICATIONS · BRITANNICA HOUSE · WALTHAM CROSS · HERTS · ENGLAND

Contents

Printed and bound in Great Britain by Jarrold & Sons Ltd, Norwich

ISBN 0 903505 31 2

© D G HESSAYON 1990

CHAPTER 1

FRUIT IN THE GARDEN

Botanists know exactly what they mean when they talk about 'fruit'. A fruit for them is the seed-bearing organ of a plant. Luscious Pears and juicy Oranges are of course included — but so are grains of Wheat, Walnuts and dried Peas!

For the gardener the word 'fruit' has a much more restricted and vaguer meaning — and there is no general agreement where the classification should start and finish. All fleshy seed-bearing organs which are either cooked or eaten fresh for dessert are included. But do you include nuts (which are not fleshy) and rhubarb (which is not truly a fruit)? It's up to you, but they are not included in this book.

Some fruits are traditionally picked from hedgerows — Elderberries, Sloes, Blackberries and hips of Shrub Roses. For practical purposes such sources can be ignored — if you want fruit without paying for it, you will have to grow your own.

Growing fruit in the garden is decorative, interesting ... and rewarding when you consider shop-prices. It is therefore not surprising that the story of fruit growing in the garden is as old as gardening itself. What is surprising is the sophistication of the subject in those early days. In the 16th century numerous varieties of Apples grafted on to Crab Apple rootstocks were grown in British gardens and there were "Peares of all sortes". In addition the textbooks of the day described white and red Peaches, Cherries, Bullaces, Quinces, Raspberries, white and red Strawberries, Currants, Mulberries, Medlars, Bilberries, Grapes, Gooseberries, Damsons, Apricots, Plums ... a list which would do credit to a specialist catalogue of today.

These Elizabethan books also bemoaned the fact that British gardeners did not grow as many fruit trees and bushes as Continental gardeners — a criticism which could probably be made to this day. Only one U.K garden in three grows fruit, and there are two basic reasons for this lack of universal appeal. First of all, there is the view that fruit growing is difficult and time-consuming. This, of course, is not true — once planted and established the fruit garden gives more for less effort than the vegetable plot. Perhaps some textbooks are to blame — descriptions of pruning often make it sound as complex and delicate as brain surgery. Secondly, there is the view that fruit growing is space-demanding. Visions of spreading trees, ladders for picking and the thought of room-sized fruit cages deter the gardener with a pocket-handkerchief plot, but fruit trees these days need take up no more space than rose bushes.

Things are now changing, and in recent years there has been an upsurge of interest in growing fruit. There are a number of reasons for this increase in domestic fruit culture. The garden centre with its container-grown plants has enabled trees, canes and bushes to be seen in flower and in fruit, and these containers are available for planting all the year round. In addition the introduction of dwarfing stocks has meant that Apple, Pear, Plum and Cherry can be grown as trees in small gardens. Catalogues are so much more exciting these days — there are new types of fruit such as the Kiwi Fruit and Cape Gooseberry plus new growth forms such as the 'Ballerina' Apple tree.

Fruit should be grown in every garden. A separate fruit garden is ideal, of course, but you need both space and money for such a feature. But soft fruit is quite at home in the vegetable plot, and non-vigorous tree fruit can be grown as specimen plants in the lawn or shrub border.

The great fascination is to be able to pick the produce in peak condition straight from the tree or bush. Another plus point is that you can grow delicious varieties which aren't found in the shops.

An introductory chapter should end on a high note with words of encouragement and enthusiasm, but this one ends with a note of caution. Planting a fruit tree or bush is a long-term investment, which means that you should read the appropriate chapter carefully *before* looking through the catalogue. Then choose carefully, making sure that both the fruit type and variety are suitable for your particular conditions. For example, few varieties of Pears are suitable for northern and midland gardens despite the glowing praise for them in some catalogues.

Never guess that a variety will be suitable — do check. You might like *Cox's Orange Pippin, Golden Delicious* or *Granny Smith* based on shop-bought experience, but none of these Apple varieties is a good choice for the garden. You might think that the compact tree in the garden centre won't be a problem in your small garden, but do check the rootstock before buying. You might think that the Raspberry canes look healthy, but check that they are certified virus-free. As stated earlier, fruit growing in the garden can be decorative, interesting and rewarding, but it can also be disappointing if you blunder into it without knowing what you are doing. The purpose of this book is to guide you along the right road.

Choosing the right type

Fruit-bearing plants come in all shapes and sizes. In the right setting, a stately Apple tree with stout and spreading branches is not out of place in a large garden — nor is a row of Alpine Strawberries nestling under the Roses. To make some sense out of this vast array of trees, shrubs and canes a variety of classifications have been proposed. Set out below is one of the simpler ways of dividing up the various types of fruits which are grown in Britain.

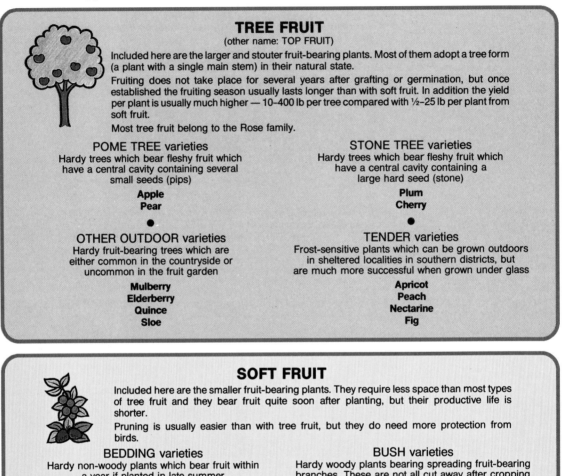

TREE FRUIT
(other name: TOP FRUIT)

Included here are the larger and stouter fruit-bearing plants. Most of them adopt a tree form (a plant with a single main stem) in their natural state.

Fruiting does not take place for several years after grafting or germination, but once established the fruiting season usually lasts longer than with soft fruit. In addition the yield per plant is usually much higher — 10–400 lb per tree compared with ½–25 lb per plant from soft fruit.

Most tree fruit belong to the Rose family.

POME TREE varieties
Hardy trees which bear fleshy fruit which have a central cavity containing several small seeds (pips)

Apple
Pear

●

OTHER OUTDOOR varieties
Hardy fruit-bearing trees which are either common in the countryside or uncommon in the fruit garden

Mulberry
Elderberry
Quince
Sloe

STONE TREE varieties
Hardy trees which bear fleshy fruit which have a central cavity containing a large hard seed (stone)

Plum
Cherry

●

TENDER varieties
Frost-sensitive plants which can be grown outdoors in sheltered localities in southern districts, but are much more successful when grown under glass

Apricot
Peach
Nectarine
Fig

SOFT FRUIT

Included here are the smaller fruit-bearing plants. They require less space than most types of tree fruit and they bear fruit quite soon after planting, but their productive life is shorter.

Pruning is usually easier than with tree fruit, but they do need more protection from birds.

BEDDING varieties
Hardy non-woody plants which bear fruit within a year if planted in late summer

Strawberry

●

CANE varieties
Hardy woody plants bearing long and slender shoots. They bear fruit in the second year after planting

Raspberry
Blackberry

Hybrid berries — crosses between Raspberry, Blackberry and/or Dewberry:

Boysenberry   **Marionberry**
Dewberry   **Silvanberry**
Hildaberry   **Sunberry**
Japanese Wineberry   **Tayberry**
John Innes   **Tummelberry**
King's Acre Berry   **Veitchberry**
Loganberry   **Youngberry**

BUSH varieties
Hardy woody plants bearing spreading fruit-bearing branches. These are not all cut away after cropping

Gooseberry
Worcesterberry
Blackcurrant
Red & White Currant

Heathland berries — require very acid soil:

Lowbush Blueberry   **Cranberry**
Highbush Blueberry

●

TENDER varieties
Frost-sensitive or warmth-loving plants which require greenhouse culture in the North and Midlands

Cape Gooseberry
Grape
Kiwi Fruit
Melon

CHAPTER 2

TREE FRUIT

The tree you propose to plant will bear fruit for 20–60 years, depending on the type and location. You can choose one which will grow knee-high or as tall as a house — the factors again are type and location. Obviously the choice is vast, so get to know the basic facts before you buy.

The usual growth pattern is the **free-standing tree** — here you will find a central trunk with a crown of branches radiating in all directions. Where space is limited a **supported tree** can be grown — see page 10 for details.

The eventual height of the tree will be determined by type, growing conditions and by the rootstock on which the variety has been grafted. The growth pattern is determined by pruning and training — details are given in the instructions for individual fruits.

Pick the sunniest spot available — full sun and a mild climate are essential for the tender types. The soil should be reasonably deep, not prone to waterlogging and ideally it should be slightly acid. If the site is exposed, you will have to provide some protection from strong winds — see page 31. Frost can be a serious menace at blossom time — if you live in a frost-prone area, choose a late-flowering variety or one with high frost tolerance. Planting a supported tree against a south-facing wall saves ground space as well as helping in the battle against frost. This method of cultivation should be used for the tender types of tree fruit.

Having chosen the fruit you wish to grow and the spot where it will live (remember the effect of its shadow on other plants when picking the site), it is now time to choose the variety. The usual advice is to go for dessert (eating) varieties rather than culinary (cooking) varieties where space is short. Most tree fruits require a pollinating partner to ensure satisfactory fruit set. You will have to plant a partner if fruit trees are not common in your area — seek advice or read the appropriate section in this book. Where several varieties are to be grown pick ones which will provide an extended cropping period.

So choose your fruit tree from the following pages. The tender ones may only be for the lucky few, but the hardy types should succeed almost anywhere apart from upland and very wet localities.

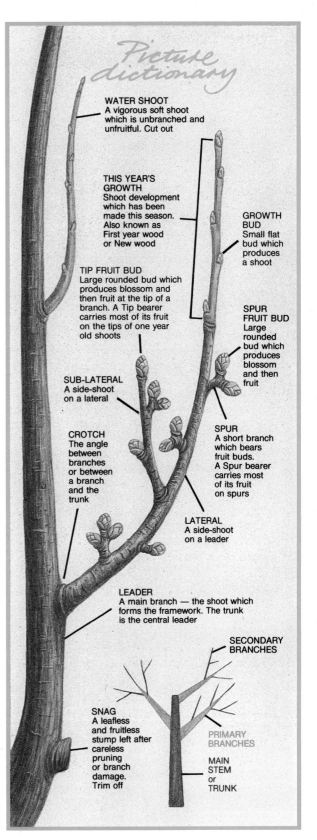

Picture dictionary

WATER SHOOT
A vigorous soft shoot which is unbranched and unfruitful. Cut out

THIS YEAR'S GROWTH
Shoot development which has been made this season. Also known as First year wood or New wood

GROWTH BUD
Small flat bud which produces a shoot

TIP FRUIT BUD
Large rounded bud which produces blossom and then fruit at the tip of a branch. A Tip bearer carries most of its fruit on the tips of one year old shoots

SPUR FRUIT BUD
Large rounded bud which produces blossom and then fruit

SUB-LATERAL
A side-shoot on a lateral

SPUR
A short branch which bears fruit buds. A Spur bearer carries most of its fruit on spurs

CROTCH
The angle between branches or between a branch and the trunk

LATERAL
A side-shoot on a leader

LEADER
A main branch — the shoot which forms the framework. The trunk is the central leader

SECONDARY BRANCHES

SNAG
A leafless and fruitless stump left after careless pruning or branch damage. Trim off

PRIMARY BRANCHES

MAIN STEM or TRUNK

Buying

You should buy fruit trees only from a supplier who you know to be reputable — an often quoted (and often ignored) piece of advice. Do avoid mail order bargains from unknown nurseries — if you must buy through the post then do order from a company with a good reputation and put your order in early. The widest selection of varieties is available in autumn. By early spring some of the old favourites and new introductions are sold out.

If possible go along personally to buy your plants so that you can discuss your choice. Make sure that you find out the type of rootstock used — see the appropriate sections of this book for recommended stocks.

There are no hard and fast rules for the best age of trees for planting. If you really know about pruning then choose a 1 year old feathered maiden — you will save money and you can be sure that it will be properly trained. On the other hand you should buy a 2 or 3 year old tree if you have little or no practical experience — the basic framework will have been created by the nurseryman. These trained and partly trained trees are the type usually on offer — 1 year old maidens are stocked by only a few garden centres.

The tree you buy will have been dug up at the nursery and damp peat packed around the bare roots before transportation — a bare-rooted tree designed for planting in the dormant season. You will have to buy a container-grown plant if you have missed the traditional November–March planting season. Look at the container carefully before you buy — see below. Give it the tug test. Lift the tree by holding the base of the main stem and pulling gently upwards. Don't buy the tree if the soil ball readily moves out of the container.

Planting material

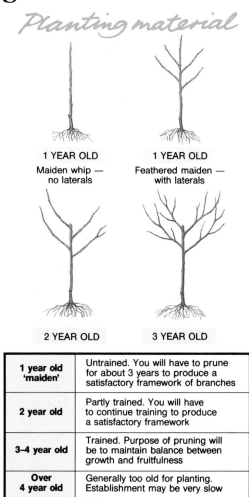

1 YEAR OLD
Maiden whip —
no laterals

1 YEAR OLD
Feathered maiden —
with laterals

2 YEAR OLD

3 YEAR OLD

1 year old 'maiden'	Untrained. You will have to prune for about 3 years to produce a satisfactory framework of branches
2 year old	Partly trained. You will have to continue training to produce a satisfactory framework
3–4 year old	Trained. Purpose of pruning will be to maintain balance between growth and fruitfulness
Over 4 year old	Generally too old for planting. Establishment may be very slow

The things to look for

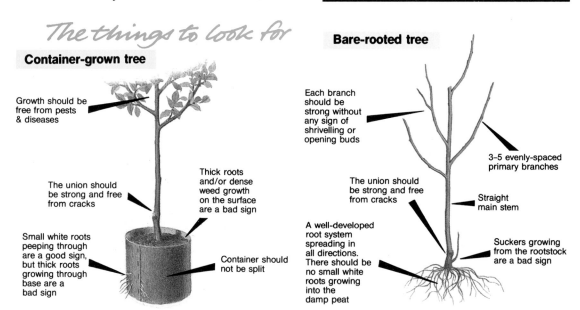

Container-grown tree

Growth should be free from pests & diseases

The union should be strong and free from cracks

Small white roots peeping through are a good sign, but thick roots growing through base are a bad sign

Thick roots and/or dense weed growth on the surface are a bad sign

Container should not be split

Bare-rooted tree

Each branch should be strong without any sign of shrivelling or opening buds

3–5 evenly-spaced primary branches

The union should be strong and free from cracks

Straight main stem

A well-developed root system spreading in all directions. There should be no small white roots growing into the damp peat

Suckers growing from the rootstock are a bad sign

Planting

Having bought a good plant by following the guidance on the previous page, you must now give it a good home. Do not plant in a spot which has recently housed the same type of fruit — do not replace an old Apple tree with another Apple, a Plum with a Plum etc.

Planting of bare-rooted plants takes place between early November and the end of March. The preferred time is November whilst the soil is still warm. Soil conditions are as important as the calendar — the ground must be neither frozen nor waterlogged.

Getting the soil ready

You should dig the site at least a month before the proposed time of planting. Double digging is recommended to aerate the topsoil and break up the subsoil. See The Garden Expert (page 12) for details. If the trees are to be widely spaced there is no need to dig the whole area. Dig a 3 ft square plot where each planting site is to be — remove all perennial weeds during this soil preparation. For closely planted trees dig the whole length of the area to be planted.

Most soils can be successfully prepared in this way — do add plenty of organic matter if the soil is sandy or heavy. Very heavy clays and shallow chalks can be a difficult problem — the only satisfactory plan here is to add topsoil rather than trying to double dig.

Getting the tree ready

If planting has to be delayed for a few days keep the tree in an unheated but frost-free garage or shed. Do not remove packing around roots until planting day

Plunge roots in a bucket of water for about 2 hours if they appear dry or if the stems are shrivelled. Roots must never be allowed to dry out before planting — keep them covered until you are ready to set the plant in its planting hole

Cut back any damaged or very long roots to about 12 in.

Putting in the stake

Bare-rooted tree

Stage 2
Plant firmly, as described on page 8. The stem should be about 3 in. away from the stake

Stage 3
Fix a tie near the top of the stake for a bush. Standards need an additional tie lower down. Buy a proprietary tie — leave loose and then tighten after a few weeks when the tree has settled. Adjust as stem thickens

Top of the stake should be just below the lowest branch

Stage 1
Drive the stake in firmly — to at least 1 ft below the bottom of the planting hole

Buy a stake which has been treated with a preservative. Place it on the side from which the prevailing wind blows

Container-grown tree

Stage 1
Plant firmly, as described on page 8

Stage 3
Fix tie — adjust as stem thickens

Stage 2
Drive stake into the soil on the side *away* from which the prevailing wind blows

Digging the hole

The first step is to mark out the planting stations with canes to make sure that the trees will be spaced out as planned. Next, the planting hole for each tree must be dug, and the commonest mistake is to dig a hole which is too deep and too narrow to house the roots properly. Another mistake is to try to turn tree planting into a one-person job. You will find it much more efficient to have someone to fill in the hole whilst you hold the plant in the desired position.

It is essential that the union between rootstock and grafted stem is kept well above ground level. The best plan is to aim to have the old soil mark at the top of the planting hole.

Fork over the bottom of the planting hole and form a low mound at the base. A stake is now essential if a free-standing tree (see page 10) is to be grown — supported types have their own type of support. The stake should remain in position for 4–5 years — with M27 and M9 rootstocks the stake should remain as a permanent feature throughout the life of the tree.

Do not use the soil removed from the hole for planting the tree — use a planting mixture instead.

PLANTING MIXTURE

Make up the planting mixture in a wheelbarrow on a day when the soil is reasonably dry and friable — 1 part topsoil, 1 part moist peat and 3 handfuls of Bone Meal per barrow load. Keep this mixture in a shed or garage until you are ready to start planting.

It is just as important to use a planting mixture for filling the hole when planting a container-grown tree. Roots hate to move from a peat-based compost into a mineral soil which is practically devoid of organic matter. The recommended planting mixture provides a suitable bridge between the two.

Planting continued

Planting a bare-rooted tree

① The old soil mark on the stem should be level with the bottom of the board

Set a board across the top of the hole to ensure correct planting depth

The hole should be wide enough to allow the roots to be spread evenly

② Work a couple of trowelfuls of the planting mixture around the roots. Shake the plant gently up and down — add a little more planting mixture. Firm this around the roots with the fists. Do not press too hard

③ Half-fill the hole with more planting mixture and firm it down. Depending on the size of the plant, do this by gentle treading or by pressing with the fists. On no account should you tread heavily. Start firming at the outer edge of the planting hole, working gradually towards the centre

④ Add more planting mixture until the hole is full. Firm once again and then loosen the surface. Spread a little soil around the stem to form a low dome

When planting is finished, build a shallow ring of soil. This will form a water-retaining basin

Planting a container-grown tree

① Dig a planting hole which is large enough and deep enough for the soil ball to be surrounded by a 3–4 in. layer of planting mixture

The hole should be deep enough to ensure that the top of the soil ball will be about 1 in. below the soil surface after planting

3–4 in. layer of planting mixture

② Water the container thoroughly before planting

Cut down the side of the container when it is stood on the base of the hole. Remove very carefully

③ Examine the exposed surface of the soil ball. Very gently cut away circling or tangled roots but never break up the soil ball

④ Fill the space between the soil ball and the sides of the hole with planting mixture. Never use ordinary soil. Firm down the planting mixture with your hands

After planting a shallow water-retaining basin should remain

After planting

Proper after-care is just as important as good planting. Once the new tree is in place it should be watered in thoroughly. In spring place a mulch of rotted manure, garden compost, bark, peat or black polythene sheeting around the tree — this mulch should extend about 18 in. from the stem.

During the first growing season keep the soil moist and occasionally spray the leaves on warm evenings. Remove all blossom in the first spring after planting. Check the ties at least once a year — make sure the trunk is not being strangled.

APPLES

We grow more Apples both commercially and in the garden than any other fruit tree — the Apple, unlike the Pear, is completely at home in this country. There are four basic types, but the first two are of little interest to the home fruit grower. The Cider Apple with its massive yields (up to 1000 lb per tree) has no place on our plot, although the Crab Apple with its colourful fruits is grown as a decorative tree and is sometimes used for making jelly.

The choice for the gardener is between the dessert (eating) varieties and the culinary (cooking) varieties, although just a few are dual-purpose. The variety you pick can be bought in a number of growth forms (see page 10) and the rootstock used will largely determine the eventual height (see page 11). A mature dwarf bush will grow about 6 ft high and provide about 40 lb of fruit — a mature standard will reach 20–25 ft and give yields of 200–400 lb.

The usual advice is to grow a bush if space is reasonably plentiful. If space is limited then a dwarf bush or a row of cordons is a much better choice. An espalier is the favoured supported form to clothe a wall or fence. We may have to add to this standard advice — the introduction of the compact columnar tree (page 10) is a new trouble-free form for the small garden and the step-over tree (page 10) is a recent introduction which casts little shade in the tiny plot.

Whichever form you choose, plant correctly in properly prepared soil. Finding a suitable site rarely offers a problem, but even the long-suffering Apple has its pet hates. Salt-laden sea air creates a problem and so does a shallow alkali soil. Culinary varieties are more successful than dessert types when things are not quite right, such as rainfall over 40 in. per annum, altitude over 500 ft, partial shade, nitrogen-rich soil or partly-impeded drainage.

Plant at the recommended distance (page 21) even though it will seem that the trees are far too widely spaced at first. Follow the rules of correct care set out in this section and even a small number of trees can provide you with fruit from August right through to May.

Many gardeners make do with the old trees they acquired with the house. You can undertake a rejuvenation programme (see page 24) which takes about three seasons, but it is often better to start again, choosing a fresh spot in the garden for the new trees.

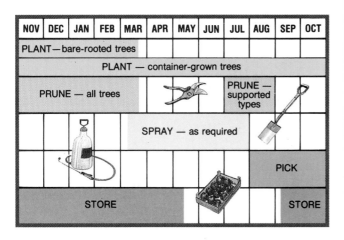

NOV	DEC	JAN	FEB	MAR	APR	MAY	JUN	JUL	AUG	SEP	OCT
PLANT — bare-rooted trees											
		PLANT — container-grown trees									
PRUNE — all trees						PRUNE — supported types					
				SPRAY — as required							
										PICK	
	STORE									STORE	

Tree Types

FREE-STANDING TYPES

BUSH
The most popular type — bushes have an open centre and a short trunk (bushes 2–2½ ft, dwarf bushes 1½–2 ft). They soon come into fruit and are easy to maintain. The mature size depends on the rootstock — 6 ft high on M27 to 18 ft on MM106. Not suitable for planting in the lawn.

STANDARD
Large trees grown on semi-vigorous or vigorous root-stocks — they are only suitable where there is plenty of space and top yields are required. The standard tree has a 6–7 ft high trunk — the half standard trunk is 4–4½ ft. These 15–25 ft tall trees are difficult to care for.

Apples can be trained in various ways — the choice depends on the needs of the gardener. Some books divide the various growth types into 'unrestricted' and 'restricted', but this rather vague concept makes the classification of the dwarf pyramid and spindle-bush rather difficult.

It is more straightforward to think of **free-standing** and **supported** types. Free-standing trees are grown in the open without any horizontal supports — maintenance is usually straightforward once the framework has been established. A supported tree is grown against a fence, framework of wire or a wall and is pruned in summer. Such types require more work than a bush and the yield is lower.

PYRAMID
A pyramid is similar to a bush but the central leader is maintained to give a broadly conical shape. The dwarf pyramid (up to 7 ft high with a 4 ft spread) is a good choice for a tub or small plot, but it requires careful summer pruning.

SPINDLEBUSH
A variation of the pyramid — the basic difference is that the side branches are permanently tied down so that they are kept almost horizontal. Not for the garden — the tall central stake and the surrounding ring of vertical strings make it unsightly.

NEW

COMPACT COLUMN
The compact column was introduced in 1989 as the Ballerina tree and immediately aroused great interest. There is a single main stem with hardly any side branches, which means that no pruning is required. The height after 5 years is about 8 ft, and the unique growth habit makes it suitable for lawns, tubs, borders, hedging etc. Four varieties are offered — *Bolero* (green early dessert Apple), *Polka* (red/green mid-season dessert Apple), *Waltz* (red/green late dessert Apple) and *Maypole* (purple/red May-flowering Crab Apple). The rootstock is MM106.

SUPPORTED TYPES

CORDON
A single-stemmed tree which is planted at 45° and tied to a permanent support system such as a fence. A dwarfing rootstock is generally used and vigorous varieties are usually avoided. An excellent way of growing several varieties in a restricted space.

ESPALIER
The pairs of branches are stretched horizontally to form a series of tiers at 18 in. intervals. It is more decorative than the cordon, but it takes up more space and it is more difficult to maintain. Buy trees which have already been trained.

FAN
An attractive form when planted against a wall, but it needs space — a height of 6 ft and a spread of 10 ft. Careful training is essential. Not a popular tree form for Apples — the fan is much more widely used for Cherries, Plums and Peaches.

NEW

STEP-OVER
An old idea which attracted interest when re-introduced in 1986. A single-tier espalier is grown along a wire support stretched about 12 in. above ground level. Extremely dwarfing rootstock is used, and the result is an Apple edging for bed or border.

Rootstocks

Apples generally grow badly on their own roots. This has been known for hundreds of years and grafting desirable varieties on to rootstocks has been practised for centuries. But it is only since the end of World War II that the dwarfing rootstock has been widely introduced to the home gardener, and this has made tree fruit growing possible in small gardens.

The rootstocks we use these days were developed at East Malling Research Station (the M series) and Merton (the MM series). The use of a dwarfing stock brings about all sorts of advantages. Trees come into fruit more quickly and the Apples are usually more brightly coloured. Picking becomes a simple task and pruning is much less complex. Spraying is possible with simple equipment.

It would seem that dwarfing stock should be an automatic choice, but this is not so. Very dwarfing stock needs fertile soil, regular watering and yields are much lower. Thus, it is necessary to choose semi-dwarfing stock or even vigorous stock for poor soil planting.

M27
EXTREMELY DWARFING
A recently introduced root-stock which after 10–15 years produces a bush which is only 6 ft high. Obviously a good choice for pot culture, and for a dwarf bush or cordon of a vigorous variety. It is the rootstock used for step-over trees — see page 10. Perma-nent staking is necessary — the branches may have to be supported. Good soil and regular feeding, watering and weeding are essential.

M9
VERY DWARFING
An established dwarfing root-stock, producing a bush which is about the size of a small room when mature. It will grow under average soil conditions but needs good soil to thrive. It is popular for dwarf bushes, dwarf pyramids, cordons and small espaliers. M9 is a good choice for a small garden with fairly good soil. Permanent staking is necessary, and so is routine feeding and watering.

The effect of the rootstock

Rootstock	Mature tree		Age of tree when first fruits appear	Age of tree when full cropping capacity is reached
	Approximate height	Approximate yield		
M27	5–6 ft	15–25 lb	2–3 years	4–5 years
M9	8–10 ft	35–45 lb	3–4 years	5–6 years
M26	10–12 ft	65–75 lb	3–4 years	5–6 years
MM106	14–18 ft	90–110 lb	4–5 years	7–8 years
MM111 M2	18–25 ft	160–360 lb	6–7 years	8–9 years

M26
DWARFING
A rootstock which produces an effect which is quite similar to M9. It is rather more vigorous and a little stronger all round. The bush tends to be about 2 ft taller and wider and staking is only needed for about 5 years. This is a good stock for average soil conditions where compact growth is required — the crop is appreciably greater than on an M9 tree.

MM106
SEMI-DWARFING
Called semi-vigorous in some catalogues — it is the most widely used of all rootstocks. The unlabelled tree at the garden centre is probably on MM106 — it is the best choice for bushes to be grown in the average garden under average conditions. MM106 is nearly always used for the weaker varieties where more dwarfing stocks would produce under-sized bushes. This rootstock can be used for half standards but it is rather too vigorous for cordons unless the soil is poor.

MM111 & M2
VIGOROUS
There is no place for these rootstocks in most gardens — the resulting tree is far too large and wide-spreading. Trees come into fruit very slowly, and on good soil you will need ladders and extra tools for pruning, spraying and picking. However, they have a number of special uses. MM111 is the right choice for a standard to be grown in a large garden or for a medium-sized bush to be grown on poor soil such as an infertile loamy sand.

Varieties A-Z

There are hundreds of varieties to choose from. Some are available at almost every nursery and others are restricted to just one or two specialist catalogues. Listed here are 56 of them — the ones you are most likely to find in the garden centre or mail order list. The Apples described are certainly not a 'recommended' or 'best-buy' selection — a few of them are a poor choice.

Read the descriptions carefully to see if the variety is right for you — there is no such thing as the 'perfect' Apple. Avoid very vigorous types such as *Bramley's Seedling* if space is limited. Choose an early or mid-season fruiting variety (see below) if you live in a northern district and reject a canker-prone type if your ground stays cold and wet in spring. Frost is an important consideration. If your garden seems more prone than most to suffer from frost then you should choose a mid-season/late- or late-flowering variety (see Pollination Groups). Alternatively look through the A-Z list for an Apple with good frost resistance — do avoid *Cox's Orange Pippin* and *Bramley's Seedling*. When choosing a culinary variety, think of the end-product you require — *Newton Wonder* cooks down to a golden fluff whereas *Lane's Prince Albert* keeps its shape.

Pick your Apples in peak condition — commercial fruit is often picked too early. Remember the general rule — home-grown 'English' varieties (*Cox's Orange Pippin, Worcester Pearmain* etc) taste better than shop-bought ones, but home-grown 'Foreign' varieties (*Granny Smith, Sturmer Pippin* etc) taste worse.

You will find some odd words in the descriptions — look them up in the glossary as they may affect your decision. Biennial bearing means that you can have a very disappointing crop every other year. Tip bearing means that most of the fruit is borne at the end instead of along the length of the branch which is the much more usual spur-bearing habit. The months listed in the A-Z descriptions refer to southern England — add on a couple of weeks for the North. For Apples which need to be stored note that the start of the period of use may be up to 2 months after the recommended time for picking.

FRUIT SIZE	Diameter of fruit
Very large	over 3½ in.
Large	2¾–3½ in.
Medium	2 –2¾ in.
Small	less than 2 in.

FRUITING SEASON	Picking time	Storage period
Early	July — Early September	Nil — eat within 7 days
Mid-season	September — October	Limited — 2–3 weeks
Late	October — November	Prolonged — 1–6 months depending upon variety

Pollination Groups

A few Apples are self-fertile, capable of setting some fruit with their own pollen — examples include *James Grieve* and *Arthur Turner*. In practically all cases, however, it is necessary to have a pollination partner nearby — another variety which flowers at approximately the same time, enabling cross-pollination to take place.

In urban areas where Apples occur in many gardens there is often no need to provide a pollination partner in your own garden — there are usually enough suitable ones in surrounding plots. But if Apples are not common in your area then it will be necessary to plant a suitable pollen provider in your garden.

Apples are classified into 4 flowering season groups — see below. A pollination partner is a variety which is ideally in the same group or else in the one immediately above or just below the group which includes the Apple in question.

The so-called Triploid varieties pose a special problem. Here the variety is an extremely poor pollinator, so 2 non-Triploid varieties need to be grown nearby to act as pollination partners — these pollinate both the Triploid variety and each other.

A Early flowering	BEAUTY OF BATH EGREMONT RUSSET GEORGE CAVE IDARED IRISH PEACH LORD LAMBOURNE REV W WILKS	ST EDMUND'S PIPPIN VISTA BELLA
		AT Triploid — needs *two* partners RIBSTON PIPPIN
B Mid-season flowering	ARTHUR TURNER BOUNTIFUL CHARLES ROSS COX'S ORANGE PIPPIN DISCOVERY EARLY VICTORIA ELSTAR EPICURE FIESTA FORTUNE GRANNY SMITH GREENSLEEVES GRENADIER JAMES GRIEVE JESTER KATY	KIDD'S ORANGE RED LANE'S PRINCE ALBERT MERTON KNAVE REDSLEEVES SPARTAN STURMER PIPPIN SUNSET WORCESTER PEARMAIN
		BT Triploid — needs *two* partners BLENHEIM ORANGE BRAMLEY'S SEEDLING CRISPIN JUPITER
C Mid-season/ late flowering	ANNIE ELIZABETH ASHMEAD'S KERNEL ELLISON'S ORANGE GALA GOLDEN DELICIOUS GOLDEN NOBLE HOWGATE WONDER LAXTON'S SUPERB LORD DERBY	ORLEANS REINETTE PIXIE TYDEMAN'S LATE ORANGE WINSTON
		CT Triploid — needs *two* partners JONAGOLD
D Late flowering	AMERICAN MOTHER EDWARD VII NEWTON WONDER	**DT** Triploid — needs *two* partners SUNTAN

Family Trees

The need for a pollination partner can create a difficulty in a small garden where there is room for only one tree. Growing a family tree can be the answer. Here 2–4 different but compatible varieties are grafted on to one tree — ensuring cross-pollination plus a prolonged cropping period. A choice of rootstocks and an extensive range of varieties are available in this form.

Typical offerings include
Charles Ross/Grenadier/Worcester Pearmain
Discovery/Fortune/Sunset
Cox's Orange Pippin/James Grieve/Spartan

Avoid combinations which include *Bramley's Seedling* or *Golden Delicious* as these varieties tend to take over.

Type:	Dessert
Fruit size:	Medium
Skin colour:	Yellow, flushed and striped with crimson
Pollination group:	D
Picking time:	Late September
Period of use:	October–November

AMERICAN MOTHER

An age-old American variety introduced into Britain over 100 years ago. Eating qualities are excellent — sweet, juicy and distinctly aromatic. Despite its listing as a dessert Apple, *American Mother* has long been a favourite for apple pies in the States. Growth habit is upright and resistance to scab is good. Cropping is irregular and full sun is needed.

American Mother

Type:	Culinary
Fruit size:	Large
Skin colour:	Golden, flushed speckled and striped with pinkish-red
Pollination group:	C
Picking time:	Mid October
Period of use:	December–May

ANNIE ELIZABETH

No cooking Apple has better keeping qualities than old Annie — it lasts for months in store. An upright tree which spurs freely and is suitable for northern climes. The flesh is acid and crisp — texture is rather dry. *Annie Elizabeth* has been around for a long time and was once popular with commercial growers, but it is no longer in the top-seller lists.

Type:	Culinary
Fruit size:	Large
Skin colour:	Greenish-yellow, flushed orange-brown
Pollination group:	Partly self-fertile: B
Picking time:	August–September
Period of use:	August–October

ARTHUR TURNER

Arthur Turner is not recommended by all the experts, but it certainly has its share of plus points. The pink blossom is outstanding — no Apple provides a finer display. Growth is upright and this variety is reliable in northern districts. Crops are heavy and the rather dry texture of the fruit makes it an excellent baking Apple. Quite freely available.

Arthur Turner

Type:	Dessert
Fruit size:	Medium
Skin colour:	Yellowish-green, mostly covered with mid-brown russet
Pollination group:	C
Picking time:	Mid October
Period of use:	December–March

ASHMEAD'S KERNEL

Nearly 300 years old and still regarded as one of the best late dessert Apples. The yellow flesh is crisp and the flavour is rated as superb. Scab resistance is good and the fruit has excellent keeping qualities. Quality is not matched by quantity — it is a light and erratic cropper which cannot be recommended for exposed northern gardens.

Type:	Dessert
Fruit size:	Small–medium
Skin colour:	Pale yellow, flushed and speckled with bright red
Pollination group:	A
Picking time:	Early August
Period of use:	Early August

BEAUTY OF BATH

Once a very popular early dessert Apple, but commercial growers now choose better varieties. The tree has a spreading habit — the taste is sweet but somewhat tart and nothing special. You will find it in numerous catalogues but it is no longer recommended by the experts. Premature fruit drop is a problem and cropping is slow to start.

Beauty of Bath

Type:	Dessert/Culinary
Fruit size:	Large
Skin colour:	Golden, flushed and striped with dull red and fine brown russet
Pollination group:	BT
Picking time:	Early October
Period of use:	November–January

BLENHEIM ORANGE

After nearly two centuries it is still regarded as the best of all dual-purpose Apples. The creamy flesh is crisp and dry with an excellent nutty flavour. Mildew resistance is good and yields are heavy. Growth is very vigorous — make sure it is on dwarfing stock. Succeeds in the North. It is a biennial bearer and scab can be a problem.

Type:	Culinary
Fruit size:	Large
Skin colour:	Pale green, striped with orange-red
Pollination group:	B
Picking time:	Late September
Period of use:	September–January

BOUNTIFUL

The first new cooking Apple for decades — a good choice for people who want large fruit but haven't the space for a *Bramley's Seedling*. This compact variety pollinates freely and does not suffer from mildew. Heavy crops are produced and *Bountiful* can be bought as a cordon. Fruit is quite sweet for a cooker — extra sugar is not required.

Bountiful

TREE FRUIT: APPLES

Bramley's Seedling

Cox's Orange Pippin

Crispin

Discovery

BRAMLEY'S SEEDLING

By far the most popular cooking Apple. The reason is easy to see — heavy crops of extra-large fruit with creamy flesh which is juicy and full of flavour. But think before making it your first choice — it is too vigorous for small gardens and it is often a biennial bearer. Neither scab nor frost resistance are good. A partial tip bearer.

Type:	Culinary
Fruit size:	Very large
Skin colour:	Yellowish-green, lightly striped with red
Pollination group:	BT
Picking time:	Mid October
Period of use:	November–March

CHARLES ROSS

Some Apple varieties are chosen for their outstanding flavour — this one's claim to fame is the beauty of the fruit. Large, round, colourful and showy — a popular sight on the show bench. The flesh is sweet and juicy at first but becomes dry and flavourless with long storage. This eater/baker is widely available and does well in limy soils.

Type:	Dessert/Culinary
Fruit size:	Large
Skin colour:	Yellowish-green, flushed and striped with orange-red
Pollination group:	B
Picking time:	Mid September
Period of use:	October–December

COX'S ORANGE PIPPIN

Regarded by most people as the best of all eating Apples — aromatic, juicy, crisp, superb flavour etc. Still, it is in most cases one for your weekly shopping list rather than the garden. It is not suitable for northern districts and even in the South it is temperamental and susceptible to frost and disease. It needs good soil and knowledgeable attention.

Type:	Dessert
Fruit size:	Medium
Skin colour:	Golden, flushed with orange-red. Patches of brown russet
Pollination group:	B
Picking time:	October
Period of use:	October–January

CRISPIN

A post-war variety from Japan, grown for its very heavy cropping potential. The fruit is distinctly oblong and ribbed, and the flesh is crisp, pleasant and rather tart. A good one for eating straight from the tree, or the fruit can be stored for up to 4 months. Growth is vigorous — make sure that it has a dwarfing rootstock.

Type:	Dessert/Culinary
Fruit size:	Large
Skin colour:	Yellowish-green
Pollination group:	BT
Picking time:	Mid October
Period of use:	November–February

DISCOVERY

An early variety with firmer flesh and better keeping qualities than most others which ripen in August–September. It is earlier and better than its parent *Worcester Pearmain*. Disease resistance and frost tolerance are good, and the moderate growth habit makes it suitable for the smaller garden. It can be slow to start cropping — a spur and tip bearer.

Type:	Dessert
Fruit size:	Small-medium
Skin colour:	Yellow, almost entirely covered with bright crimson
Pollination group:	B
Picking time:	August
Period of use:	August–September

EARLY VICTORIA

Early Victoria (also known as *Emneth Early*) is the first cooker of the season. Fruit are ready for picking in late July and the greenish-white flesh cooks to a sweet fluff. Trees are very hardy and yields are high. Growth is upright and compact — the major problem is that thinning of the trusses is essential or biennial bearing and small fruits will result.

Type:	Culinary
Fruit size:	Medium
Skin colour:	Yellowish-green
Pollination group:	B
Picking time:	July
Period of use:	July–August

EDWARD VII

Late to flower and late to fruit — this hardy variety is a good choice for northern areas or gardens with a frost pocket. Growth is compact and upright, so it is on the recommended list for small gardens. Scab resistance is good. The acid flesh turns pink after cooking. *Edward VII* is only a moderate cropper, and is often slow to start bearing fruit.

Type:	Culinary
Fruit size:	Large
Skin colour:	Yellowish-green
Pollination group:	D
Picking time:	Mid October
Period of use:	December–April

EGREMONT RUSSET

You will find this one in nearly all the catalogues. It has been around for a hundred years but it's still one of the best russets you can buy. The skin is rough and the flesh is crisp. Flavour is very good — nutty and sweet. Growth is upright and the fruit is rather small. An advantage is the frost tolerance of its blossom, but bitter pit can be a problem.

Type:	Dessert
Fruit size:	Small-medium
Skin colour:	Golden. Large patches of pale brown russet
Pollination group:	A
Picking time:	Late September
Period of use:	October–December

ELLISON'S ORANGE

A hardy Apple which is easy to grow. It is praised to the skies in some catalogues, and is sometimes listed as *Red Ellison*. Scab and frost resistance are good, but it is still not really a good choice —the fruit is very juicy but the rather odd aniseed flavour is not enjoyed by everybody. Canker can be a problem, and so can biennial bearing.

Type:	Dessert
Fruit size:	Medium
Skin colour:	Greenish-yellow, flushed and striped with red
Pollination group:	C
Picking time:	Mid September
Period of use:	September–October

ELSTAR

A new one from Holland which is not yet in the textbooks and is restricted to the catalogues of specialist fruit growers. *Elstar* is expected to become a popular variety — it crops heavily, stores well and both juiciness and flavour are outstanding. Thin fruitlets to avoid biennial bearing — not a tree for beginners.

Type:	Dessert
Fruit size:	Medium
Skin colour:	Greenish-yellow, flushed with bright red
Pollination group:	B
Picking time:	October
Period of use:	October–January

EPICURE

You will find it in numerous catalogues — often listed as *Laxton's Epicure*. A good choice for beginners and cold districts — it is both hardy and easy to grow. The fruit is prettily striped and juicy, but it tends to be small and the flavour rapidly deteriorates after picking. A compact tree with few branches.

Type:	Dessert
Fruit size:	Small
Skin colour:	Yellow, striped with red
Pollination group:	B
Picking time:	Mid August
Period of use:	Mid August–September

FIESTA

An outstanding new variety for people who would like to grow *Cox's Orange Pippin* but can't. Cox is one of the parents and all of the aroma and nuttiness are present. The flavour, however, is not quite as good despite the claim in a few catalogues. The main points are that *Fiesta* is reliable and it crops heavily. Growth is rather pendulous.

Type:	Dessert
Fruit size:	Medium-large
Skin colour:	Yellow, flushed and striped with bright red
Pollination group:	B
Picking time:	Early October
Period of use:	October–March

FORTUNE

Fortune (Laxton's Fortune) is a popular variety which has a place in most catalogues. It appeals because it has a compact growth habit, is easy to grow and the fruit is sweet and juicy. However, it's not a winner these days — problems include canker, biennial bearing and a loss of crispness soon after picking.

Type:	Dessert
Fruit size:	Medium
Skin colour:	Golden-yellow, flushed and striped with red
Pollination group:	B
Picking time:	Early September
Period of use:	September–October

GALA

Not widely available, although you will find it in some of the specialist catalogues. *Gala* is sometimes praised for its shiny red skin and crisp, sweet flesh, the degree of redness depends on the amount of sunshine. It crops heavily but you can do better. *Gala* is prone to both scab and canker and the fruit can be quite small if not thinned.

Type:	Dessert
Fruit size:	Medium
Skin colour:	Yellow, heavily flushed with red
Pollination group:	C
Picking time:	October
Period of use:	October–January

Egremont Russet

Ellison's Orange

Epicure

Fortune

TREE FRUIT: APPLES

George Cave

Greensleeves

Grenadier

Howgate Wonder

GEORGE CAVE

Regarded by some as the best of the early varieties. *George Cave* crops heavily and regularly, the first fruits being ready in late July in favourable districts. Do not wait too long before picking — early fruit drop can occur. The fruit is described as refreshing — soft, juicy and acidic, but with no special merit. A tip and spur bearer.

Type:	Dessert
Fruit size:	Small-medium
Skin colour:	Green, flushed and striped with red
Pollination group:	A
Picking time:	August
Period of use:	August

GOLDEN DELICIOUS

Don't be tempted to plant this one because you like the shop-bought fruit, with its characteristic ribs and the bumps at the crown. *Golden Delicious* needs sunnier climes than Britain to give of its best — flavour and size will disappoint after a poor summer. Yields are usually heavy and the fruit stores well. A good pollinator for other varieties.

Type:	Dessert
Fruit size:	Medium
Skin colour:	Greenish- or golden-yellow
Pollination group:	C
Picking time:	Late October
Period of use:	November–February

GOLDEN NOBLE

Highly praised in many textbooks as one of the best cookers. The flesh becomes a golden froth with a delicious flavour, but you will have to turn to a specialist fruit grower if you want to buy one. It succeeds in cool districts and crops regularly, but it is susceptible to scab and canker. A tip and spur bearer.

Type:	Culinary
Fruit size:	Medium-large
Skin colour:	Yellow. Pale russet may be present
Pollination group:	C
Picking time:	Early October
Period of use:	October–December

GRANNY SMITH

A fine eating Apple when bought from the greengrocer — but not when grown in the garden. A reliable and heavy cropper, but you need a hot summer, a favoured locality, late picking and prolonged storage to produce fruit fit for eating rather than for cooking. Keeping quality is outstanding — the fruit can sometimes be kept until May.

Type:	Dessert/Culinary
Fruit size:	Medium
Skin colour:	Green, sometimes flushed and striped with brown
Pollination group:	B
Picking time:	Late October
Period of use:	January–April

GREENSLEEVES

An outstanding modern variety — this is the one to grow if you are a *Golden Delicious* fan. The tree is hardy, reliable, self-fertile and easy to manage. Fruit appears early in the life of the tree and very heavy crops can be expected. Unfortunately the refreshing flavour soon fades in store. A tip and spur bearer.

Type:	Dessert
Fruit size:	Medium
Skin colour:	Pale green turning to pale yellow
Pollination group:	B
Picking time:	September
Period of use:	September–November

GRENADIER

Grenadier is the standard early cooking Apple seen on the greengrocers' shelves — green, flattish and distinctly ribbed. It is also a popular garden variety as it is hardy, crops heavily and has a compact growth habit. Scab resistance is good and it cooks down to a white fluff with an excellent flavour. Poor storage quality is the major problem.

Type:	Culinary
Fruit size:	Medium-large
Skin colour:	Yellowish-green
Pollination group:	B
Picking time:	Mid August
Period of use:	August–September

HOWGATE WONDER

A good choice if you live in the North or in a frosty area and if you don't mind a vigorous, spreading tree in your garden. Crops are very heavy and the extra large, striped fruit is suitable for the autumn horticultural show. Unfortunately the flavour is not as good as many of the catalogues indicate — it is often insipid.

Type:	Culinary
Fruit size:	Very large
Skin colour:	Greenish-yellow, flushed and striped with pale red
Pollination group:	C
Picking time:	October
Period of use:	November–March

Type:	Dessert/Culinary
Fruit size:	Medium-large
Skin colour:	Yellow, mostly flushed with bright red
Pollination group:	A
Picking time:	Late October
Period of use:	November–April

IDARED

Idared has two important features to its credit — unfortunately good flavour is not one of them. The first feature is the excellent keeping quality of the fruit in store — Apples picked in October can be used in late spring. In addition they can be used for cooking as well as for eating fresh. The flesh is white.

Idared

Type:	Dessert
Fruit size:	Small-medium
Skin colour:	Yellow, flushed and striped with orange and red
Pollination group:	A
Picking time:	Late August
Period of use:	August–September

IRISH PEACH

You will find this one in a number of guides to recommended varieties, but not in many catalogues. This recommendation is based on the outstanding flavour and juiciness of fruit picked straight from the tree. The lack of popularity is based on its reluctance to reach the fruiting stage, the poor quality of stored fruit and its tip-bearing nature.

Type:	Dessert
Fruit size:	Medium-large
Skin colour:	Yellow, speckled and striped with orange
Pollination group:	Partly self-fertile: B
Picking time:	Early September
Period of use:	September–October

JAMES GRIEVE

An excellent choice, especially for a difficult site, if you want a reliable and hardy early variety. It crops heavily and regularly, and the soft-textured fruit is both juicy and tangy. Thinning is often necessary and the keeping quality is rather poor. Does better in the North than in western areas, where canker may be a problem.

James Grieve

Type:	Dessert
Fruit size:	Medium
Skin colour:	Yellowish-green, heavily flushed with red
Pollination group:	B
Picking time:	September
Period of use:	October–November

JESTER

One of the modern varieties raised at East Malling. A good garden Apple, but it has been overshadowed by *Jupiter* which was introduced at the same time. *Jester* may become popular — it spurs freely, has a compact growth habit and the fruit is crisp and juicy. The main claim to fame is the frost resistance of its blossom.

Type:	Dessert
Fruit size:	Large-very large
Skin colour:	Greenish-yellow, lightly flushed and mottled with red
Pollination group:	CT
Picking time:	Mid October
Period of use:	November–March

JONAGOLD

A modern Apple from the U.S with *Golden Delicious* and *Jonathan* as its parents. Fruit quality is excellent — crisp, juicy and full of flavour. The colour is sometimes insipid, and its vigour and spreading habit may be a problem in a small garden. Yields are very high and young trees quickly come into fruit.

Jupiter

Type:	Dessert
Fruit size:	Medium
Skin colour:	Golden-yellow, mostly flushed and striped with red
Pollination group:	BT
Picking time:	Mid September
Period of use:	October–March

JUPITER

Introduced in 1982 as the variety which had all the flavour of *Cox's Orange Pippin* and none of its unreliability. Cropping is very heavy and growth is vigorous — make sure that it is grafted on dwarfing stock. It is quite easy to find a supplier, but its Cox-substitute role is being taken over by others like *Sunset* and *Fiesta*.

Type:	Dessert
Fruit size:	Small-medium
Skin colour:	Greenish-yellow, heavily flushed with bright red
Pollination group:	B
Picking time:	Early September
Period of use:	September–October

KATY

Katy, Katja or *Katya*. This early variety came to us from Sweden — not surprisingly it is a good choice for northern gardens. It is similar in many ways to its parent *Worcester Pearmain*, but *Katy* is generally considered to be a better choice these days. Cropping is heavy and regular — fruit is juicy and refreshing.

Katy

TREE FRUIT: APPLES

Kidd's Orange Red

Laxton's Superb

Lord Derby

Newton Wonder

KIDD'S ORANGE RED

This New Zealand variety was expected to become popular because it is similar to *Cox's Orange Pippin* in flavour and texture but has none of its cultural problems. It is a heavy and regular cropper and this variety spurs freely. It is suitable for northern gardens and has quite good resistance to disease. However, it never became a best seller.

Type:	Dessert
Fruit size:	Small-medium
Skin colour:	Yellow, heavily flushed with red. Patches of pale brown russet
Pollination group:	B
Picking time:	Early October
Period of use:	November–February

LANE'S PRINCE ALBERT

One of the small group of popular cooking Apples which you will find in most catalogues. It has many good points. The tree is hardy, compact and spurs freely. The fruit keeps better than *Bramley's Seedling* and does not break up when cooked. Still, it has its problems. It is susceptible to mildew and has too little vigour for poor soil.

Type:	Culinary
Fruit size:	Large
Skin colour:	Grass-green, striped with dull red
Pollination group:	B
Picking time:	Early October
Period of use:	November–March

LAXTON'S SUPERB

Perhaps the most widely grown of all late dessert varieties. There are some good points — the flowers have above-average frost resistance and the fruit stores well. But you can do better these days. It is a biennial bearer, susceptible to scab and a little too vigorous for the small garden. Thinning is usually necessary.

Type:	Dessert
Fruit size:	Medium-large
Skin colour:	Greenish-yellow, flushed with dark red. Patches of russet
Pollination group:	C
Picking time:	Early October
Period of use:	November–February

LORD DERBY

This old Apple is still quite widely available but no longer appears in the lists of recommended varieties. It does not have the keeping qualities you would expect from a cooker picked in September or October, but the variety has several good points. It succeeds in cold and wet areas and has good disease resistance. Flesh turns pink when cooked.

Type:	Culinary
Fruit size:	Large
Skin colour:	Green
Pollination group:	C
Picking time:	Late September
Period of use:	October–December

LORD LAMBOURNE

This mid-season variety is highly recommended by many experts. The reason is that it can be relied upon to crop both heavily and regularly almost anywhere. Its compact growth habit makes it suitable for small gardens and the brightly-coloured fruit is sweet, juicy and aromatic. A tip and spur bearer which spurs very freely.

Type:	Dessert
Fruit size:	Medium
Skin colour:	Greenish-yellow, flushed and striped with red
Pollination group:	A
Picking time:	Mid September
Period of use:	October–November

MERTON KNAVE

This brightly-coloured Apple has never become really popular — you will have to look for it in a specialist catalogue. *Merton Knave* is not difficult — it can be grown anywhere and its blossom is fairly frost resistant. The growth habit is weeping and it spurs freely. The problem is that the fruit flavour is only fair.

Type:	Dessert
Fruit size:	Medium
Skin colour:	Greenish-yellow, almost entirely flushed with bright red
Pollination group:	B
Picking time:	Late August–September
Period of use:	September

NEWTON WONDER

This very vigorous Apple is not really suitable for small gardens. It is recommended for its heavy yields of fine-flavoured fruit, but it is a biennial bearer and prone to bitter pit. The fruit is juicy, acid and boils down to a golden fluff. Not really a dual-purpose variety, but stored fruit can be used as a dessert Apple.

Type:	Culinary
Fruit size:	Very large
Skin colour:	Golden-yellow, flushed and striped with red
Pollination group:	D
Picking time:	Mid October
Period of use:	November–December

Type:	Dessert
Fruit size:	Medium-large
Skin colour:	Yellow, flushed orange-red. Patches of grey-brown russet
Pollination group:	C
Picking time:	Mid October
Period of use:	November–January

ORLEANS REINETTE

An 18th century variety still offered for sale because of its excellent fruit quality — crisp flesh and a delicious nutty flavour. The catalogues, however, tend to make light of its problems. Yields are rather low and irregular — it is a biennial bearer and is prone to scab in wet soils. This one does not store well — fruit often shrivels in store.

Orleans Reinette

Type:	Dessert
Fruit size:	Small-medium
Skin colour:	Yellowish-green, flushed and striped with red
Pollination group:	C
Picking time:	Mid October
Period of use:	December–March

PIXIE

You will have to search for this one, which is a shame. The fruit quality is exceptional — attractive, crisp, aromatic, juicy, refreshing etc. The problem is that they are rather small, but this should not really discourage gardeners. The growth properties of the variety are good — cropping is prolific and disease resistance is high. It must be thinned.

Type:	Dessert
Fruit size:	Medium
Skin colour:	Yellowish-green, almost entirely flushed with bright red
Pollination group:	Partly self-fertile: B
Picking time:	Late August
Period of use:	August–September

REDSLEEVES

Will *Redsleeves* be a leading early variety in the 1990s? Only time will tell, but the East Malling Research Station report certainly sounds promising. Growth is compact, and the fruit is crisp and juicy. Disease resistance is claimed to be excellent and it is reported to need very little pruning. Apples can be stored for up to a month.

Rev W Wilks

Type:	Culinary
Fruit size:	Very large
Skin colour:	Pale green, flushed and striped with dark pink
Pollination group:	A
Picking time:	Early September
Period of use:	September–November

REV W WILKS

A compact, short-rooted cooking variety which is specially recommended for small gardens. Disease resistance is good and it is surprising that such a small tree can give high yields of very large fruit. Quality is good — juicy and tangy with a reputation for being an excellent baker. No variety is perfect — *Rev W Wilks* is a biennial bearer.

Type:	Dessert
Fruit size:	Medium
Skin colour:	Yellow, flushed and striped with dull red. Patches of russet
Pollination group:	AT
Picking time:	Late September
Period of use:	October–January

RIBSTON PIPPIN

As you would expect from a parent of *Cox's Orange Pippin*, the russeted fruit of this variety is firm, aromatic and fine-flavoured. *Ribston Pippin* is not widely available as it does have its problems. The tree is prone to canker and the fruit drops easily. It crops regularly but yields are not always heavy. A fruit with a fine past but limited future.

Type:	Dessert
Fruit size:	Small-medium
Skin colour:	Golden, lightly flushed with orange. Patches of brown russet
Pollination group:	A
Picking time:	Mid September
Period of use:	September–October

ST EDMUND'S PIPPIN

Choose this one if you want a russet early in the season. The fruit quality is very high with a distinct tangy sweetness. The texture is firm. The growth habit is compact and cropping is regular. Thinning may be necessary when overcropping takes place. In some years yields are low. A tip and spur bearer — unsuitable for growing as a cordon.

St Edmund's Pippin

Type:	Dessert
Fruit size:	Medium
Skin colour:	Yellow, almost entirely flushed with dark red
Pollination group:	B
Picking time:	Early October
Period of use:	November–January

SPARTAN

This is one for the *Red Delicious* or *McIntosh* fan. The smooth-skinned red fruit is white-fleshed, crisp and very juicy. The hardy tree yields moderately well and spurs freely, but canker can be a problem. So can fruit size — thinning is essential if there is an abundance of fruitlets. This variety responds well to feeding.

Spartan

Sturmer Pippin

Sunset

Tydeman's Late Orange

Worcester Pearmain

STURMER PIPPIN

A popular shop-bought variety, but don't grow it in the garden unless you live in a warm western district. Leave the fruit on the tree as long as possible — following a good summer you can enjoy excellent fruit in the new year — crisp, greenish flesh and a refreshing flavour. Growth is compact — cropping is regular.

Type:	Dessert
Fruit size:	Medium
Skin colour:	Pale green, flushed with brown. Small patches of russet
Pollination group:	B
Picking time:	November
Period of use:	January–April

SUNSET

The usual choice where a Cox-like Apple is required. This offspring of *Cox's Orange Pippin* has nearly all of the quality of its illustrious parent with hardly any of the bad points. It is hardy, compact and has very good disease resistance. It crops heavily and regularly but the fruit is rather small. With care will keep until January.

Type:	Dessert
Fruit size:	Small-medium
Skin colour:	Golden, flushed and striped with red. Small patches of russet
Pollination group:	B
Picking time:	Late September
Period of use:	October–December

SUNTAN

Another Cox-like variety. It scores over *Sunset* by producing larger fruit which can be stored until early spring. It also flowers later so that it escapes frost damage. However, the fruits are more acidic than *Sunset* and they are prone to bitter pit. In addition growth is much more vigorous and two pollinators are needed.

Type:	Dessert
Fruit size:	Medium-large
Skin colour:	Yellowish-green, flushed and striped with red. Patches of russet
Pollination group:	DT
Picking time:	Mid October
Period of use:	November–February

TYDEMAN'S LATE ORANGE

The fruit is very similar in texture, colour and taste to its parent *Cox's Orange Pippin*. This variety is easy to grow — spurs are freely produced and the blossom is quite resistant to frost. The storage qualities are excellent — much better than *Cox*, but yields are only moderate. Thinning is necessary and it is a biennial bearer.

Type:	Dessert
Fruit size:	Small-medium
Skin colour:	Golden, flushed and striped with dull red. Patches of russet
Pollination group:	C
Picking time:	Mid October
Period of use:	December–April

VISTA BELLA

A new red dessert Apple with a single claim to fame — it can be picked from the tree and eaten before the end of July. It is reasonably crisp and juicy but the flavour is insipid. The fruit cannot be stored as it soon goes soft. Yields are not high and it is a biennial bearer. Don't be put off — picking bright red Apples in July is worth a few problems.

Type:	Dessert
Fruit size:	Medium
Skin colour:	Bright red
Pollination group:	A
Picking time:	Late July
Period of use:	July–mid August

WINSTON

A late dessert Apple which is an improvement on *Laxton's Superb*. The flavour and colour are better and so is the resistance to disease. In addition it will set fruit without a pollination partner. Still, this hardy and easy-to-grow variety is not widely listed in the catalogues — perhaps the problem is the need to thin the trusses in June.

Type:	Dessert
Fruit size:	Small-medium
Skin colour:	Yellowish-green, flushed and striped with red
Pollination group:	Partly self-fertile: C
Picking time:	Mid October
Period of use:	December–April

WORCESTER PEARMAIN

An old favourite — hardy, reliable and resistant to mildew. The trick is to leave the fruit on the tree until they are fully ripe — in that way the flavour and aroma are enhanced. There are problems — it is susceptible to both scab and canker, and it is a tip bearer. It is slow to start bearing fruit — choose *Discovery* or *Katy* instead.

Type:	Dessert
Fruit size:	Small-medium
Skin colour:	Yellowish-green, almost completely flushed with bright red
Pollination group:	B
Picking time:	Early September
Period of use:	September–October

Planting

Follow the basic rules for planting set out on pages 7–8. Before putting in the tree the soil should have been limed if it is very acid and some form of windbreak should have been created (see page 31) if the site is exposed.

Remember to plant to the old soil mark — the union with the rootstock should be about 4 in. above ground level. The bulge formed by this union should be on the upper surface when planting cordon Apples. Plant cordons in North-South rows with the trees pointing North. Make sure that all stakes and supports are in position before planting — cordons need canes set at 45°.

**WALL SUPPORT
FOR FANS**

Vine eye firmly secured to the wall

Galvanised wire pulled taut between vine eyes

6 in.

4 ft

At least 3 in. between wire and wall

**FENCE SUPPORT
FOR CORDONS, ESPALIERS & FANS**

4 in. x 4 in. post — make sure it has been treated with a wood preservative

6 in. for fans
18 in. for cordons & espaliers

Tighten straining bolt

8–12 ft

Pull wire taut before driving home the staples

heavy-gauge galvanised wire

The post must be fixed securely. Bury 2 ft deep — support with a stout angled strut

TREE TYPE	SPACE BETWEEN TREES	SPACE BETWEEN ROWS	YIELD PER MATURE TREE
Standard	30 ft	30 ft	200–400 lb
Half standard	20 ft	20 ft	100–250 lb
Fan	15 ft	—	15 – 25 lb
Bush	15 ft	15 ft	60–120 lb
Espalier	14 ft	6 ft	20 – 30 lb
Dwarf bush — M27 rootstock — other stocks	5 ft 9 ft	8 ft 15 ft	12 – 16 lb 40 – 60 lb
Spindlebush	7 ft	14 ft	60–120 lb
Dwarf Pyramid	5 ft	8 ft	10 – 14 lb
Step-over	5 ft	6 ft	5 – 6 lb
Cordon	2½ ft	6 ft	5 – 7 lb
Compact Column	2 ft	6 ft	10 – 20 lb

Feeding & Mulching

A starved tree cannot support a large crop — lack of nutrients can also affect next year's harvest. There are several complex feeding programmes for Apples, but a simple and well-tried method is to sprinkle 2 oz of Growmore per sq. yard in early spring around the soil under the branches. In April put a mulch of compost or rotted manure around the base of the trunks — keep away from the bark.

Watering

Newly-planted trees must be thoroughly watered when the weather is dry. This need for irrigation is less with established trees, but even here you will have to water if there is a drought. Failure to do so when the tree is in fruit will result in a smaller crop and a reduction in the number of fruit buds next year. Use a hosepipe held close to the ground — apply 10 gallons per sq. yard and repeat every 2 weeks until the dry weather is over.

Pruning

The purpose of pruning during the first 4 years of the tree's life is **training** — the creation of the basic framework which will ensure satisfactory cropping in later years. With bushes and standards this calls for fairly severe cutting back of the branches in order to produce an open-centred and freely-branched tree. In addition you must remove poor quality wood — weak twigs, dead or badly diseased shoots etc.

After 4 years the purpose of cutting out wood is **maintenance pruning** — the creation of a regular supply of new fruiting wood balanced with the need to retain as much existing fruiting wood as possible. This pruning is generally much less severe than training, but you must continue to remove all dead wood, crossing branches and so on.

All this is winter pruning, designed to *encourage* shoot growth. However, the main time to prune cordons, espaliers and dwarf pyramids is in summer, and the role of cutting out wood here is to *inhibit* shoot growth.

PRUNING KNIFE
is useful for cleaning up ragged pruning cuts. Excellent for pruning thin branches, but only if you are experienced in its use

LONG-HANDLED PRUNER
for stems ½–1½ in. across — many gardeners prefer them to a pruning saw for dealing with thicker stems

TWO-BLADED SECATEURS
with proper care will cut cleanly for many years. The cut must be made at the centre of the blades — maximum diameter ½–¾ in.

PRUNING SAW
is used for branches which are more than ½ in. across — essential for large branches

BUSHES & STANDARDS

Training a 2 year old tree

Cut back strong branches to half of their length

Cut back weak branches to a third of their length

Cut out snags

Prune in winter after planting — keep 3–5 primary branches

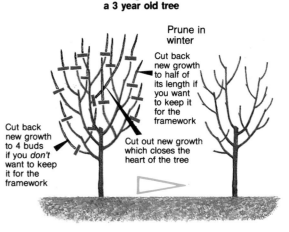

Training a 3 year old tree

Prune in winter

Cut back new growth to half of its length if you want to keep it for the framework

Cut back new growth to 4 buds if you *don't* want to keep it for the framework

Cut out new growth which closes the heart of the tree

Pruning an established tree

The simplest way to look after your mature tree is to follow the Regulation System in winter:

Spur-bearing variety
Remove dead and badly diseased wood. Cut back crossing branches and vigorous laterals crowding into the centre. Then:

Inside the head — leave leaders alone. Cut back each lateral which is growing into and beyond the branch leader

Outside the head — leave both leaders and laterals alone

Overcropping and undersized fruit may become a problem. If this has happened, thin some of the fruiting spurs and cut out some laterals

Tip-bearing variety
Remove dead, diseased and overcrowded wood. Then:

Cut back some leaders — leave alone all laterals with fruit buds at their tips

CORDONS

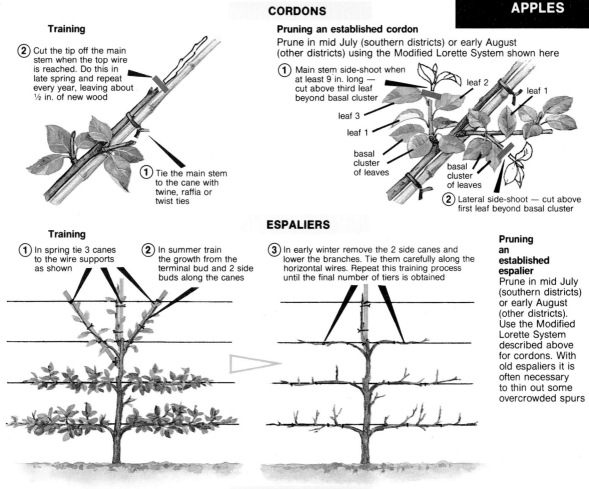

Training

2 Cut the tip off the main stem when the top wire is reached. Do this in late spring and repeat every year, leaving about ½ in. of new wood

1 Tie the main stem to the cane with twine, raffia or twist ties

Pruning an established cordon

Prune in mid July (southern districts) or early August (other districts) using the Modified Lorette System shown here

1 Main stem side-shoot when at least 9 in. long — cut above third leaf beyond basal cluster

leaf 2

leaf 1

leaf 3

leaf 1

basal cluster of leaves

basal cluster of leaves

2 Lateral side-shoot — cut above first leaf beyond basal cluster

ESPALIERS

Training

1 In spring tie 3 canes to the wire supports as shown

2 In summer train the growth from the terminal bud and 2 side buds along the canes

3 In early winter remove the 2 side canes and lower the branches. Tie them carefully along the horizontal wires. Repeat this training process until the final number of tiers is obtained

Pruning an established espalier
Prune in mid July (southern districts) or early August (other districts). Use the Modified Lorette System described above for cordons. With old espaliers it is often necessary to thin out some overcrowded spurs

DWARF PYRAMIDS

The dwarf pyramid is a compact, high-yielding tree type when grown in open ground, reaching about 7 ft tall and bearing a distinct Christmas tree shape. It has not become popular with gardeners as it requires careful and regular pruning in summer, but it has proved to be the ideal tree type for pot culture. See page 25 for a simplified pruning programme for this tree type.

The pruning cut

Sloping cut

¼ in.

Outward-pointing dormant bud

All pruning cuts must be clean — pare off any ragged parts. Sharp secateurs are essential — press downwards, don't just squeeze. Cuts more than ½ in. across should be painted with Arbrex to protect them from frost and damp. It is impossible to avoid making some wrong cuts when pruning and as a result snags of dead wood will form above some of the new shoots. Cut off these dead bits as they develop.

LOPPING

The removal of a large branch from the trunk of a tree. Call in a tree surgeon if the job is larger than your experience.

2 Saw downwards to sever the main part of the branch

1 Make a shallow saw cut on the underside of the branch about 4 in. away from the trunk

Saw off the stub — make the cut almost flush with the trunk

Pare away the rough edges with a pruning knife. Paint the cut surface with Arbrex

Bird control

As with all tree fruits, Apples have a bird problem. Fruit buds are attacked in winter and the opening blossom is at risk in spring. Cordons in cages are, of course, kept out of harm's way, but virtually all Apples are grown in the open. Neither bird scarers nor spray-on repellents are really effective and the range of physical protectants (netting, paper bags around the fruit, cardboard collars around the fruit stalks etc) are rarely practical. Apples do not suffer as badly as Plums, Pears or Cherries, and so the usual course of action is to do nothing and trust to luck.

Weed control

Weed control should begin before planting — pick out and destroy all perennial weed roots when preparing the planting hole. Weeds and grass should be kept away from the stem after planting — a clean ring with a radius of 18–24 in. should be maintained. Weeds within this area compete for nutrients, water etc and also encourage diseases. Hoeing, hand pulling and mulching are non-chemical answers. The most widely used herbicides are paraquat/diquat and glyphosate. Paraquat/diquat burns off the foliage, so keep it off the leaves and avoid drift. It is quick-acting — glyphosate acts more slowly but it does kill or inhibit perennial weeds.

Picking

The appearance of the first windfalls indicates that the time for picking is near. The colour of the fruit will have started to change and with most varieties the pips will have begun to change from white to brown. However, by far the best guide is to lift the fruit gently in the palm of your hand and give it a slight twist. It is ripe if the Apple comes away easily with the stalk attached.

Harvest the fruit at daily intervals rather than trying to gather them all at once. Pick the brightest coloured ones first and handle them gently — place them in a cloth- or straw-lined container. Never tug the Apples away from the tree — this can seriously damage the spurs.

Apples gathered for storage should not be over-ripe — if they are the fruit will rot in store. Most late varieties should be off the tree by late October. Eat or cook bruised or insect-damaged fruit within a day or two — don't try to store them.

Storage

Early varieties cannot be stored, but mid-season Apples can be kept for a few weeks and the late ones will last for months. Storage life depends on variety and on the conditions — for maximum storage you need a cool, dark and airy store which is not too dry.

There are 2 basic storage techniques. The traditional method is to use a series of trays which are either built or stood on top of each other with space for ventilation between them. You can use wooden orchard boxes, polystyrene containers or inexpensive fibre trays. Wrap each fruit in oiled paper and place folded side down in the tray.

A more recent technique is to store the fruit in clear polythene bags, placing about 5 lb of Apples in each one. Do not mix varieties. Perforate the bag with a few small holes, bend the top over without excluding all the air and place folded side down in the store. Whichever method you use, remember to inspect the fruit regularly and remove rotten ones immediately.

Rejuvenating neglected trees

1 The problem often occurs when a keen gardener moves house. In the new garden there are a few old Apple trees — crusty-barked, diseased and ugly. A mass of branches form a criss-crossed jungle of wood and leaves, and the fruit is undersized and pest-ridden.

2 Are the neglected trees worth saving? Even with skill and good luck it will take several seasons to restore productivity, and the work is hard. If the main branches are badly cankered, get rid of them. Only consider saving a tree if the framework is sound and healthy.

3 The first step in a rejuvenation programme is to consider spacing. Removal of one or more trees will be necessary if overcrowding is a problem, but remember that you may be removing an important pollen provider (see page 12).

4 The next step is to start to open up and reduce the size of each overgrown tree. It will be necessary to cut out some wood each winter for 3 years — to do all this surgery in a single season would seriously shock the plant.

5 In the first winter remove all dead, diseased and broken branches. Paint all large pruning cuts with Arbrex. Next, cut out some of the over-tall branches in the heart of the tree. Also remove some of the branches which are crossing others.

6 When cutting back a branch do make sure that the piece remaining is large and stout enough to support worthwhile growth in future. Spray with tar oil winter wash — follow the spring and summer spray programme set out on page 50.

7 Continue this de-horning (removal or cutting back of stout and over-sized branches) for the next 2 seasons. In addition you should cut out overcrowded secondary branches so as to produce an open-centred tree with its main branches spaced about 2 ft apart.

8 Feed and mulch each season as outlined on page 21. The effect of neglect may be that yields are still disappointing after the rejuvenation programme. Look at the chart on page 26 for the likely causes of poor yield — take remedial action.

Apples in pots

The introduction of dwarfing rootstocks such as M27 and M9 has made the cultivation of Apples in containers a practical proposition. There are several advantages. Space saving is the obvious one — Apples on the balcony, patio or tiny plot. But there are other important ones. You can move the pots indoors or cover with netting to protect against birds, frost and high winds. Free drainage can be ensured and pruning becomes a simple job. Finally, you can take the plant with you when you move.

Still, there are drawbacks. Watering every day is essential in dry summer weather although winter watering should not be necessary. Yields are not high (7–12 lb) and repotting in February is necessary every other year. Feeding is also essential — use Flower Maker or other high-potash feed at fortnightly intervals from blossom time to shortly before harvest.

Choose a 2 year old plant. Select from the A-Z list (pages 13–20) — popular types for pot culture include *Blenheim Orange, Discovery, Egremont Russet, Fiesta, Greensleeves, James Grieve, Katy, Lane's Prince Albert, Spartan* and *Sunset.* Grow as a dwarf pyramid (see below) — alternatively buy a dwarf bush.

Plant in a 12–15 in. container. Wood is ideal, but you can use a terracotta pot. Choose a heavy compost such as Baby Bio Multicompost or JI3. Stake firmly and place the pot in a reasonably sunny spot away from strong winds. Unimpeded drainage is essential — if necessary place the pots on bricks.

You will have to protect the containers during very frosty weather in winter — move them indoors or surround each one with insulating material. At fruiting time thinning (page 26) is nearly always essential. Finally, you should be able to enjoy your pot-grown Apple tree for many years, but don't expect it to last for 50 years like its open-garden relative.

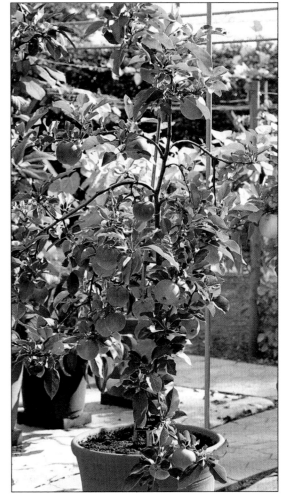

Pruning

**Training
a 2 year old tree**

Cut back leader to 6 in. from where it arises from central trunk

Prune in winter after planting — maintain all sound primary branches

Cut back upper branches to 6 in. from where they arise from central trunk

Cut out weak branches not needed for the framework

Cut back lower branches to 10 in. from where they arise from central trunk

**Pruning
an established tree**

Cut back leader to a bud on the opposite side of last year's direction — this maintains vertical habit

Prune in summer — seek to maintain the conical shape

Cut back all the new branches to 6 in. from where they arise from last year's wood

Cut out weak branches not needed for the framework

Causes of poor yields

● IMPATIENCE Your newly-planted bush cannot be expected to produce fruit for a couple of seasons after planting. Any blossom appearing in the first season should be removed, although letting a single fruit develop for tasting seems to do little harm. Fruiting starts slowly — you will not obtain top yields until the tree is 4–7 years old.

● POOR PRUNING & CARELESS PICKING Strong warnings have appeared on earlier pages. Over-severe pruning of a mature tree will result in abundant new growth in the following summer, and this will be at the expense of fruiting. Cutting off all the tips of laterals is disastrous with tip-bearing varieties. Pulling unripe fruit from the spurs can cause damage and a serious drop in yield next year.

● OVERCROPPING The tree can only support a limited number of large and well-shaped fruit. A heavy crop of Apples should be thinned or the resulting fruit will be small and next year's crop will be very light.

● FROST The effect of a severe frost on open blossom can be disastrous — see page 55. Reduce risk by choosing late-flowering varieties.

● PESTS & DISEASES Many Apple troubles spoil the quality of the fruit, but some lead to lower yields. Typical examples are birds, canker, brown rot and honey fungus. Treat pests and diseases promptly — see pages 50–57.

● BIENNIAL BEARING Some varieties (see the A–Z guide) have an inherent tendency to crop heavily one season and then very lightly 12 months later. However, nearly all other varieties will behave in the same way if not fed, not watered and not thinned. If biennial bearing is a problem, try bud rubbing in spring before the expected heavy-cropping season.

● POOR LOCATION OR POOR PLANTING Water-logging and poor soil result in poor growth and disappointing yields. There is little you can do with the established tree — tackle the problem before planting and at planting time. Other fruit inhibitors include exposed sites, upland locations and sunless spots.

● BLOSSOM DROP & FRUIT DROP A small amount of these problems will do no harm, but when severe the crop will be seriously reduced. See pages 55 and 57. The absence of a suitable pollination partner is a likely cause.

● OVERVIGOROUS GROWTH Too much nitrogen can result in lush and extensive leaf and stem growth with little or no blossom and fruit formation. Another cause is over-severe pruning. Feeding weekly with a high-potash fertilizer such as Flower Maker or Tomato Food will help, but more drastic action may be necessary. Growing grass around but not up to the trees will help. Cut back some vertical branches in late summer (*not* winter). Try arching and then tying down some of the branches ('festooning'). If all else fails, try bark ringing.

● STARVATION All fruit trees require feeding — a heavy crop is a drain on the soil's reserves. See page 21 for details.

Wait until the June drop — the time in late June-early July when the tree naturally sheds some of the fruitlets. If the trusses are still crowded, carry out thinning.

① Remove the King Apple (large, central fruit) if it is misshapen

② Remove small and damaged fruits to leave 2 Apples per truss. Use scissors

Rub away about half the fruit buds from the spurs

Bark ringing is suitable for Apples and Pears but not stone fruits

4 in.

¼ in. wide strip of bark removed in early summer. Cover wound with adhesive tape and paint over with Arbrex. Remove tape in autumn

PEARS

Pears are obviously closely related to Apples. They are trained into the same range of tree types and the basic rules of pruning are just the same. The planting technique is identical and many pests and diseases can move from one to the other.

There are many differences, however, and these may be either merely interesting or very important to know. These differences include:

- Pears generally live longer. Fifty years is the normal life span for an Apple tree, but a Pear should live for a century or more.

- Pears are more temperamental. Dessert types need more sun than Apples and they detest cold easterly winds. Young foliage is blackened and torn on exposed sites — you will need some form of windbreak under such conditions.

- Pears have different soil requirements. They will thrive in heavier soil than their more popular rival, but they are less happy in sandy soil, chalky soil and in salt-laden air.

- Pears are more sensitive to frost. Blossom appears 2–4 weeks before Apple blooms open, which is a welcome sight but it means that the chance of frost damage is greater.

- Pears usually give lower yields and are slower to come into fruit (4–8 years). Read page 26 if the yields seem to be abnormally low.

- Pears are grown on a more limited range of rootstocks. An Apple tree will reach 5 ft or 25 ft depending on the rootstock. Nearly all Pears are grown on Quince rootstocks. Quince A is the popular one, producing trees which grow about 10–20 ft high. Quince C has a dwarfing effect, but this is slight. Trees come into fruit a little earlier and the mature height is about 2 ft less — Quince C also needs a richer soil than Quince A. Pear rootstocks are still used, but only for standards — not for garden cultivation.

- Pears are less able to withstand drought but they are generally less prone to pests and diseases. There is one notable exception — birds, such as bullfinches, find the fruit buds of Pears more attractive than those of Apples.

- Pears have far fewer varieties in the catalogues and at the garden centres. You can expect to find only one third or a quarter of the number of Apple varieties in the Pear list and suitable choices for most gardeners are very few. Don't pick a cooker — use firm dessert Pears instead.

- Pears are more likely to need a pollination partner in your garden. *Conference* is partly self-fertile but it prefers and most others positively need a pollination partner — see page 28 for details.

- Pears have a more limited storage life. You can enjoy a wide variety of late Apples from store until well into spring, but there is hardly a dessert Pear which can be kept until after Christmas.

Varieties A-Z

You can look through the whole list of varieties if you can provide a warm and sheltered site — if not it would be wise to choose from *Conference, Beth* and *Concorde.* Many of the others described here may sound attractive, but they can be unreliable in cooler areas or in a poor season.

Pears are much less popular than Apples in gardens, which means that you probably have to provide a suitable pollination partner in your own plot. If space is limited, choose several different cordons. Or you can plant a family tree. The basic type carries the big three — *Conference, Doyenné du Comice* and *Williams' Bon Chrétien.*

Pollination Groups

A Early flowering	LOUISE BONNE DE JERSEY PACKHAM'S TRIUMPH SECKLE	
B Mid-season flowering	BETH BEURRE HARDY BEURRE SUPERFIN CONFERENCE DURONDEAU FERTILITY IMPROVED JOSEPHINE DE MALINES	THOMPSON'S WILLIAMS' BON CHRETIEN
		BT Triploid — needs *two* partners JARGONELLE MERTON PRIDE
C Late flowering	CONCORDE DOYENNE DU COMICE GORHAM	ONWARD WINTER NELIS

BETH

A new star of the Pear world, but not for commercial growers. This excellent English-bred variety is too small and variable in shape for them, but it is a good choice for you. Yields are high and cropping is regular — the white flesh has a melting texture. The upright tree soon comes into fruit. Definitely one for the 1990s.

Type:	Dessert
Fruit size:	Small–medium
Skin colour:	Pale yellow. Spots of russet
Pollination group:	B
Picking time:	Late August
Period of use:	September

BEURRE HARDY

Highly recommended for the orchard but not the best choice for a small garden — it is strong-growing, slow to bear fruit and only fairly hardy. *Beurré Hardy* is not always a regular cropper, but the conical fruit are juicy with a distinctive flavour, and the leaves turn bright red in autumn. Pick fruit whilst quite hard — leave it to ripen in store.

Type:	Dessert
Fruit size:	Medium–large
Skin colour:	Greenish-yellow, flushed with red. Large patches of russet
Pollination group:	B
Picking time:	Mid September
Period of use:	October

BEURRE SUPERFIN

A variety grown for its better-than-average fruit quality — the white flesh is melting and very sweet. The yields are not as high as some of the catalogues claim and the growth habit is moderate. Do not store for long — the fruit starts to rot once the flesh becomes soft. Shape is long-conical. Scab can be a problem.

Type:	Dessert
Fruit size:	Medium
Skin colour:	Golden-yellow. Patches of russet
Pollination group:	B
Picking time:	Late September
Period of use:	October

CONCORDE

A new Pear from East Malling Research Station. "A perfect garden variety" according to one noted nurseryman, but only time will tell. It has the right parents — *Conference* ensures reliability, heavy cropping and an early start to fruiting, and *Doyenné du Comice* provides very good flavour and melting, juicy flesh. Well worth a trial in your garden.

Type:	Dessert
Fruit size:	Medium
Skin colour:	Pale green
Pollination group:	C
Picking time:	Late October
Period of use:	November–December

CONFERENCE

Conference remains the No.1 choice because of its reliability under less than perfect conditions. It is self-fertile, but a nearby pollination partner will ensure a better crop. The fruits are long and narrow with juicy but firm flesh. Flavour is satisfactory but not outstanding. Good in the North, but susceptible to scab and wind damage.

Type:	Dessert
Fruit size:	Medium
Skin colour:	Olive green. Large patches of russet
Pollination group:	Partly self-fertile: B
Picking time:	Late September
Period of use:	October–November

Beth

Concorde

Conference

Type: Dessert	
Fruit size: Medium–large	
Skin colour: Golden-yellow, flushed brownish-red	
Pollination group: C	
Picking time: Mid October	
Period of use: November–December	

DOYENNE DU COMICE

The Queen of Pears if you are looking for flavour — the texture and taste are truly outstanding. A poor choice, however, if you are looking for a reliable tree for less than favourable conditions. It needs warmth, shelter from winds, a nearby pollination partner such as *Beth* or *Concorde* and spraying against scab. An irregular cropper.

Type: Dessert	
Fruit size: Medium–large	
Skin colour: Yellow, flushed red. Patches of russet	
Pollination group: Partly self-fertile: B	
Picking time: Late September	
Period of use: October–November	

DURONDEAU

The compact growth habit makes this variety a suitable choice for a small garden. It has a good reputation for regularity and heavy cropping, and as a bonus the leaves turn fiery red in autumn. The long fruits store well and the flesh is juicy. Flavour is nothing special. Self-fertile in warm districts. Not really popular despite its charms.

Type: Dessert/Culinary	
Fruit size: Small	
Skin colour: Yellow. Large patches of russet	
Pollination group: Partly self-fertile: B	
Picking time: Late September	
Period of use: October	

FERTILITY IMPROVED

Flavour is only fair and the texture is rather gritty, but *Fertility Improved* still has its fans. It is a dual-purpose variety and is both hardy and a heavy cropper. It is self-fertile, but a nearby pollination partner will ensure a better crop. Disease resistance is good, but canker can be a problem. Grows anywhere, but that grittiness is a problem.

Type: Dessert	
Fruit size: Small–medium	
Skin colour: Pale yellow. Large patches of russet	
Pollination group: C	
Picking time: Early September	
Period of use: September–October	

GORHAM

Quite a popular Pear, but there really isn't a great deal going for it. *Gorham* is a regular cropper, but yields are rather light and fruit size is not large. The flavour is good but unusual — "musky" according to the catalogues. Growth is distinctly upright and spurs form readily. An excellent pollinator. Less prone to scab than its parent *Williams'*.

Type: Dessert	
Fruit size: Medium	
Skin colour: Greenish-yellow, flushed brownish-red	
Pollination group: BT	
Picking time: Early August	
Period of use: August	

JARGONELLE

The best of the earlies, although the growth habit is straggly. *Jargonelle* is a very old variety which produces good quality fruit. It is a tip bearer, so take care when pruning. Good points include high yields and a hardy constitution which makes it suitable for the North — bad points are the very short fruiting season and the lack of fertile pollen.

Type: Dessert	
Fruit size: Small	
Skin colour: Greenish-yellow. Russet around stalk area	
Pollination group: B	
Picking time: Mid October	
Period of use: December–January	

JOSEPHINE DE MALINES

The best of the late varieties — you can enjoy the fruit at the start of the New Year. Quality is very good — the pale pink flesh is sweet and perfumed. Yields are high but growth is weak and weeping. It is a tip bearer with a rather delicate constitution — *Josephine* needs a warm situation in order to ensure a good set of fruit.

Type: Dessert	
Fruit size: Small–medium	
Skin colour: Yellowish-green, flushed and spotted with red	
Pollination group: A	
Picking time: Late September	
Period of use: October	

LOUISE BONNE DE JERSEY

Rated highly in the flavour league — the flesh is white, melting and sweet. Growth is upright and moderately vigorous — yields are respectable. Blossom appears early, but it is reasonably frost-tolerant. The blossom is attractive and so is the long, colourful fruit. This variety will not pollinate *Williams'* nor *Seckle*.

Doyenné du Comice

Fertility Improved

Gorham

Louise Bonne de Jersey

Merton Pride

Onward

Williams' Bon Chrétien

Winter Nelis

MERTON PRIDE

A high quality Pear — the creamy flesh is juicy and the flavour is excellent. A good cropper, but *Merton Pride* sometimes becomes a biennial bearer — see page 26. Check that the plant has been 'double worked' to ensure compatibility with the Quince rootstock. The fruits are conical and this variety appears in many recommended lists.

Type:	Dessert
Fruit size:	Medium–large
Skin colour:	Pale green. Patches of russet
Pollination group:	BT
Picking time:	Early September
Period of use:	September

ONWARD

A new Pear which is highly regarded. *Doyenné du Comice* is one of the parents, but the two varieties will not pollinate each other. Fruit quality is excellent. The problem with *Onward* is the short period of use — storage qualities are poor which means that the crop is finished by early October. Still, an excellent new variety.

Type:	Dessert
Fruit size:	Medium–large
Skin colour:	Yellowish-green, flushed with pink. Patches of russet
Pollination group:	C
Picking time:	Mid September
Period of use:	Late September

PACKHAM'S TRIUMPH

A *Williams'* type Pear which crops later in the season. Both cropping and keeping qualities are good — the conical, irregular-shaped fruit is very juicy and sweet. Tree growth is compact and upright — a reasonable choice but the early flowering habit makes it susceptible to frost. A variety recommended for milder districts.

Type:	Dessert
Fruit size:	Medium
Skin colour:	Yellow, flushed with orange
Pollination group:	A
Picking time:	Mid October
Period of use:	November–December

SECKLE

Blooms early, but the flowers are fairly frost-resistant. The small red fruit are delicious, but both vigour and cropping are usually disappointing. An old variety which has slipped out of the recommended lists and is no longer generally offered. It will not pollinate *Williams'* nor *Louise Bonne de Jersey*.

Type:	Dessert
Fruit size:	Small
Skin colour:	Reddish-brown, spotted with white
Pollination group:	Partly self-fertile: A
Picking time:	Late September
Period of use:	October–November

THOMPSON'S

Another old variety which is disappearing from the catalogues. There is nothing wrong with the fruit — the flesh is white, melting and sweet. The foliage turns red to provide an autumn display, but cropping is irregular and *Thompson's* is distinctly unhappy on an exposed site. Grow it only if flavour is all-important.

Type:	Dessert
Fruit size:	Large
Skin colour:	Golden-yellow. Small patches of russet
Pollination group:	B
Picking time:	Late September
Period of use:	October–November

WILLIAMS' BON CHRETIEN

Popular as a shop-bought fruit and as *Bartlett* Pears in tins. As a garden tree this old English variety is a regular cropper and hardy enough for northern districts. The quality of the oval, smooth-skinned fruit is very good but storage qualities are poor and so is disease resistance. Will not pollinate *Seckle* nor *Louise*.

Type:	Dessert
Fruit size:	Medium–large
Skin colour:	Pale yellow, striped and spotted with pale red
Pollination group:	B
Picking time:	September
Period of use:	September

WINTER NELIS

Winter Nellis or *Winter Nelis* — the catalogues can't agree. They do agree that this Pear is a fine late variety with fruit in good condition for Christmas or even later. Growth is slender and arching but cropping is heavy. Flowers late and blossom has good frost resistance — this makes *Winter Nelis* one of the best northern varieties.

Type:	Dessert
Fruit size:	Small–medium
Skin colour:	Green. Patches of russet
Pollination group:	C
Picking time:	Late October
Period of use:	November–January

Planting & Pruning

The site for Pears should be chosen with a little more care than for Apples. Some shelter from cold winds is essential. In northern districts choose a spot close to a wall — the microclimate will be warmer and less windy. Follow the basic rules for planting set out on pages 7–8. Plant to the old soil mark — the union with the rootstock should be about 4 in. above ground level.

Pears can be grown as bushes, dwarf pyramids, cordons, espaliers and fans in the same way as Apples. For pruning details see pages 22–23. The usual practice is to buy bushes as 2 year old trees and supported types such as cordons as 3 year old ones. Very few nurseries name the rootstock on the label — it is most likely to be Quince A. Do not plant standard or half standard Pear trees in an average-sized garden — they are far too vigorous and far too much trouble.

TREE TYPE	SPACE BETWEEN TREES	SPACE BETWEEN ROWS	YIELD PER MATURE TREE
Standard	30 ft	30 ft	100–250 lb
Half standard	20 ft	20 ft	50–125 lb
Fan	15 ft	—	12 – 24 lb
Bush	15 ft	15 ft	50–100 lb
Espalier	14 ft	6 ft	15 – 25 lb
Dwarf bush	8 ft	15 ft	20 – 40 lb
Spindlebush	7 ft	14 ft	40 – 80 lb
Dwarf pyramid	5 ft	8 ft	8 – 12 lb
Cordon	2½ ft	6 ft	4 – 6 lb

Windbreaks

Pears flower earlier than Apples, and at this time few pollinating insects are present. Turbulent air around the trees will deter them, so you should consider a windbreak if the site is exposed. A solid wall or fence over which the wind can blow will actually increase air turbulence — use a plastic windbreak through which the air can pass. A nearby hedge will provide a useful windbreak — it will gently reduce the wind speed for a distance of 15–30 times the height of the hedge.

Feeding & Mulching
see page 21

Watering
see page 21

Bird control
see page 24

Weed control
see page 24

Maypoling

A heavy crop can cause one or more branches to break. Support heavily laden branches by propping them up with a forked pole or by maypoling as shown below.

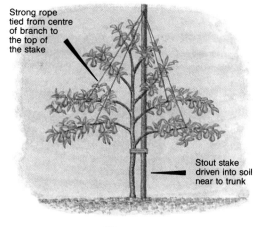

Strong rope tied from centre of branch to the top of the stake

Stout stake driven into soil near to trunk

Picking

A Pear is ripe if it readily parts from the tree when lifted gently in the palm of the hand and given a slight twist. Skill is required to judge the correct time of picking. With early-ripening varieties the fruit should be removed when they are full-sized but before they have reached the fully-ripe stage described above. Cut the stalks and leave the fruit for a few days for the full flavour to develop. Eat as they ripen — do not attempt to store. Later varieties are ripened in store. Pick when they come away from the tree quite easily.

Storage

You can follow the general rules described for Apple storage on page 24, but the experts prefer a slightly different technique. Pears are best stored in slatted trays and they should not be wrapped. The stalks should be intact and the need for careful handling and the rejection of bruised or damaged fruit is even greater than with Apples. The atmosphere around the stored fruit can be drier and warmer than in the Apple store — 45°F is quite acceptable. Ripeness is indicated by a softening near the stalk. Bring the ripe fruit into the kitchen for a few days to complete the ripening process.

PLUMS

Plums are the most popular of the stone fruits and they are also the easiest to grow. However, Plums are not for everyone. They flower very early in the season and that means cropping can be very disappointing and irregular in low-lying or exposed sites. Choose the highest spot in the garden and a position which gets lots of sun if you plan to grow a dessert Plum or Gage.

A standard or half standard has no place in the ordinary garden. Even a bush or pyramid on the popular St Julien A rootstock can reach 20 ft or more when mature. This would be a problem in a small garden. One way of tackling the problem would be to choose a specimen grafted on to Pixy (see below). Perhaps the best way of saving space is to grow the Plum as a fan against a south-facing wall. Note that Plums are not grown as espaliers nor cordons. An added advantage of the fan growth form is the ease with which netting can be used to protect the buds and fruit from birds.

Cropping should start when the tree is about 5 years old — earlier if Pixy rootstock is used. The mature tree is easily cared for, but the dreaded silver leaf disease is a constant threat. Choose your plant with care — some fruit are sweet and others are sour. There are several distinct types as described below.

MATURE BUSH 15–25 ft high	DESSERT PLUM	CULINARY PLUM	GAGE
	Sweet — eaten fresh. Fleshy fruit — trees smaller and less hardy than culinary varieties. Most popular variety: *Victoria*	Rather tart — used for cooking. Fruit less fleshy than dessert varieties — trees more tolerant of poor conditions. Most popular variety: *Czar*	Smaller, rounder and sweeter than dessert Plums. Yields are not high. Rather tender — grow as a fan against a south wall

MATURE BUSH 10–15 ft high	BULLACE	DAMSON	MIRABELLE
	Sharp flavour — used for cooking. Fruit left until late autumn before picking. Choose a Damson variety instead	Spicy tart flavour — used for cooking, jam- and wine-making. A hardy tree which succeeds where a Plum would fail	Similar in shape to Bullace, but sweeter and golden-yellow. Found in the textbooks but not in the catalogues

MATURE BUSH 20–30 ft high	MYROBALAN (CHERRY PLUM)
	A decorative Plum used as a specimen tree and for hedging — attractive blossom in March. Cherry-like fruit in July which can be used for cooking or jam-making

Rootstocks

The most widely used rootstock is **St Julien A** — this is the one to choose if conditions are less than ideal. A newer dwarfing form (**Pixy**) is becoming quite popular as it produces bushes with a mature height of only 10–15 ft. You do need good soil and good growing conditions for Pixy-rooted Plums — some nurserymen do not recommend this rootstock for northern districts.

Other stocks are available. **Myrobalan B** is far too vigorous for ordinary gardens. **Brompton** comes to fruit quickly and resists suckering, but it is much more vigorous than St Julien A. **Mussel** produces a more compact tree than either Myrobalan B or Brompton.

Varieties A-Z

Pollination Groups

A Early flowering	None listed here — early frosts can cause havoc. Some are offered in the catalogues: Ariel Ontario Farleigh Damson Warwickshire Drooper
B Mid-season flowering	CZAR PERSHORE YELLOW DENNISTON'S SUPERB PURPLE PERSHORE EARLY LAXTON RIVERS' EARLY EDWARDS PROLIFIC MERRYWEATHER SANCTUS HUBERTUS OPAL VICTORIA
C Late flowering	CAMBRIDGE GAGE KIRKE'S BLUE EARLY TRANSPARENT MARJORIE'S SEEDLING GAGE OULLIN'S GOLDEN GIANT PRUNE GAGE

Plums are one of the earliest fruit trees to open their flowers in the spring, which means that pollination is sometimes disappointing. Hand pollination of a well-grown Plum is worth while — see page 41.

Many Plums are self-fertile, including the most popular dessert variety (*Victoria*) and the most widely grown cooker (*Czar*). Others need a pollination partner chosen from the same or an adjacent group — see the table on the left. Buy 2 or 3 year old partly-trained trees and if the site is unfavourable choose varieties in the late flowering group. *Victoria* remains a good overall choice — it is reliable and flavour is acceptable, but it is susceptible to silver leaf disease.

Type:	Bullace
Use:	Culinary
Fruit size:	Very small
Skin colour:	Blue–black
Pollination group:	Self-fertile
Period of use:	November

BULLACE
Search all the catalogues and you will find a supplier, but it really isn't worth growing. The yellow variety (*Shepherd's Bullace*) is even more difficult to find. The sharp-flavoured fruits have to be left on the thorny branches until late autumn in order to allow early frosts to mellow the acidity. The wild form grows in hedgerows.

Bullace

Type:	Gage
Use:	Dessert/Culinary
Fruit size:	Small
Skin colour:	Yellowish–green, flushed with red
Pollination group:	Partly self-fertile: C
Period of use:	Early September

CAMBRIDGE GAGE
Very similar to the old *Greengage* but more reliable and a heavier cropper. The flesh is yellowish–green and juicy — flavour is very good. Growth is vigorous, but this variety cannot be recommended for cold areas. Unlike the traditional *Greengage* it does set some fruit without a partner. You will find *Cambridge Gage* in nearly all the catalogues.

Cambridge Gage

Type:	Myrobalan
Use:	Culinary
Fruit size:	Small
Skin colour:	Red or yellow
Pollination group:	Self-fertile
Period of use:	Late July

CHERRY PLUM
The Cherry Plum is not really a 'fruit' tree — it is usually grown as a hedge or as a round-headed decorative tree. The shiny leaves are not distorted by greenfly in the same way as ordinary Plums. The flesh of the small fruits is yellow and juicy — they are used for bottling or stewing and occasionally for eating fresh.

Type:	Plum
Use:	Culinary
Fruit size:	Medium
Skin colour:	Dark purple
Pollination group:	Self-fertile: B
Period of use:	Early August

CZAR
The cooking variety most people choose — the oval fruits have yellowish–green flesh which has a good acidic flavour. *Czar* can be used as a dessert Plum when fully ripe. It is one of the most reliable varieties in less-than-perfect areas as its frost resistance is high, but *Czar* has low disease resistance. Growth is upright.

Czar

Type:	Gage
Use:	Dessert
Fruit size:	Large
Skin colour:	Greenish-yellow, streaked with dark green
Pollination group:	Self-fertile: B
Period of use:	Late August

DENNISTON'S SUPERB
Listed with the Gages but it is really a Plum. *Denniston's Superb* has a good reputation for hardiness and reliability — growth is upright and vigorous. The transparent flesh is sweet and the skin often has a red flush. Yields are high and this variety is widely recommended for midland and northern regions.

TREE FRUIT: PLUMS

Early Laxton

Early Transparent Gage

Marjorie's Seedling

Merryweather

EARLY LAXTON

The first of the popular varieties to ripen — the round and firm fruits are picked before the end of July. A dessert variety — the flavour is acceptable but certainly not outstanding. *Early Laxton* is sometimes used for cooking — the golden flesh is juicy. A compact variety with none of the vigour of *Denniston's Superb* nor *Marjorie's Seedling*.

Type:	Plum
Use:	Dessert
Fruit size:	Small
Skin colour:	Yellow, flushed with pink
Pollination group:	Partly self-fertile: B
Period of use:	Late July

EARLY TRANSPARENT GAGE

Choose this one for flavour — the golden, melting flesh is very sweet. Don't expect bumper crops — growth is neat and upright, and the round fruits are small. Still, it is a reliable variety and a regular cropper — no years of plenty and then famine with this one. *Early Transparent Gage* is available from specialist fruit nurseries.

Type:	Gage
Use:	Dessert
Fruit size:	Small
Skin colour:	Yellow, spotted with red
Pollination group:	Self-fertile: C
Period of use:	August

EDWARDS

A new variety which has created a good deal of interest. The fruit is very large, ripening when the *Victoria* season is over. It is primarily used for stewing and bottling, but it is suitable for dessert purposes when fully ripe. The flesh is creamy white. Crops are heavy — it is too early to comment on disease resistance.

Type:	Plum
Use:	Culinary
Fruit size:	Very large
Skin colour:	Blue
Pollination group:	B
Period of use:	September

GIANT PRUNE

An awful name, but a reliable variety which is a prolific cropper. The fruit is long and oval, and it keeps much better than the average Plum. The flesh is purple — excellent for cooking but also acceptable for eating fresh. The growth habit is moderate and both frost and disease resistance are better than average.

Type:	Plum
Use:	Culinary
Fruit size:	Large
Skin colour:	Dark red
Pollination group:	Self-fertile: C
Period of use:	September

KIRKE'S BLUE

All the suppliers sing the praises of the eating qualities of this dark-coloured Plum. The greenish-yellow flesh is firm but juicy with an outstandingly sweet flavour. The tree is easy to train as growth is compact, but there are drawbacks. Yields are often disappointing and it needs a sheltered spot in the garden if it is to thrive.

Type:	Plum
Use:	Dessert
Fruit size:	Large
Skin colour:	Dark purple
Pollination group:	C
Period of use:	Early September

MARJORIE'S SEEDLING

Marjorie's Seedling is an excellent choice if you want a late Plum which can be used for cooking and eating fresh. The oval fruit has yellow flesh and is moderately sweet when fully ripe. Growth is both vigorous and upright, and the blossom season is late enough to miss early frosts. Picking starts at the end of September but can continue until mid October.

Type:	Plum
Use:	Dessert/Culinary
Fruit size:	Large
Skin colour:	Purple
Pollination group:	Self-fertile: C
Period of use:	Late September

MERRYWEATHER

This Damson has the characteristic features you would expect from this group — blue-black skin, yellow flesh which is juicy and acidic, and a hardy constitution. *Merryweather* is an excellent all-round performer and you will find it in most catalogues, but the other popular Damson (*Shropshire Damson*) is a better choice where space is limited.

Type:	Damson
Use:	Culinary
Fruit size:	Large for a Damson
Skin colour:	Blue-black
Pollination group:	Self-fertile: B
Period of use:	Late September

Type:	Plum
Use:	Dessert
Fruit size:	Medium
Skin colour:	Reddish-purple
Pollination group:	Self-fertile: B
Period of use:	Late July

OPAL

A new variety to rival *Early Laxton* for the early Plum crown. *Opal's* flavour is better — there is a distinct Gage-like texture and taste. A feature noted in the catalogues is the ease with which the yellow flesh parts from the stone. *Opal* has not had time to establish a long-term reputation. It is easy to manage but the buds are extremely attractive to birds.

Opal

Type:	Gage
Use:	Dessert/Culinary
Fruit size:	Large
Skin colour:	Golden-yellow, spotted with green or brown
Pollination group:	Self-fertile: C
Period of use:	Mid August

OULLIN'S GOLDEN GAGE

The best choice of all, according to some experts. It is not a true Gage — it is a Gage-like Plum. The fruit is large and round and the yellow transparent flesh is moderately but not outstandingly sweet. The fruit is excellent for bottling and freezing as well as for eating fresh. Growth is vigorous, upright and reasonably healthy.

Type:	Plum
Use:	Culinary
Fruit size:	Medium
Skin colour:	Golden-yellow
Pollination group:	Self-fertile: B
Period of use:	Mid August

PERSHORE YELLOW

Here is the one for yellow Plum jam and golden pie filling. An excellent cooker, but the flavour is rather insipid for eating fresh. The tree is one of the most reliable you can choose. Advantages include good frost resistance, regular cropping and heavy yields. It is self-fertile, so no pollination partner has to be provided.

Oullin's Golden Gage

Type:	Plum
Use:	Culinary
Fruit size:	Medium
Skin colour:	Bluish-purple
Pollination group:	Self-fertile: B
Period of use:	Mid August

PURPLE PERSHORE

The purple equivalent of *Pershore Yellow*. The same excellent cooking qualities are there, but this time you get purple stewed fruit, jam or tart filling. Some experts feel that the flavour is superior to the yellow variety. The same desirable growth properties are found — good disease resistance, prolific cropping and reliability.

Type:	Plum
Use:	Culinary
Fruit size:	Small
Skin colour:	Bluish-purple
Pollination group:	B
Period of use:	Early August

RIVERS' EARLY PROLIFIC

Everyone agrees that this rather small and spreading tree lives up to its name — it is both early and prolific. The round or oval fruit are quite small but they are golden-fleshed and juicy with a moderately good flavour. It can be used as a dessert variety when the fruit is fully ripe. The best or worst of the earlies — the experts can't agree.

Purple Pershore

Type:	Plum
Use:	Dessert/Culinary
Fruit size:	Medium
Skin colour:	Bluish-purple
Pollination group:	Partly self-fertile: B
Period of use:	Early August

SANCTUS HUBERTUS

A new variety from Belgium which promises to take over from *Rivers' Early Prolific*. The fruit is larger and there is a heavy grey bloom. The flowers are partly self-fertile. The flavour is good enough to make it a dual-purpose Plum and the tree is easy to manage. Unfortunately there are very few suppliers, but this should change.

Type:	Plum
Use:	Dessert/Culinary
Fruit size:	Large
Skin colour:	Pale red
Pollination group:	Self-fertile: B
Period of use:	Late August

VICTORIA

Still the most popular Plum with both amateur and commercial growers. Flesh is yellowish-green. "If you can grow only one, this is it" say many catalogues. However, do think twice. It is a reliable and heavy cropper, but thinning is often essential to avoid biennial bearing. Its disease resistance is poor and flavour is only average.

Victoria

Planting

Plums need a moisture-retentive but free-draining soil. Light soils which easily dry out must be enriched with humus. November is the best time for planting. Staking will be required for 5–6 years.

TREE TYPE	SPACE BETWEEN TREES	SPACE BETWEEN ROWS	YIELD PER MATURE TREE
Standard	25 ft	25 ft	50–100 lb
Half standard	20 ft	20 ft	30 – 60 lb
Fan	15 ft	—	12 – 24 lb
Bush	14 ft	14 ft	30 – 50 lb
Pyramid	12 ft	12 ft	30 – 50 lb

Pruning

There are 2 basic points to remember — do not prune in winter and paint all cuts with Arbrex. These measures are necessary to reduce the risk of silver leaf infection.

BUSHES

Training a 2 or 3 year old tree

Prune in March. The simplest procedure is to follow the plan for Apples — see page 22. The goal is to have 3–5 strong branches at the 2 year old stage — these branches should be as near to horizontal as possible. At the 3 year stage there should be about 8 strong primary and secondary branches which are well-spaced.

Pruning an established tree

Prune in June–late July. Keep pruning to a minimum. The sole purpose of cutting out wood at this stage is to keep the tree healthy and to reduce overcrowding. Remove dead, broken and diseased branches. Cut back overcrowded branches. Suckers growing around the base should be removed at this stage. Pull them up — do not cut off with secateurs.

FANS

Create the framework of the tree by following the instructions for Peaches — see page 44.

In spring rub away buds growing towards or away from the wall

In July pinch the side-shoots back to 6 leaves

After harvest cut back the side-shoots to half their length

Seasonal care

Bird damage can be severe. Both buds in spring and fruit in summer are at risk. Cover the tree with netting if practical.

Water regularly in dry weather — apply up to 5 gallons per sq. yard every 10 days until the dry weather breaks. Avoid heavy watering at irregular intervals, as fruit splitting can result.

Hoe to keep down weeds around the base of the tree, but avoid hoeing deeply at all costs. Surface root damage will result in sucker formation.

Fruit overcrowding results in small, tasteless fruit and biennial bearing. Thin with scissors in early June and again at the end of the month if the crop is heavy — leave fruit 3–4 in. apart. Support overladen branches by post support or by maypoling — see page 31.

Feeding & Mulching

See page 21. Plums require more nitrogen than Apples — apply a late spring application of a nitrogen-rich liquid fertilizer such as Leaf Maker.

Picking & Storage

A Plum is ripe when it parts easily from the tree. With Plums the stalk usually remains on the branch — with Gages and Damsons the stalk comes away with the fruit. Pick dessert varieties when thoroughly ripe — go over the tree several times. Culinary varieties should be harvested while the fruit is still slightly unripe — use within 1–2 weeks.

Dessert Plums will keep for only a few days. They can be kept for 2–3 weeks in a cool place if picked when still unripe and with the stalks attached. Remove stones from Plums before freezing.

CHERRIES

Until quite recently there was no point in trying to grow a sweet Cherry in an average-sized garden. The spring blossom was attractive, but the tree would grow steadily until it became a monster with a spread and height of about 40 ft. This meant that proper maintenance was extremely difficult, and the need for a pollination partner meant that two trees had to be grown. At least the chore of picking was unnecessary — without protection the fruit merely served as living bird food.

Things began to change in the late 1970s when the self-fertile *Stella* was introduced. At about the same time Colt rootstock enabled trees to be maintained at 15–20 ft. Grown as a pyramid it is possible to restrict growth to about 10 ft and it is even practical to grow *Stella* grafted on to Colt in a pot on the patio. Treat it in the same way as a pot-grown Apple, but prune in April instead of winter — see page 25.

The speed of change has begun to quicken. *Compact Stella* has been introduced — a less vigorous sport of *Stella*. New self-fertile varieties have come over from Canada — you will find *Cherokee* and *Sunburst* in one or more specialist catalogues. Even more interesting is the dwarfing rootstock Inmil (GM9). The promise is for trees that grow to a maximum height of 6–7 ft — and that means netting the branches and reaching the fruit will no longer be a problem. Cherries on this rootstock are beginning to appear in the catalogues, but some growers are awaiting the outcome of further trials before introducing Inmil-grafted Cherries.

Until the sweet Cherry revolution described above it was traditional to choose an acid Cherry variety for garden cultivation. Growth is much more compact and the most popular variety (*Morello*) is self-fertile. Trees begin to bear fruit after only 3 or 4 years and the acid Cherries grow quite happily in some shade. This means that *Morello* can be trained as a fan against a north-facing wall.

So Cherry-growing is a practical proposition nowadays, and you don't have to restrict yourself to an acid variety. All you need for a sweet Cherry fan is an 8 ft high wall in full sun and the application of netting when birds are active.

SWEET (Dessert) CHERRY

Sweet — eaten fresh. Flesh is either soft and very juicy or firm and moist. Skin colour ranges from pale yellow to near black. Traditionally very vigorous and self-incompatible, but semi-vigorous and self-fertile trees are now available.

ACID (Sour or Culinary) CHERRY

Sour — used for cooking, bottling, jam, wine-making etc. Flesh may be white, pink or red. *Morello* is the usual choice, but other self-fertile acid varieties such as *Nabella* are available.

DUKE CHERRY

A cross between the sweet and acid Cherry — the flavour is intermediate between the two. Flesh is juicy. *May Duke* is the only variety you are likely to find.

Rootstocks

Until the mid 1970s we had to make do with the vigorous rootstock **Malling F12/1**. Trees grown on this stock require a lot of space and you have to wait a number of years before fruiting begins. The introduction of the dwarfing rootstock **Colt** has resulted in trees which grow to only about half the height of an F12/1-grafted Cherry. Not a dwarf tree, but still practical as a fan for the average garden.

An even more dwarfing rootstock (**Inmil** or **GM9**) has recently been introduced from Belgium. *Stella* and *Morello* on GM9 are now available, but its long-term behaviour in the U.K is not yet known.

Varieties A-Z

Choose a self-fertile variety. Pick the well-established *Stella* if you want a sweet variety, or you can choose one of the new ones — *Compact Stella* or *Sunburst. Morello* is the acid Cherry chosen by nearly everyone although you could try the recently-introduced *Nabella.*

Other varieties require a pollination partner, and the situation with Cherries is complex. Take care to pick a suitable partner — it will have to flower at approximately the same time and it will also have to be compatible. Not all varieties with the same time of flowering are compatible, so with Cherries a specific partner is usually named.

Pollination Partners

Stella, Noir de Guben or Merchant can be used
to pollinate nearly all the varieties listed below.
Specific pollinators, where one is needed, are shown here:

Variety	Pollen Provider
COMPACT STELLA	Self-fertile
EARLY RIVERS	Governor Wood, Noir de Guben
GOVERNOR WOOD	Napoleon Bigarreau, Stella
MAY DUKE	Partly self-fertile
MERCHANT	Early Rivers, Noir de Guben
MERTON BIGARREAU	Governor Wood, Morello
MERTON GLORY	Merton Bigarreau, Morello
MORELLO	Self-fertile
NABELLA	Self-fertile
NAPOLEON BIGARREAU	Morello, Stella
NOIR DE GUBEN	Early Rivers, Merton Glory
STELLA	Self-fertile
SUNBURST	Self-fertile
VAN	Merton Glory, Stella

Compact Stella

Merchant

Merton Bigarreau

COMPACT STELLA

A compact form of *Stella* which is less vigorous and less spreading. All of the basic properties of the most popular sweet Cherry are there. It readily forms spurs and both bushes and fans grafted on to Colt (but not on to GM9) are available.

Type:	Sweet
Fruit size:	Large
Skin colour:	Dark red
Picking time:	Late July

EARLY RIVERS

Introduced over 100 years ago and still popular. A black Cherry noted for both its earliness and fruit size. Both skin and flesh are very dark and flavour is excellent. Cropping is both heavy and regular, but its vigour and spreading habit can be a problem.

Type:	Sweet
Fruit size:	Very large
Skin colour:	Near black
Picking time:	Mid June

GOVERNOR WOOD

A yellow-fleshed Cherry with a good but not out-standing flavour. Either yellow or red may be the predominant colour of the skin and crops are usually very heavy. A popular variety — you should have no difficulty in finding a supplier.

Type:	Sweet
Fruit size:	Medium-large
Skin colour:	Dark red, flushed with yellow
Picking time:	Early July

MAY DUKE

Generally agreed to be the best of the duke Cherries. It is compact with only moderate vigour like an acid variety, but it should be pruned in the same way as a sweet Cherry. The flavour is tart but not unpleasant. Cropping is only moderate.

Type:	Duke
Fruit size:	Large
Skin colour:	Dark red
Picking time:	Mid July

MERCHANT

A new variety with a number of virtues. The fruit is large and the yields are heavy, and there is some resistance to bacterial canker. It is not self-fertile, but it will pollinate all the other varieties listed here. Not yet widely available.

Type:	Sweet
Fruit size:	Very large
Skin colour:	Dark red or near black
Picking time:	Early July

MERTON BIGARREAU

This large, black Cherry contains flesh which is dark red and firm. The flavour is outstanding and *Merton Bigarreau* is a heavy cropper. This variety from the John Innes Institute has no important drawbacks, but it has higher-than-average vigour.

Type:	Sweet
Fruit size:	Large
Skin colour:	Near black
Picking time:	Mid July

Type:	Sweet
Fruit size:	Very large
Skin colour:	Yellow, flushed with red
Picking time:	Late June

MERTON GLORY

This is the one to choose if you want an outstandingly large yellow Cherry early in the season. The white flesh is firm and the fruit is heart-shaped rather than round. Growth is distinctly upright and trees are quite widely available.

Merton Glory

Type:	Acid
Fruit size:	Large
Skin colour:	Near black
Picking time:	August

MORELLO

By far the most popular acid Cherry — until recently the only self-fertile one. It can be picked at the very sour, dark red stage for stewing or it can be left under netting until near black and bitter-sweet. The flesh is dark red — growth is compact and spreading.

Type:	Acid
Fruit size:	Medium
Skin colour:	Near black
Picking time:	August

NABELLA

A new one from Germany — a black self-fertile acid variety. It is claimed that yields are high and growth is compact, but *Morello* is also blessed with these virtues. "Excellent flavour" according to the supplier — try it if you are novelty-minded.

Morello

Type:	Sweet
Fruit size:	Medium-large
Skin colour:	Pale yellow, flushed with dark red
Picking time:	Early August

NAPOLEON BIGARREAU

One of the great Bigarreau or fleshy varieties, introduced into Britain 150 years ago. Renowned for generations for its firm, very sweet flesh. It is a heavy cropper and you will have no trouble in finding a supplier. Sometimes sold as *Bigarreau Napoleon*.

Type:	Sweet
Fruit size:	Large
Skin colour:	Near black
Picking time:	Early July

NOIR DE GUBEN

The outstanding point with *Noir de Guben* is its high resistance to bacterial canker. The drawback is the less-than-average yield. The firm, red flesh has an acceptable flavour and it makes a good pollination partner for all the varieties listed here.

Napoleon Bigarreau

Type:	Sweet
Fruit size:	Large
Skin colour:	Dark red
Picking time:	Late July

STELLA

The first self-fertile sweet Cherry — the No.1 choice for garden use. Growth is vigorous — upright at first and later spreading. The flavour is good and the flesh is juicy. A good pollinator for other Cherries. Fruit may be dark red or near black.

Type:	Sweet
Fruit size:	Large
Skin colour:	Near black
Picking time:	Early July

SUNBURST

A new one from British Columbia — the first self-fertile and black sweet Cherry. Similar to *Stella* in general growth habit, but the fruit is much darker. The U.K supplier claims "a gorgeous flavour". Try it and see — you won't need a pollination partner.

Stella

Type:	Sweet
Fruit size:	Large
Skin colour:	Dark red
Picking time:	Late July

VAN

Van is chosen for its reliability. Cropping is both regular and heavy, but growth is very vigorous. Not a good choice where space is limited. The dark red flesh is firm — the flavour is sweet and some consider it to be superb.

Planting

Sweet Cherries need a sheltered site in full sun — acid varieties are less fussy. Both types need deep soil which should be moisture-retentive but free-draining. Don't bother to grow Cherries in shallow or sandy soil. November is the best time for planting.

TREE TYPE	CHERRY TYPE	ROOTSTOCK	SPACE BETWEEN TREES	SPACE BETWEEN ROWS	YIELD PER MATURE TREE
Standard	Sweet	F12/1	35 ft	35 ft	100 lb
Half standard	Sweet	F12/1	25 ft	25 ft	70 lb
Bush	Sweet	F12/1	25 ft	25 ft	50 lb
Fan	Sweet	F12/1	20 ft	—	25 lb
Bush	Sweet	Colt	15 ft	15 ft	35 lb
Fan	Sweet	Colt	15 ft	—	20 lb
Bush	Acid	F12/1	20 ft	20 ft	40 lb
Fan	Acid	F12/1	20 ft	—	20 lb
Bush	Acid	Colt	15 ft	15 ft	30 lb
Fan	Acid	Colt	15 ft	—	20 lb
Pyramid	Sweet	Colt	12 ft	12 ft	25 lb

Pruning

Do not prune in winter and paint all cuts with Arbrex. These measures are necessary to reduce the risk of silver leaf and bacterial canker infection.

SWEET CHERRY : BUSHES

Follow the rules laid down for Plum bushes (page 36) for both the training of young trees and the pruning of established trees.

SWEET CHERRY : FANS

Follow the training procedure given for Peach fans — see page 44. With established fans follow the diagrams on page 36. In April rub away unnecessary buds and in July pinch back the tips of new shoots. In September shorten these shoots again, leaving 3 or 4 buds.

ACID CHERRY : BUSHES

Follow the training procedure given for Plum bushes — see page 36. With established trees remove dead, diseased and broken branches in spring but leave healthy old wood. Fruit will only develop on young shoots, so each year after harvest remove some of the poor-yielding branches in order to stimulate new growth.

ACID CHERRY : FANS

Follow the training procedure given for Peach fans — see page 44. With established fans remove inward- or outward-facing buds in April. Fruit will only develop on young shoots, so each year after harvest cut back each fruited stem to the replacement shoot at its base — see Peach pruning for details.

Seasonal care

Hessian or netting draped over the bush or fan in spring will help to protect the blossom from frost damage. Avoid damaging the blossom.

Netting to prevent bird damage is essential for sweet and duke Cherries — with unprotected trees, bullfinches devour many buds in winter and early spring — ripe fruits are removed by other birds in summer. Unnetted *Morello* Cherries should be harvested at the unripe red-fruit stage to avoid the inevitable attack on ripe fruit.

Water regularly in dry weather — apply up to 5 gallons per sq. yard every 10 days until the dry weather breaks. Avoid heavy watering at irregular intervals as fruit splitting can result.

Keep grass away from the trunk. For the first 4 years it is wise to keep the grass about 2–3 ft away from the base of the tree.

Feeding & Mulching

See page 21 — both annual feeding and mulching are necessary for Cherries. Acid varieties require more feeding than sweet ones — apply a later spring application of a nitrogen-rich liquid fertilizer.

Picking & Storage

Sweet Cherries should be left on the tree until they are ripe — try one or two in order to tell if the sweet and juicy stage has been reached. Harvest immediately if fruits are starting to crack. Eat as soon as possible after picking, although sweet Cherries can be frozen. Red and black ones are best — the yellow ones tend to become discoloured in the deep freeze. Use in fruit salad when thawed.

Use scissors or secateurs when harvesting acid Cherries — pulling off fruits can encourage the entry of disease. Cut off with the stalk attached.

PEACHES & NECTARINES

Peaches can be successfully grown in England. This delicious fruit is well-known in both its shop-bought and canned form — less well-known is its smooth-skinned sport, the Nectarine. There is no point in pretending that the cultivation of both of these fruits outdoors is anything but a gamble in most areas. In East Anglia and most of the South East the chance of success is quite high — in the Midlands and the North it is quite low.

Hardiness is not the problem — a cold winter is actually helpful. Trouble may start as early as February when the blossom opens — pollinating insects are scarce and frosty nights are plentiful. High rainfall and high winds are distinctly harmful, and there must be a hot and sunny summer to ensure successful ripening of the fruit.

Plan carefully if you want to take the gamble. Unless the site is extremely favourable, choose a Peach and not a Nectarine — Nectarines are more delicate and yields are much lower. Next, grow as a fan and not as a bush. Bushes are much easier to care for and give higher yields, but fans benefit greatly from the extra warmth and extra frost- and wind-protection provided by the wall. This wall should face South or South-West — don't even bother to try to grow a Peach if it faces in any other direction.

Choose a tried-and-tested variety such as *Peregrine* or *Rochester* — it should have a picking time of mid September or earlier for southern counties — mid August or earlier for midland regions. The earlier the ripening time, the greater the chance of success. Peaches and Nectarines are self-fertile, and that means a pollination partner is not necessary. Follow the cultural rules laid down in the following pages, and remember to carry out a peach leaf curl spraying programme every year — see page 53. As you can see from the above information and from the pruning instructions on page 44, there is no easy way to grow Peaches and Nectarines.

Perhaps the most straightforward technique is to grow *Duke of York* or *Peregrine* on St Julien A or Pixy rootstock in a 15 in. pot. Move the pot indoors from February until the danger of frost is past — then keep on a warm and sheltered patio. After harvest cut back all the branches that have borne fruit to a point where a new shoot has arisen.

Growing under glass

Growing a Peach or Nectarine under glass removes many of the problems which the outdoor tree has to face. The best location is undoubtedly the wall of a lean-to greenhouse — this wall must face South-West, South or South-East. Plant a partly-trained fan in well-prepared border soil and then create the basic framework against the supporting wires by following the rules on page 44. Prune the established indoor fan in the same way as an outdoor one.

Close up the house in January, then ventilate if the temperature reaches 60°–65°F. High humidity is essential — spray the floor and mist the foliage in sunny weather. Regular watering is also necessary — in summer that may mean once or even twice a day. Feed regularly with a high-potash fertilizer such as Tomato Food from the start of flowering until the fruit is almost full-sized. Keep pests and diseases in check — peach leaf curl won't be a problem but red spider mite and greenfly will.

Keep the house cool after harvest. Open up the ventilators and don't worry if winter temperatures fall to freezing point.

Rootstocks

Peaches and Nectarines are nearly always grafted on to **St Julien A** — a semi-vigorous rootstock which produces fans and bushes with a 15 ft spread. Both **Brompton** and **Peach Seedling** are vigorous stocks which are used by professional growers but are not recommended for the home gardener.

Plants grafted on to the dwarfing stock **Pixy** are more difficult to find, although compact trees are produced which grow only 6–8 ft high and wide. These dwarfs come into fruit very quickly, but the yield is quite small and the need for good soil and good growing conditions is greater.

Hand pollination

Peach and Nectarine blossom opens very early in the season when pollinating insects are scarce, so it is a good idea to give Nature a helping hand. Dab the flowers gently with a ball of cotton wool or a soft-bristled brush every day or two from the time the buds open until the petals fall. Hand pollination is, of course, essential for Peaches and Nectarines grown under glass — close the ventilators and dampen the floor afterwards in order to encourage fertilization.

Varieties A-Z

Duke of York

Early Rivers

Humboldt

AMSDEN JUNE

The first Peach to ripen — a great advantage in our climate. But *Amsden June* is not a heavy cropper and the fruit is not an attractive colour. Still, the creamy-white flesh inside the round Peach does have a good flavour. Grow outdoors or under glass.

Type:	Peach
Fruit size:	Medium
Skin colour:	Greenish-white, flushed with red
Picking time:	Mid July

BELLEGARDE

A variety with lots of virtues — the fruit is large or very large, the flesh a deep yellow and the flavour is extremely good. The tree gives high yields but there is a major drawback. It ripens very late and so is only really suitable for the greenhouse.

Type:	Peach
Fruit size:	Large
Skin colour:	Golden-yellow, flushed with dark red
Picking time:	Mid September

DUKE OF YORK

If you don't choose *Peregrine* or *Rochester* for reliability then it should be *Duke of York* for fruit quality. The pale yellow flesh is very juicy and the flavour is deliciously refreshing. It crops heavily and does well on a south-facing wall.

Type:	Peach
Fruit size:	Large
Skin colour:	Yellow, heavily flushed with crimson
Picking time:	Mid July

EARLY RIVERS

Early Rivers and the rather similar *John Rivers* are the first Nectarines to ripen. The yellow flesh is juicy and the flavour is good. Fruit is borne freely, but despite its earliness this variety is not as popular as *Lord Napier*.

Type:	Nectarine
Fruit size:	Large
Skin colour:	Yellow, streaked with red
Picking time:	Late July

ELRUGE

You will have to search the catalogues for this one, as its late-ripening habit demands a very favourable spot outdoors. Good when grown under glass. The nearly round fruit has almost white flesh with a good flavour like all Nectarines.

Type:	Nectarine
Fruit size:	Medium
Skin colour:	Pale green, flushed with dark purple
Picking time:	Late August

HAYLES EARLY

This one crops very heavily and is early enough to make it a sound choice for growing outdoors. Its prolific nature means that thinning is essential in a good season. The flesh is melting rather than firm and the flavour is average.

Type:	Peach
Fruit size:	Medium
Skin colour:	Yellow, flushed and blotched with red
Picking time:	Late July

HUMBOLDT

Don't choose this one for outdoors — *Lord Napier* is much more reliable. The situation is different when growing in the greenhouse — *Humboldt* is a very heavy cropper, producing fruit with golden flesh and a distinctive rich flavour.

Type:	Nectarine
Fruit size:	Large
Skin colour:	Orange, flushed with red
Picking time:	Late August

LORD NAPIER

The most popular Nectarine for growing at home. It ripens reasonably early and the white flesh is aromatic and full of flavour. It is both a regular and heavy cropper. *Lord Napier* deserves its popularity and is the one to choose for outdoors.

Type:	Nectarine
Fruit size:	Large
Skin colour:	Yellow, flushed with red
Picking time:	Early August

Type:	Peach
Fruit size:	Large
Skin colour:	Crimson
Picking time:	Early August

Type:	Nectarine
Fruit size:	Medium–large
Skin colour:	Yellow, flushed with red
Picking time:	Early September

Type:	Peach
Fruit size:	Medium
Skin colour:	Yellow, heavily flushed with dark red
Picking time:	Mid August

Type:	Peach
Fruit size:	Medium
Skin colour:	Yellow, flushed with dark red
Picking time:	Mid August

Type:	Peach
Fruit size:	Large
Skin colour:	Yellow, flushed with dark red
Picking time:	Late August

PEREGRINE

The No.1 Peach choice by gardeners, and also the best choice according to some experts. It has the features you want — the flesh is juicy with an excellent flavour and the tree is reliable. Yields are high and nothing succeeds better against a wall outdoors.

PINE APPLE

Early autumn ripening rules out this Nectarine for growing outdoors, but it is an excellent choice for greenhouse cultivation. The yellow flesh is melting in texture and the rich flavour is outstanding. A hint of Pineapple, according to the catalogues.

RED HAVEN

A round Peach with a good reputation for reliability in southern counties. It crops well and the fruit is attractive. The yellow flesh is firm but juicy with a distinct red tinge around the stone. The flavour is good but not outstanding.

ROCHESTER

Rochester nearly matches *Peregrine* in popularity and is usually considered to be the best all-round variety. The flavour is not as good but the yellow flesh is firm and juicy and the tree is thoroughly reliable. It flowers rather late, thereby missing early frosts.

ROYAL GEORGE

Not an early ripening Peach, so it's for southern walls only. You will find it in a number of catalogues because of its virtues. Crops are heavy and the round fruits have juicy aromatic flesh with a very rich flavour. Good under glass.

Peregrine

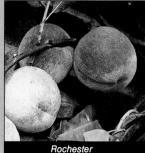
Rochester

Planting

A sheltered, sunny site is essential — the soil should be free-draining but also moisture-retentive. November is the best time for a bare-rooted plant — early autumn for a container-grown one. Plant a fan about 9 in. away from the wall — slope the stem slightly inwards when planting.

TREE TYPE	FRUIT TYPE	ROOTSTOCK	SPACE BETWEEN TREES	SPACE BETWEEN ROWS	YIELD PER MATURE TREE
Bush	Peach	Brompton	20 ft	20 ft	50 lb
Bush	Peach	St Julien A	15 ft	15 ft	40 lb
Bush	Peach	Pixy	10 ft	10 ft	25 lb
Fan	Peach	St Julien A	15 ft	—	20 lb
Fan	Nectarine	St Julien A	12 ft	—	10 lb
Fan	Peach	Pixy	8 ft	—	10 lb

Pruning

Do not prune in winter and paint all cuts with Arbrex. These measures are necessary to reduce the risk of silver leaf and bacterial canker infection.

BUSHES

Prune in spring. Follow the training procedure for Plum bushes — see page 36. Remove all blossom which appears in the season after planting.

For pruning of established trees follow the routine given for acid Cherry bushes — see page 40.

FANS

Training a 2 or 3 year old tree

Buy a partly-trained 2 or 3 year old tree with 8 or more branches. Starting from scratch with a maiden will save a little money, but it will mean a lot of extra work and the loss of a season or two.

(3) Spread out the remaining canes to form a well-shaped fan — tie to the wires

(1) Tie each branch ('rib') to a cane

(2) Tie the canes of the 2 primary branches to the wires at an angle of 45° to the ground

(4) In February cut about one-third off each rib, pruning back to a bud. More ribs will develop — tie into wires to cover whole area evenly

Pruning an established tree

In spring remove any shoots growing inwards or outwards. Then pinch out growth buds on each flowering lateral to leave one at the base, one in the middle and one at the top

In May cut back each shoot to 6 leaves

After harvest cut out the fruited lateral — tie in the replacement lateral

Seasonal care

Hessian or netting placed over the fan or bush in early spring should be used to protect the blossom from frost damage. Remove netting during the day to allow insects to pollinate the flowers.

Netting is also necessary to prevent birds from stripping buds in winter and damaging ripening fruit in summer.

Water regularly in dry weather — apply up to 5 gallons per sq. yard every 10 days until there is prolonged rainfall. Never let the soil around the roots dry out — this is especially important with a newly-planted tree close to the house.

Thinning will be necessary if the crop is heavy. Begin when the fruit is marble-sized and continue until it is the size of a walnut. Thin at intervals until there is just one fruit at 6-9 in. intervals.

Feeding & Mulching

See page 21 — Peaches require annual feeding and mulching. In addition to the spring application of Growmore it is beneficial to use a high-potash feed occasionally during the fruit swelling stage.

Picking & Storage

A Peach or Nectarine is ripe when the flesh around the stalk is soft — the skin also bears a reddish flush. Handle carefully — lift up the fruit in the palm of your hand and twist gently. If ripe it will come away easily. Fruit can be stored in a cool place for about a week — lay them unwrapped in a box lined with tissue.

Peaches can be bottled, dried or frozen — remove the stones before freezing.

APRICOTS

There are many similarities between Apricots and Peaches, some of which are obvious. The trees have the same height, spread and general appearance — the fruit of both are stone-hearted, downy-skinned and golden or red with sweet and succulent flesh. Our climate makes their cultivation outdoors a risky business — with both Apricots and Peaches the standard advice is to grow the tree as a fan against a sunny and protected wall in the South and Midlands, and to grow the tree in a cold greenhouse if you live in Wales or the North.

Frost protection outdoors is essential in most seasons and bird protection is desirable. The blossom is self-fertile so a partner is not required, although the earliness of the flowering season means that hand pollination is recommended. Pot culture is practical — grow *Moorpark* grafted on to St Julien A or Pixy. Begin with a partly-trained tree in a 15 in. pot — cut back the main branches by about one half each early spring until a satisfactory framework has been built up. In subsequent years after harvest cut all branches which have borne fruit back to a side branch. Keep the pot in a greenhouse or conservatory all year round or stand outdoors on a warm patio.

Alongside the many similarities there are several important differences between Apricots and Peaches. Bacterial canker and silver leaf are not serious threats, so pruning is safe in late winter or early spring. Even more important is the ability of Apricots to bear fruit on spurs borne by older wood as well as on 1 year old wood like Peaches. Because of this pruning is quite a simple task. Soil requirements are also rather different — Apricots need more humus and more lime — the ideal locality is in deep and slightly chalky loam.

The choice of varieties is much more restricted than the Peach list. Many catalogues just contain *Moorpark*, an Apricot which came to England over 200 years ago. It is perhaps the most reliable variety you can choose — pick one of the newer ones if you are adventurous.

Growing under glass

Apricots flower even earlier than Peaches, so spring frosts can easily ruin the outdoor crop. Even in southern districts you cannot rely on regular fruit production — you get a decent crop of Apricots only when the spring is mild and when frost protection is provided.

Growing under glass is much more reliable, and you can choose between cultivating a fan against the south-facing wall of a lean-to or growing it as a dwarf bush in a pot. Pot-grown plants give lower yields than fans, but they are much less trouble.

Any of the varieties described overleaf is suitable. Follow the general cultivation rules set out for Peaches on page 41.

Rootstocks

Apricots are grown on Plum rootstocks. Both **Brompton** and **Mussel** are too vigorous for garden use — the most popular stock is the semi-vigorous **St Julien A** which produces a bush about 15 ft high or a fan which spreads to a similar distance. The dwarfing rootstock **Pixy** is beginning to appear in the catalogues.

Hand pollination

See page 41.

Planting

A sheltered sunny site is essential. Good drainage is vital — add well-rotted organic matter if the ground is short of humus. Liming will be necessary if the soil is acid. November is the best time for planting a bare-rooted plant.

TREE TYPE	ROOTSTOCK	SPACE BETWEEN TREES	SPACE BETWEEN ROWS	YIELD PER MATURE TREE
Bush	St Julien A	15 ft	15 ft	40 lb
Bush	Pixy	10 ft	10 ft	25 lb
Fan	St Julien A	15 ft	—	20 lb

Varieties A~Z

Alfred

Moorpark

ALFRED

The fruit is smaller than *Moorpark*, but it ripens earlier and the tree is less prone to die-back. Flesh is orange and juicy. There are two drawbacks — flowers appear early and the tree tends to be a biennial cropper.

Type: Apricot	
Fruit size: Medium	
Skin colour: Orange, flushed with pink	
Picking time: Early August	

FARMINGDALE

An American variety which has earned a good reputation over here as an outdoor Apricot. It ripens early and the flesh has an excellent flavour. It crops heavily and exhibits some resistance to die-back. Definitely worth trying.

Type: Apricot	
Fruit size: Medium	
Skin colour: Golden-yellow, flushed with red	
Picking time: Late July	

MOORPARK

By far the most popular variety and the only one offered by many nurseries. The orange flesh of this round variety has a very good flavour and the tree is renowned for its reliability — but it is prone to die-back.

Type: Apricot	
Fruit size: Large	
Skin colour: Golden-yellow, flushed with red	
Picking time: Late August	

NEW LARGE EARLY

The oval fruit is larger and ripens earlier than *Moorpark* — the flavour is good but not as sweet as *Farmingdale*. Reputed to be robust and hardy with good die-back resistance. Not many nurseries offer this one.

Type: Apricot	
Fruit size: Large	
Skin colour: Pale orange, flushed with red	
Picking time: Early August	

Pruning

BUSHES

Plant a 2 or 3 year old partly trained tree. Follow the training procedure for Plum bushes — see page 36. Prune in early February.

For pruning of established trees follow the routine given for acid Cherry bushes — see page 40.

FANS

Plant a 2 or 3 year old partly trained tree. Follow the training procedure for Peach fans — see page 44.

For pruning of established trees follow the routine given for Plum fans — see page 36.

Seasonal care

Hessian or netting placed over the fan or dwarf bush in early spring should be used to protect the blossom from frost damage. Support the net away from the flowers to avoid harming them. Remove during the day.

Water regularly in dry weather — apply up to 3 gallons per sq. yard every 10 days until there is prolonged rainfall. Never let the soil dry out — this is especially important with a newly-planted tree and when the fruits are beginning to swell.

Thinning will be necessary if the crop is heavy. Wait until the average fruit is about the size of a cherry and then remove the smallest and most crowded ones. Repeat the process until the fruits are 2–3 in. apart.

Feeding & Mulching

See page 21. Each spring mulch the plants with a 1 in. layer of organic matter.

Picking & Storage

Apricots become soft several days before they are ready for picking. Harvest them when they come away easily from the tree. Handle gently — the fruit bruises very easily. Keep indoors for about a day before eating. Apricots store much better than Peaches — they can be kept for several weeks in a cool place. Lay them unwrapped in a box lined with tissue.

Apricots can be bottled, dried or frozen — remove the stones before freezing.

FIGS

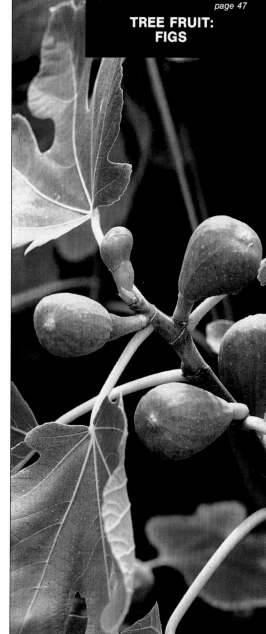

Figs are a strange fruit — their cultivation involves techniques which you will find nowhere else in this book. It is not even easy to classify them. Tree fruit in this and several other textbooks — soft fruit in some catalogues.

Figs are quite easy to grow. They are not grafted on to rootstocks and they do not need a pollination partner. Any soil will do as long as it drains reasonably freely, and the trees can withstand the winters in southern and western counties. Spraying is not necessary as pest and disease attack are rare. This ease, however, only applies to the tree as an ornamental plant — it is difficult to induce a Fig tree to produce a worthwhile crop every year. Read this section before deciding to buy one — like most gardeners you will probably decide that a Peach, Grape vine or Melon would be a much more desirable exotic.

The first problem concerns root growth — if left unrestricted the tree grows too vigorously and few fruit develop. To prevent this the roots are restricted by planting in a 15 in. pot or in a lined pit — see below. Pot-grown Figs can be trained as a fan against a wall or maintained as a dwarf bush — bush Figs can be kept in a greenhouse or else left outdoors for most of the year and then brought indoors during the leafless period when frosts threaten.

A sheltered wall facing the South or South-West is the place for a Fig. Greenhouse culture is feasible — you will get two crops instead of one each year if you can maintain a temperature of 55°F from January onwards. But do think carefully — Figs are leafy and cast a lot of shade.

Another problem is winter protection for outdoor crops. This year's Figs were present last year as tiny (embryo) fruits. These embryo fruits and young shoots must be individually covered during winter.

During the growing season the crop needs regular attention. Frequent watering is essential — during dry weather in summer you will have to irrigate twice a week. Shoots have to be pruned in June and unwanted Figs have to be removed in late September — see page 48. Obviously Figs are *not* for the lazy gardener, but they are a worthy challenge for the keen gardener who wants to see just how delicious a home-grown Fig can be. There are two types — the green varieties which have greenish skin and pale flesh, and the purple varieties with brown or purple skin and red flesh. For outdoor cultivation the reliable *Brown Turkey* is the usual choice — under glass the superb-tasting *Bourjasotte Grise* is worth trying.

Planting

Choose a well-sheltered spot which is exposed to the sun. Plant fans 12-15 ft apart. November to March is the recommended planting period — March is the best time.

The traditional method is to construct a Fig pit, as shown here. An easier method is to plant in a large tub or a 15 in. pot. Make sure that the container has adequate drainage holes, crock well and use a soil-based compost. In both pits and pots you should plant very firmly.

The pot can be stood in a sunny sheltered part of the garden, to be moved into a shed when frost threatens. If the Fig is to be grown against a wall as a fan then the pot should be sunk up to its rim in the earth close to the wall.

Repotting will be necessary every 2-3 years — do this in late winter.

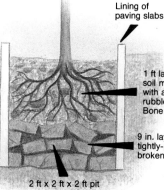

Lining of paving slabs

1 ft layer of soil mixed with a little rubble and Bone Meal

9 in. layer of tightly-packed broken bricks

2 ft x 2 ft x 2 ft pit

Varieties A-Z

Brown Turkey

White Marseilles

BOURJASOTTE GRISE

This one is strictly for growing in the greenhouse — it is too tender for outdoors. The fruits are rounder than the other varieties listed here and the flavour is better — probably the richest and sweetest Fig you can grow. Good for pot cultivation.

Type:	Green Fig
Fruit size:	Medium–large
Skin colour:	Pale green
Picking time:	September

BROWN TURKEY

For many years this has been the No.1 choice — it is suitable for outdoors or under glass. A reliable and heavy cropper producing oval fruit — the red flesh has a rich and sweet flavour. Usually the only Fig offered in the catalogue.

Type:	Purple Fig
Fruit size:	Medium–large
Skin colour:	Brownish-red. Blue bloom
Picking time:	August–September

BRUNSWICK

Not as popular as *Brown Turkey*, but it does come next in the rankings. An oval-shaped fruit like *Brown Turkey*, but it is larger and also ripens about a couple of weeks earlier. The flavour is very good but the tree is not as reliable as its rival and the yields are lower.

Type:	Green Fig
Fruit size:	Very large
Skin colour:	Greenish-yellow, flushed with brown
Picking time:	Mid August

WHITE MARSEILLES

This variety ripens at about the same time as *Brown Turkey*, but that is the only similarity. The fruit of *White Marseilles* is distinctly Pear-shaped, and the whitish flesh is almost transparent. It has a good reputation for pot culture.

Type:	Green Fig
Fruit size:	Large
Skin colour:	Pale green
Picking time:	August–September

Pruning

Buy a 2 or 3 year old partly trained tree. For a bush follow the training procedure for Apple bushes — see page 22. For a fan follow the training procedure for Peach fans — see page 44.

Pruning of established bushes and fans takes place in June. All young shoots should be pinched back so that only 5 leaves remain — this will encourage new fruiting shoots to form. In the case of fans tie these shortened growths to the wires.

Thin out the fruits in late September. The embryo Figs which should be retained are close to the end of the shoots and are about pea-sized. These will develop into fruit for picking next year. At this late September stage all the ripe fruit will have been picked, but you will also find some cherry-sized Figs which will not ripen — remove them.

In spring clean up the tree. Remove branches killed by frost and on a fan remove buds which are pointing directly inwards or outwards from the wall.

Seasonal care

Winter protection of young shoots and embryo fruits is vital. Move a pot-grown plant into a shed, garage or greenhouse. For plants which can't be moved indoors it will be necessary to tie a covering of straw or bracken loosely around the tender parts. Put on this cover in late autumn — remove gradually during April and May.

Regular watering is essential as the tree has restricted root growth. The root ball must never be allowed to dry out — adequate moisture is especially important when the fruits are swelling in early summer. Watering can be reduced as harvesting approaches.

In late summer it is usually necessary to hang a net over the tree to protect the ripening fruit from birds.

Feeding & Mulching

Do not overfeed. Apply a light dressing of Growmore in spring and spread an organic mulch over the soil surface. When the fruits start to swell apply a high-potash liquid fertilizer.

Picking & Storage

A Fig is ready for harvest when the stalk weakens and the fully-coloured fruit hangs downwards. There will be other tell-tale signs — the skin may be cracked or there may be a drop of nectar at the base. Gather the fruit carefully — it will keep in a cool place for several weeks. Figs can be dried in the airing cupboard. Turn daily — drying will take 4–7days.

MULBERRIES

The place for a Mulberry tree is in a large lawn where its gnarled branches and stately head can be admired. It is remarkably trouble-free and the flowers are self-fertile, and harvesting couldn't be easier. All you have to do is spread a sheet below the branches in August or September when the fruits have started to fall. Shake the branches gently, and on to the sheet drop the large Raspberry-like fruits — dark red or nearly black with a sweetish but tart flavour. Eat fresh or use for making jam, jellies or wine.

All of this sounds most appealing, but do think of the drawbacks before buying a Mulberry for your garden. Space can be a problem — the eventual height and spread will be about 20 ft. You will need patience as well as a large garden — growth is slow in the early years and the tree is slow to produce leaves in the spring. Worst of all, you will have to wait about seven years before you can taste the first fruits. Locality can also be a problem — Mulberries are disappointing in shady northern gardens and in heavy, water-retentive soil.

Still, Mulberries have been grown in Britain for hundreds of years and they are still worth considering for southern areas. Buy a 3–5 year old trained tree and plant in March — choose a Black Mulberry and not the insipid-tasting White Mulberry. Stake for the first few years and prune as little as possible —the branches bleed when cut. During the first two winters shorten some of the lateral branches not wanted for the main framework — in subsequent years merely cut out dead, broken or crossing branches in winter. With old trees the brittle branches may break — propping up with forked poles may be necessary.

QUINCES

Even if you have no use for the fruit it is worthwhile growing a Quince tree. The gnarled and contorted trunk and branches, the grey bark and the leathery, dark green leaves give the tree a distinctly oriental look. In June the attractive white or pale pink blossoms appear, 1½–2 in. in diameter, and then come the large (5–6 in. long) fruits. Pear- or Apple-shaped and aromatic, but too tart and gritty to be eaten raw. Quinces make delicious jellies and also pie-fillings when combined with Apple. The word 'marmalade' is derived from *marmalo* — the Portuguese name for Quince.

This is a plant for the South and Midlands. A moist soil is preferred and you will need sufficient space for a tree which will grow about 12 ft high. Plant between November and March, or any time of the year if it is a container-grown specimen. Choose a 2–4 year old trained plant — *Vranja* (large, Pear-shaped) is the popular variety, but you may also find *Champion* (large, Apple-shaped) and *Portugal* (large, early, orange, Pear-shaped). The popular shrub known as Japanese Quince or Japonica is much smaller and quite different to a true Quince.

During the first few years cut back the main leaders in winter so as to remove about a half of the previous year's growth. Keep the centre of the bush open. Once the mature framework is established, prune as little as possible — simply remove dead or crossing branches in winter.

Pick the fruits in October before the first frosts arrive. Store them in trays in a cool, dark place until the Quinces change from green to yellow. This will take 4–8 weeks.

The major pests and diseases

STAGES OF FRUIT DEVELOPMENT		WHEN TO SPRAY
BUD SWELLING		◀ NO NEED TO SPRAY
BUD BREAK		◀ NO NEED TO SPRAY
BUD BURST		◀ SPRAY
MOUSE EAR		◀ NO NEED TO SPRAY
GREEN CLUSTER		◀ SPRAY
PINK BUD (Apples) **WHITE BUD** (Pears)		◀ SPRAY
BLOSSOM TIME Early to mid May (Apples) Late April to early May (Pears)		◀ DO NOT SPRAY
PETAL FALL When nearly all petals have fallen		◀ SPRAY
FRUITLET Mid June		◀ SPRAY
FRUITLET Early July		◀ SPRAY

APPLES

Greenfly • Codling moth • Caterpillars
Scab • Mildew • Canker • Brown rot

PEARS

Greenfly • Pear & cherry slugworm
Caterpillars • Scab • Fireblight

Spraying programme

The usual plan is to spray when a pest or disease attacks — see pages 51–57. A spray programme for Apples and Pears may seem to be a chore because it involves applying several sprays during the season. The really keen fruit grower, however, follows a regular routine — a spray programme to provide automatic protection against the major and numerous minor troubles.

The mixture

Carbendazim + Fenitrothion. Tip the contents of one Supercarb sachet into about a teaspoonful of water in a small container. Stir to form a thin cream. Wash this into a bucket and make up to one gallon with water. Add 20 ml of pbi Fenitrothion and stir well. You are now ready to spray.

A medium-sized fruit tree will require about 1–2 gallons of spray. Make sure you cover the foliage and shoots thoroughly. After spraying pour away any mixture left over — do not keep it for use next time you spray.

The troubles controlled or reduced

Apple blossom weevil	Codling moth
Apple fruit rhynchites	Greenfly
Apple leaf skeletonizer	Leaf weevil
Apple sawfly	Mildew
Apple twig cutter	Scab
Blossom wilt	Sucker
Canker	Tent caterpillar
Capsid bug	Tortrix moth
Caterpillar	

PLUMS

Greenfly • Birds • Wasps • Plum sawfly
Red spider mite • Silver leaf • Brown rot

CHERRIES

Cherry blackfly • Birds • Silver leaf
Bacterial canker • Brown rot

PEACHES

Greenfly • Red spider mite • Peach leaf curl
Silver leaf • Bacterial canker • Split stone

APRICOTS

Greenfly • Red spider mite • Die-back
Silver leaf • Bacterial canker

FIGS

Canker • Grey mould (page 101) • Coral spot

QUINCES

Canker • Mildew • Brown rot

SHOT HOLE DISEASE

A fungal disease which attacks Plums, Peaches and Cherries. Brown spots appear on the leaves which turn into small holes. No other symptoms appear and the trees are not seriously affected. As only weak trees are attacked, build up their vigour by spraying with Fillip during the summer. Drought makes the trees susceptible so water in dry weather.

BACTERIAL CANKER

Pale-edged spots are the first sign of this serious disease of Plums, Cherries and other stone fruit. At a later stage gum oozes from the bark and affected branches die back. Tackle the problem quickly to save the tree. Cut out the diseased branches and paint the cuts with Arbrex. Spray the trees with Copper in August, September and October.

TREE FRUIT TROUBLES: Holes in Leaves

Holes in the foliage of fruit trees are a common sight. The culprit in spring is usually the winter moth or mottled umber moth — during late spring and summer there are a number of pests which can attack fruit trees in this way. The common causes of torn or skeletonized leaves are shown on this page, but some caterpillars which attack soft fruit (yellowtail moth, magpie moth etc — see page 97) occasionally attack Apples, Pears and Plums.

CAPSID BUG

¼ in. active bugs

The first signs of capsid damage on Apple leaves are reddish-brown spots. As the leaf expands these tear to produce ragged brown-edged holes. Damaged foliage is usually puckered and distorted. Spray with Fenitrothion or Long-last at green cluster. Repeat at petal fall to protect the fruit.

PEAR & CHERRY SLUGWORM

½ in. black grubs

Both Pear and Cherry leaves are attacked by these slimy slug-like insects between June and October. They feed on the upper surface and the foliage may be skeletonized. Spray with Hexyl if the leaves are seriously affected.

FRUIT TREE TORTRIX MOTH

Leaves are spun together or a leaf is attached to the fruit. The small active caterpillars feed within this protective cover. If touched on the head they wriggle backwards. Hand-pick spun leaves if practical. Fenitrothion or Hexyl will control them, but a thorough drenching spray is necessary.

TENT CATERPILLAR

These caterpillars produce a characteristic tent of silken webs, within which the insects feed on the foliage. The tents should be picked off and burnt if practical. Alternatively spray with Fenitrothion as soon as tents start to appear.

CATERPILLAR

MOTTLED UMBER MOTH
Smooth 'looper' caterpillar, which attacks trees in spring.

WINTER MOTH
Green 'looper' caterpillar which devours young leaves and may spin them together.

'Looper' caterpillars eat the new leaves in spring and often feed on the petals and flower stalks later in the season. Protect trees by encircling each trunk with a Boltac greaseband from September to March. If caterpillars are seen, spray with Fenitrothion.

VAPOURER MOTH
Colourful caterpillar, about 1 in. long, which feeds on the leaves from May to August. Spray with Fenitrothion.

APPLE LEAF SKELETONIZER

An occasional pest of Apples, Pears and Cherries in south-east England. The ½ in. caterpillars are yellow with black spots, and their method of feeding leads to skeletonization of the foliage. Late summer is their most active time and at this stage damaged leaves should be picked and burnt. This pest will be controlled by an apple spray programme (see page 50).

TREE FRUIT TROUBLES: Leaf & Shoot Problems

Apart from holes (page 51), all sorts of problems can occur on the foliage. Leaves may be twisted, discoloured, blistered or covered with mould. Do not waste time and money spraying against everything — just worry about the serious pests and diseases. These are blackfly on Cherries, greenfly on young trees, silver leaf on Plums, scab and mildew on Apples and Pears, leaf curl on Peaches and die-back on Apricots.

APPLE TWIG CUTTER

Blue weevil, 1/6 in. long, bites through the young shoots of Apple, Pear or Plum after egg-laying in June. These shoots wither and may remain hanging on the tree. Small trees are most at risk, and can be protected by spraying with Fenitrothion at white or pink bud. A minor pest — treatment is rarely necessary.

CLAY-COLOURED WEEVIL

Brown weevil, 1/4 in. long, gnaws the bark of woody stems. Young Apple trees are sometimes crippled by this night-feeding pest. Control is not easy — hoe the surrounding soil and spray both the tree and ground with Hexyl or Fenitrothion. Alternatively, encircle each trunk with a Boltac greaseband.

DIE-BACK

Begins at the shoot tips and progresses slowly downwards. More common in stone fruit than Apples or Pears. There are a number of reasons, including diseases such as canker. If no disease is present, waterlogging is a likely cause. Cut out dead wood. Feed with Fillip. Improve drainage.

LEOPARD MOTH

Large spotted caterpillar, about 2 in. long, which burrows for 2–3 years inside the affected branch. Leaves wilt — the branch may die. If the trunk is attacked the tree can be killed. This pest is difficult to control by chemical means — it is often necessary to cut out and burn the affected branch.

FROST

The effect of frost on the foliage becomes apparent as the leaves expand. The lower surface becomes puckered and blistered, and the skin over the blister cracks, exposing the tissue beneath. The leaves around the flower trusses are the worst affected. The leaves do not fall and there is no treatment.

WOOLLY APHID

Colonies of aphids live on stems and branches, secreting white waxy 'wool' which protects them. Their presence does little direct harm, but the corky galls they cause are a common entry point for canker spores. Brush off 'wool' with an old toothbrush and methylated spirits. Alternatively, spray with Long-last.

LEAF MIDGE

A common pest of Pears; less common on Apples. The grubs cause the edges of the leaves to roll upwards. Young foliage is more likely to be attacked than old leaves. Affected leaves may turn red and fall. Control is difficult as the grubs are protected from sprays. Pick off and burn affected leaves.

LEAFHOPPER

Pale mottled patches appear on leaves, caused by small, lively greenish insects feeding on the undersurface. Empty white skins are a tell-tale sign. They can be controlled by spraying but this is only necessary in the case of a bad attack. Suitable insecticides are Long-last, Fenitrothion and Malathion.

NUTRIENT DEFICIENCY

An abnormal change in leaf colour often indicates a shortage of an essential element. Spray the trees with a foliar feed such as Fillip. If the symptoms of iron or magnesium deficiency are severe, water MultiTonic on the soil around the trunks. Feed and mulch the tree in spring.

NITROGEN SHORTAGE
Red & yellow tints

POTASH SHORTAGE
Leaf edge scorch

MAGNESIUM SHORTAGE
Brown between veins

IRON SHORTAGE
Yellow between veins

SILVER LEAF

The most serious disease of Plums, which can also attack Apples, Cherries and Peaches. The spores enter through a wound, and the first sign is silvering of the leaves. Die-back of shoots occurs; wood is stained. Cut out dead branches 6 in. below level of infection. Paint cuts with Arbrex. Dig out tree if bracket-like toad-stools have appeared on the trunk.

Cross section of shoot

FALSE SILVER LEAF

A common disorder which looks like silver leaf at first glance. Leaves are silvery, but the effect appears all over the tree rather than progressively along a branch. A cut branch reveals that the staining of silver leaf disease is absent. The cause of false silver leaf is starvation or irregular watering. Feed regularly with Fillip and put down an organic mulch in spring.

LEAF BLISTER MITE

This microscopic mite can be a serious pest of Pears grown against walls. Leaves are spotted with yellow or red blisters which later turn black. Affected leaves fall early, and fruit may be blistered. Pick off and burn diseased leaves as soon as they are noticed.

GREENFLY

Several species of greenfly can attack Apples, Pears, Peaches and Plums — in some seasons they are a serious pest. Some greenfly cause yellowing and curling of the young leaves. The rosy leaf-curling aphid causes reddening and distortion of Apple foliage. Greenfly excrete sticky honeydew and stunt shoot growth. Spray with Long-last or Fenitrothion at bud burst. Repeat at green cluster.

RED SPIDER MITE

Fruit tree red spider mite

Bryobia mite

The first sign of red spider mite attack is a faint mottling of the upper leaf surface. In warm weather a severe infestation may occur — the leaves turn a bronze colour, become brittle and die. Examine the underside of the foliage with a magnifying glass for the tiny mites. The fruit tree red spider mite is the common species; on Pears you may find the bryobia mite. Spray with Long-last, Malathion or Derris. If necessary repeat 3 weeks later.

CHERRY BLACKFLY

Only one aphid, the cherry blackfly, attacks Cherries, but its effect can be devastating. Leaves may be severely curled and shoot growth halted. It is therefore essential to kill these pests before they become established. Spray with Malathion or Fenitrothion when they are seen.

SCAB

A serious disease of Apples and Pears, which can attack all parts of the tree. Leaves bear dark green or brown spots; twigs are blistered and fruits are badly disfigured (page 57). The best way to achieve control is to follow a regular spraying programme designed for all the major troubles (page 50). Alternatively spray with Dithane at green cluster, pink or white bud, petal fall and 14 days after petal fall. Rake up and burn fallen leaves in autumn; prune scabby shoots in winter.

MILDEW

Young leaves, shoots and flower trusses of Apples and Pears may appear grey in spring due to infection of this white powdery mould. It is a serious disease — growth is stunted, diseased flowers do not set and leaves may fall. Cox's Orange Pippin is very susceptible. Prune and burn all infected twigs. Use a spraying programme containing carbendazim. See page 50 for a suitable programme.

PEACH LEAF CURL

Large reddish blisters develop on the leaves. Apart from making the tree unsightly this serious disease of outdoor Peaches leads to early leaf fall and weakening of the tree. The fungus over-winters in the bark and between bud scales, not on fallen leaves. Spray with Dithane in mid February, 14 days later and again just before leaf fall.

TREE FRUIT TROUBLES:
Bark & Trunk Problems

Some problems of fruit tree trunks, such as scale and crown gall, are surface disorders which can be readily removed. Others, such as bacterial canker, are deep-seated and extremely serious. A few can prove fatal — potential killers include fireblight on Pears, honey fungus on Apples and canker on most tree fruits. So keep a watch for the troubles shown here.

BACTERIAL CANKER

Cankers are flat and may not be easily noticed, but the effect on stone fruit is serious. Attacked branches produce few leaves and soon die. Gum oozes from the cankers. For leaf symptoms see page 51. Cut out diseased branches; paint cuts with Arbrex. Spray trees with Copper in August, September and October.

GUMMOSIS

A disorder of Cherries and Plums — usually occurs after freezing weather. Patches of gum appear on the surface of branches and trunks. This gum arises from healthy wood — with the much more serious bacterial canker the gum oozes from diseased tissue. There is no specific cure — spray with Fillip to improve vigour.

CROWN GALL

Large, brown and warty outgrowths sometimes occur on the stems and roots of fruit trees. Attacks are usually restricted to young trees on badly drained sites. Mature trees are not harmed. Younger ones may lose vigour — cut off galls and paint the affected area with Arbrex in autumn.

FIREBLIGHT

A devastating disease of Pears which can occur on Apples. Affected shoots wilt and die. Old cankers ooze in spring. Tell-tale sign is the presence of brown, withered leaves which do not fall. Cut out all diseased wood to 2 ft below affected area. Disinfect tools. The tree is killed once the disease spreads to the trunk.

CORAL SPOT

Raised pink spots appear on the surface of affected branches. Dead wood is the breeding ground for the fungus, and the air-borne spores infect living trees through cuts and wounds. Never leave dead wood lying about. Cut out all dead and diseased branches and always paint pruning cuts with Arbrex to protect the cut surfaces.

HONEY FUNGUS

Honey fungus (root rot, armillaria disease) is a common cause of the death of Apple trees. A white fan of fungal growth occurs below the bark near ground level. On roots, black 'bootlaces' are found. Toadstools appear in autumn at the tree base. Burn stems and roots of diseased trees. Soil can be treated with Armillatox, but control is difficult.

CANKER

The bark shrinks and cracks in concentric rings. A tell-tale sign is the presence of red growths in winter. A serious disease of Apples and Pears, especially on badly drained soil. Cut off damaged twigs — cut out canker from stems and branches. Paint with Arbrex. The spray programme on page 50 supresses this disease.

PAPERY BARK

The bark becomes thin and peels off in sheets. Die-back occurs if a shoot is girdled. This form of bark canker affects Apple and Pear trees in poor condition, usually due to bad drainage. Remove loose bark — paint exposed surface with Arbrex. Improve drainage. Apply a mulch and spray the leaves with a foliar feed such as Fillip.

SCALE

Scale insects are a pest of neglected trees. These tiny shell-like creatures do not move. Uncommon outdoors, but with greenhouse fruit they may completely cover the branches with a scaly coat. All types of tree fruit can be affected. Spray with Tar Oil winter wash in December or with Malathion in late May. Prune heavily infested shoots.

Mussel scale ►

Oystershell scale ►

SPLIT BARK

A crack may appear in the bark at any time of the year. The cause can be a severe frost, but the usual culprit is a cultural problem such as poor drainage or inadequate staking. Another possible cause is heavy rain after drought. Cut away any dead wood — paint with Arbrex to keep out disease. Feed and mulch the tree to restore good health.

TREE FRUIT TROUBLES: Bud & Blossom Problems

SUCKER

The developing buds of Apples and Pears are attacked by young suckers. The blossom trusses turn brown as if attacked by frost, but careful examination reveals yellowish-white insects which look like flattened aphids. Another tell-tale sign is the presence of sticky honeydew. Spray with Long-last or Fenitrothion at green cluster.

FROST

Frost at blossom time causes the flowers to turn brown and drop off. This can, of course, be serious if little blossom has been produced, but in a year of abundant blossom the thinning effect of a slight frost is beneficial. If your garden is on a sloping site, open part of the lower boundary to air movement or you will create a 'frost pocket'. Choose a late-flowering variety.

APPLE BLOSSOM WEEVIL

A common and troublesome pest of Apples, which occasionally affects Pears. In spring the grubs feed inside developing flower buds. The stalks remain green and healthy, but the petals turn brown and fail to open. If one of these 'capped' blossoms is cut in two, a white grub or brown beetle will be found inside. This is the apple blossom weevil or the closely related and much less common pest, the apple bud weevil.

Apple blossom weevil: 'V' on back

Apple bud weevil: No 'V' on back

Spray with Fenitrothion at bud burst.

CHERRY FRUIT MOTH

These green caterpillars can be a serious pest in southern counties. They feed inside the flower buds where they eat both petals and stamens. They continue to feed on the open flowers and then inside the young fruitlets. They drop to the ground in late May. It is not usually necessary to spray against this pest, but if attacks have been heavy in the past apply Hexyl at bud burst and again at white bud.

BIRDS

Birds can be extremely destructive to flower buds, the main culprits being bull-finches and sparrows. All tree fruit can be damaged, with Cherries, Plums and Pears the worst affected. The outer bud scales are pushed aside and the central portion of each bud pecked out during late winter and spring. Unfortunately, spray repellents may not be effective as the outer sprayed portion of the bud is not eaten. The best answer is plastic netting if this is practical.

BLOSSOM WILT

In a mild, wet spring this disease can be extremely serious on Plums, when the tree appears to have been scorched. Apples and Pears can also be badly affected. The blossom trusses wilt and turn brown — shoots are killed in a bad attack. Remove infected blossoms and dead twigs in spring. In summer remove all fruit affected by brown rot (page 57). A spray programme containing carbendazim (see page 50) will help to control this disease.

BLOSSOM DROP

It is annoying to discover that a tree which was full of blossom has lost its flowers without setting fruit. To find the cause you must know whether this trouble takes place year after year or is an unusual occurrence. If it is an annual event then the most likely cause is the absence of a pollination partner. Most trees will not set fruit unless another variety with compatible pollen is growing nearby. If blossom drop does not usually occur then poor weather at flowering time is the most probable reason. Frosting of the blooms is a common problem on cold, exposed plots. Very dry air can result in poor pollination and a wet, cold spring reduces the activity of pollinating insects.

WINTER MOTH

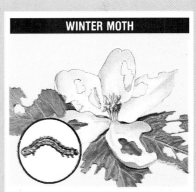

The winter moth caterpillar is a serious pest in early spring, devouring the new leaves. When the flowers are fully open the caterpillars often feed on the petals and flower stalks. The 1½ in. 'looper' caterpillars may even attack young fruitlets, biting holes in the surface. Protect trees by encircling each trunk with a Boltac greaseband from September to March. If numerous caterpillars are seen on the leaves, spray with Fenitrothion.

TREE FRUIT TROUBLES:
Fruit Problems

It is unfortunate that so many troubles can occur after the fruit has set. The most likely problems are illustrated below, but others can take their toll. Birds can be a problem, often stealing the whole crop from a Cherry tree or picking holes in ripening Apples. Greenfly attacks can result in small distorted fruit, and frost can produce corky stripes on the outside and brown watery flesh within.

SPLIT STONE

The outside of an affected Peach is holed at the stalk end and inside the stone is split and rotten. The usual cause is poor pollination or irregular watering — next year hand pollinate the flowers and spray them gently in dry weather. Keep the soil moist and apply a mulch. Apply a dressing of lime if the soil is acid.

APPLE FRUIT RHYNCHITES

Brown weevil, $\frac{1}{5}$ in. long, creates numerous small holes with its snout over the surface of developing fruit. Attacks cease in July, but affected fruit remain disfigured and distorted as they enlarge. The flesh remains sound. This pest is controlled by the spray programme described on page 50.

WASP

All types of tree fruit may be attacked by wasps. Soft-skinned types such as Plums are favoured and may be devoured; Apples and Pears usually escape if the surface is undamaged. Spraying is not effective — the only answer is to find and destroy the nest with a proprietary wasp killer. Do this job at dusk.

EARWIG

All types of tree fruit, especially the soft-skinned types, may be attacked by earwigs. Apples are attacked in late summer, the surface being holed and the flesh below eaten out. The ground below the trees should be well cultivated — if earwigs are a problem spray the ground with Hexyl in late July.

CHAFER BEETLE

The 1¼ in. brown-coloured cockchafer and the ½ in. bluish-green garden chafer are responsible for biting out holes in small Apple fruitlets in May and June. Badly bitten fruit are useless, so a severe attack can be serious. If the beetles are numerous, spray the trees with Hexyl.

PEAR MIDGE

Attacked Pear fruitlets become deformed and blackened, usually falling from the tree. Cut fruit reveals a large central cavity and numerous tiny grubs. Pick and burn blackened fruit, and keep the soil well cultivated. If it was a problem last year, spray with Hexyl at white bud.

PLUM SAWFLY

The tell-tale sign of this serious pest of Plums is a hole surrounded by sticky black 'frass'. Inside will be found the ½ in. creamy-white grub of the plum sawfly. Damaged Plums fall to the ground before maturity. Cultivate the soil around the trees and spray with Fenitrothion 7–10 days after petal fall.

PEAR STONY PIT

This is a serious virus disease of Pears — affected trees cannot be cured and have to be dug out and destroyed. Diseased fruit is small and misshapen with the surface covered with dimples and lumps. The flesh is woody and inedible. The disease usually occurs on old trees and can spread to surrounding trees.

STORAGE ROT

Most Apple rotting in store is due to bitter rot (gloeosporium). If a large quantity of fruit is to be stored, take preventive measures. Spray trees with carbendazim in August and repeat 1–2 weeks before harvest. Remove and destroy diseased fruit immediately and do not prune before February. Check stored fruit — destroy rotten ones at once.

TORTRIX MOTH

The caterpillar of the fruit tree tortrix moth spins a leaf on to the fruit and feeds underneath this cover. The summer fruit tortrix also spins on a leaf cover, and removes extensive areas of skin and surface flesh. These caterpillars can be controlled by the apple spray programme (page 50) or codling moth treatment (page 57).

SCAB

This serious disease affects Apples and Pears. Dark-coloured scabs appear on young fruit — as the fruits grow, large corky areas develop. The surface may be cracked but the flesh remains sound. Attacks are worst when the weather is warm and humid. The best way to achieve control is to follow a regular spraying programme designed for all the major troubles (see page 50). Alternatively spray with Dithane at green cluster, pink or white bud, petal fall and 14 days after petal fall. Rake up and burn fallen leaves in autumn — prune scabby shoots in winter.

BROWN ROT

Most tree fruit can be affected, but the disease is worst on Apples. The infected fruit turns brown and concentric rings of yellowish mould appear. The shrunken mummified fruit may remain on the tree throughout the winter or it may fall. This fungal disease cannot be controlled by spraying and it is necessary to destroy affected fruit as soon as they are seen on the tree or on the ground. Remember to store only sound fruit and examine them at regular intervals.

RUSSETTING

The rough scurf which sometimes forms over the surface of Apples and Pears is known as russetting. On some Apple varieties it is natural; on the smooth-skinned varieties it is a disorder which make the fruit unsightly. The eating quality is not affected. Poor growing weather is the most likely cause, especially if it occurs at petal fall. Drought, mildew, starvation, and too little organic matter in the soil are other possible causes of russetting.

BITTER PIT

Small brown areas appear in the surface tissue, each one marked by a small depression in the skin. The brown areas are occasionally scattered throughout the fruit, rendering it bitter and inedible. Bitter pit usually develops during storage. The cause of this disorder is complex, but it is linked to calcium deficiency and a period of water shortage. Mulching and watering in summer is helpful, but avoid using straw or strawy manure. Do not drastically prune trees which have been affected by bitter pit. If a regular problem try spraying with calcium nitrate at fortnightly intervals from mid June.

FRUIT DROP

Fruitlets will fall following insect damage — look for grubs in fallen Apples, Pears and Plums. But healthy fruitlets also fall — this may actually be beneficial as a heavy set must be thinned. The first drop of Apples takes place when the fruitlets are pea-sized — the usual reason is incomplete pollination due to a cold wet spring. The major shedding is the 'June drop'. There are several reasons why the fall at this time may be unusually heavy with only a sparse crop remaining. It is normal for newly-planted trees to shed most of their fruit in this way, and some varieties, such as Cox's Orange Pippin, have a notoriously heavy June drop. Irregular water supplies at the root, starvation, frost damage and overcrowding are other causes.

CAPSID BUG

Young fruitlets of Apples and Pears show reddish-brown spots following attack by these active green bugs. As the fruits enlarge, pale corky patches develop and the surface may be distorted, cracked and russetted. Despite the unsightly appearance the flesh remains sound. Leaf damage by capsid bugs is prevented by spraying at green cluster (page 51). To protect fruit, spray with Long-last or Fenitrothion at petal fall.

CODLING MOTH

The pale pink grub bores into developing fruit and feeds on the central core. Pears and Plums may be attacked as well as Apples. Grubs can be found inside the fruit in July and August; the tell-tale sign is sawdust-like 'frass' within the Apple. Spray with Fenitrothion in mid June; repeat 3 weeks later.

APPLE SAWFLY

A ribbon-like scar is produced on the surface. Later the creamy-white grub burrows down to feed on the central core which generally causes the fruit to drop in June or July. The grubs go into the ground in July. Sticky 'frass' can be seen around the hole. Spray with Fenitrothion at petal fall. Pick up and burn the fallen Apples.

CHAPTER 3

SOFT FRUIT

'Soft fruit' is a general term for a widely diverse group of plants which are generally head-high or smaller and which bear soft-skinned juicy fruit — the classification of the group is shown on page 4. Not all types fit into this definition — Grapes can be tall and Melons have a thick rind.

The increase in shop prices and the interest in home freezing have combined to make soft fruit growing much more popular than ever before. Unlike vegetables you can crop plants year after year once they are established, and unlike tree fruit there is a place for at least one example in every garden. Plant Gooseberry bushes and Raspberry canes where space permits, or plant Strawberries in a tub or window box where the garden is tiny. All are self-fertile, pruning is easier than with tree fruit and new plants quickly start to bear fruit — within a year for Melons and some Strawberries.

The attraction of luscious soft fruit from one's own garden is obvious, but beginners do run into problems because they ignore two basic points:

● **Soft fruit needs attention** You cannot neglect the plants during the year and still expect long-living and high-yielding bushes and canes. This does not mean that soft fruit care is difficult, but you must pay attention to feeding, pruning and spraying. The plants are prey to all sorts of pests and problems — keep watch and take remedial action at the first sign of trouble. Two problems overshadow all the others — birds and viruses.

● **There are not many general rules** A small number of rules apply to all types. Enrich the soil with well-rotted manure or compost before planting and feed each year after planting. Keep the bushes or canes free from weeds and make sure there is ample water around the roots after planting and when the fruits are swelling. But the differences in looking after the various types of soft fruit far outweigh the similarities. Study the planting and pruning instructions for each type — even Blackcurrant and Red Currant are treated quite differently.

So soft fruit is for everyone. The usual choice is Strawberries and Raspberries — you will find popular ones like *Cambridge Favourite* and *Glen Clova* everywhere. But do try to be a little more adventurous — there are exciting new types and varieties in the catalogues. Replacement will be necessary after a time — Strawberries should remain productive for 3–4 years and Raspberries for 10–12 years. You can propagate your own replacement stock, but do make sure the plant is virus-free before taking cuttings or runners. This is not as easy as it sounds as plants may be infected and yet show no obvious symptoms.

Buying

The rules for buying tree fruit are laid down on page 6. Some of the basics apply here — avoid 'bargains' at all costs and go to a reputable supplier. Order early before the best varieties are sold out, and choose container-grown canes or bushes rather than bare-rooted ones if you have missed the autumn-spring planting period.

The need for care when buying is greater with soft fruit than with tree fruit. Virus-infected stock will never amount to anything, so do not plant gifts from friends and always go for certified stock where the scheme applies.

Certified Stock
There is a Certification Scheme for Strawberries, Raspberries, Blackcurrants and a few varieties of Gooseberries, Red Currants and Hybrid Berries. Certified plants have been inspected and passed by Ministry of Agriculture officials as substantially free from pests and diseases, and also as true to type. Unhealthy-looking plants are rejected.

The things to look for

Label, stating the variety and details of certification

Stems should be healthy and firm. There should be a green layer under the bark — scratch the surface to find out

A well-developed root system spreading in all directions. There should be no small white roots growing into the damp peat

Site & Soil

Ideally soft fruit should be grown in full sun, but nearly all types will do reasonably well in light shade. Most localities and soils are suitable, but there are some sites which will give disappointing results. These include land exposed to strong winds or late frost; gravelly, sandy or poorly-drained soil and ground under trees. Avoid planting near fruit trees which may need spraying when soft fruit is being harvested and plant tall canes and bushes away from low-growing crops where shade could be a problem. Walls and fences can be used for bush fruit grown as fans or cordons where space is short. Strawberries can be grown in containers.

Planting

Follow the general rules set out for tree fruit on pages 7 and 8. Make sure the ground is prepared thoroughly — enrich with organic matter and remove roots of perennial weeds. Check on any special needs for the types of soft fruit to be planted — some don't like acid conditions but others will fail miserably if the land is not acidic.

Never replace an old type of soft fruit with a bush or cane of the same type — for example, do not plant Raspberry canes where you have just removed 10 year old canes of the same or a different variety of Raspberry. Find a spot where soft fruit has not been grown before if you can, or else grow a different type of soft fruit when replacing old plants.

Direction of planting

N
S

The Bird problem

Birds are a big problem. Fruit buds are attacked in winter and spring — the flowers which survive produce fruits which when ripe are again attacked. Some people plant a few extra bushes for the birds to try to get round the problem, but there are times when you will get little or no fruit if you don't do something about the bird menace.

Raspberries and Strawberries are the types most at risk. Chemical sprays are of little use and mechanical bird scarers are of limited value. The only satisfactory solution is to erect a bird cage. For Strawberries and low-growing bushes and canes a temporary cage will do, but for standard-sized bushes and canes a walk-in cage is a better idea.

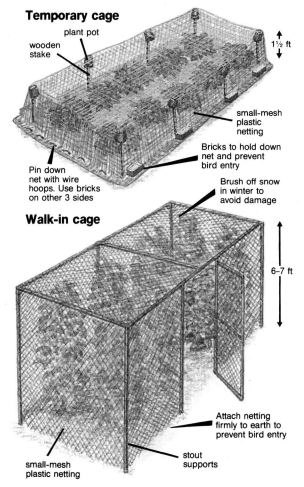

Temporary cage

plant pot

wooden stake

1½ ft

small-mesh plastic netting

Bricks to hold down net and prevent bird entry

Pin down net with wire hoops. Use bricks on other 3 sides

Brush off snow in winter to avoid damage

Walk-in cage

6-7 ft

Attach netting firmly to earth to prevent bird entry

stout supports

small-mesh plastic netting

The Virus problem

Viruses are not just another soft fruit disease — they are *the* disease which threatens the productive life of canes and bushes. Viruses are carried from plant to plant by insects such as greenfly and leafhopper and once infected the plant cannot be cured. The symptoms depend on both virus and plant type — leaves may be blotched or streaked and growth may be distorted or dwarfed. In some cases the infection may prove fatal. The usual response is for the health and fruitfulness to decline so that removal and burning of the infected plant is the only thing to do.

Tackle the virus problem by using certified stock and then spraying to keep the insect carriers under control. In this way productive cropping should continue for at least the 10 year life span we can expect from bush and cane soft fruit.

Feeding & Mulching

A spring dressing of fertilizer has 2 functions — it promotes a good crop later in the season and also encourages the production of new growth which will bear next year's crop. Treat an area extending about 3 ft from the stems — use Growmore at 2 oz per sq. yard or apply a high-potash liquid fertilizer at the manufacturer's recommended rate. Most fruit respond to foliar feeding, especially after pest damage and when the small fruits are beginning to swell. Yellowing leaves in alkaline soil are a symptom of iron or manganese deficiency. Spray the plants with MultiTonic.

The purpose of mulching is to keep down weeds and to conserve moisture. Black polythene sheeting can be used — it doesn't break down and it fully suppresses weeds. Organic mulches do not share these virtues, but they do provide nutrients and help to improve soil structure. Lay down a layer of peat, well-rotted manure or compost — this should be about 2 in. thick and it should extend for about 1 yard around the stems. Keep the ground clear for a few inches around the stems — place mulches in position immediately after weeding and feeding in spring.

STRAWBERRIES

Strawberries are the most popular soft fruit for growing at home. This should come as no surprise, as there are so many features in their favour. You don't need lots of room — you can grow them in the vegetable plot or in a container on the patio. You also don't need lots of patience — plant in August and you can be picking fruit in June or July next year. And the result is luscious and attractive fruit, each one weighing up to 2 ounces and each plant yielding 6 to 24 ounces of Strawberries.

The problem is that the season is all too fleeting. If just one popular variety is grown, picking in June or July will last for two or three weeks and then it is over. But if you have the space and choose the varieties with care, it is possible to pick Strawberries for six months of the year — from May until the arrival of the first frosts. By covering the plants with cloches in February you can pick about three weeks earlier — by growing in a heated greenhouse you can have fruits at Christmas.

The summer fruiting varieties are the most popular and dominate the catalogues. Just one large flush is produced — the early and 2nd early types are in fruit between late May and late June — the mid-season ones range from mid June to mid July and the late types are ready between early and late July. The first step is to buy young, healthy plants in late summer or early autumn — plant no later than mid September to ensure that a good root system can develop before the onset of winter.

Perpetual varieties extend the season. Several flushes are produced, the main ones being between August and October. You never get much at a single picking, but the out-of-season crop is very welcome. Recently a new group appeared — the day neutral varieties. Here fruiting is not controlled by day length and there is a simple message — pick 12 weeks after planting. In practice, however, they behave like perpetual varieties and the flavour is unfortunately indifferent. Finally, there are the alpine Strawberries, tiny berries which appear in modest amounts over a prolonged period — you will need 20–30 plants for a worthwhile crop.

Look for something different in the catalogues if you are adventurous. There are pink-flowered types and others with pink or yellow fruit. But for most of us, however, it is better to stick to old favourites and highly recommended new ones.

SUMMER FRUITING STRAWBERRY
(Other names: **Single Crop, June Bearer**)

By far the most popular group. Largest and best quality fruits found here. Cropping time between late May and late July. Single flush — a few varieties occasionally produce a second crop.
Productive life: 3–4 years

ALPINE STRAWBERRY
(Other name: **Wild**)

Fruit is very small — aromatic and sweet but not juicy. Grow in a container or as an edging. Sow seed in autumn — plant out in spring. Cropping time midsummer to late autumn. Red, yellow and white varieties are available.
Productive life: 1 year

PERPETUAL STRAWBERRY
(Other names: **Remontant, Everbearer, Autumn Fruiting, Two Crop**)

Fruit is generally smaller and less sweet than summer fruiting varieties — plants are less hardy. Cropping time June and again in late summer-autumn. Remove early flowers to increase the autumn crop.
Productive life: 2 years

DAY NEUTRAL STRAWBERRY

Only a few varieties available. Outdoors they behave like ordinary perpetuals in Britain — under glass they will produce winter fruit 12 weeks after planting. Remove early flowers in the garden to increase the autumn crop.
Productive life: 2 years

Varieties A~Z

Type:	Alpine
Fruit size:	Small
Skin colour:	Bright red
Picking time:	Midsummer-late autumn

ALEXANDRIA

Alexandria bears the largest fruits amongst the alpine Strawberries — about ½ in. long. The colourful fruits are also juicier than other alpines, but the yields are less than you will get from the more popular *Baron Solemacher*. The bushy plants do not produce runners. Flavour is excellent.

Type:	Perpetual
Fruit size:	Medium-large
Skin colour:	Medium red
Picking time:	Late summer-autumn

AROMEL

The catalogues are quite right when they say that the flavour of this variety is outstanding. It is becoming popular, but there are a few drawbacks. Crops are moderate, the leaves are susceptible to mildew and the rather soft, conical fruits are often misshapen. Water well in dry weather.

Aromel

Type:	Alpine
Fruit size:	Very small
Skin colour:	Dark red
Picking time:	Midsummer-late autumn

BARON SOLEMACHER

The most popular alpine Strawberry — this variety actually prefers partial shade to full sun. Each fruit is tiny, but they are borne in large numbers over a long period. Birds seem to leave them alone. The small bushes are erect and do not bear runners. Fine flavour.

Type:	Summer fruiting
Fruit size:	Medium-large
Skin colour:	Dull red
Picking time:	Mid July-late July

BOGOTA

There are only two reasons to consider growing *Bogota* — crops are heavy and it bears fruit after nearly all summer fruiting varieties have finished. It also freezes quite well, but the flavour is only fair and the plants are susceptible to both soil diseases and mildew.

Baron Solemacher

Type:	Summer fruiting
Fruit size:	Small-medium
Skin colour:	Dark red
Picking time:	Early July-late July

BOUNTY

This Canadian-bred variety beats its rival *Cambridge Favourite* in a couple of ways — the flavour is better and the crops are heavier. The fruit, however, is smaller and in some soils it is necessary to replant every 2 years. The firm red-fleshed Strawberries are easy to pick.

Type:	Summer fruiting
Fruit size:	Medium
Skin colour:	Orange-red
Picking time:	Mid June-mid July

CAMBRIDGE FAVOURITE

The No.1 choice for many years — it crops well and is thoroughly reliable. When virus-free it has a long productive life and there is good all-round disease resistance. Still, think about choosing elsewhere — the whitish flesh lacks full flavour and virus is now a problem.

Cambridge Favourite

Type:	Summer fruiting
Fruit size:	Large
Skin colour:	Bright red
Picking time:	Early June-late June

CAMBRIDGE VIGOUR

An old 2nd early favourite which still has its fans. Conical, firm-fleshed and full of flavour. The vigorous and upright plants produce heavy crops, but the big problem is that quality quickly deteriorates — planting every 2 years is recommended. Disease can be a problem.

Type:	Summer fruiting
Fruit size:	Large
Skin colour:	Dark red
Picking time:	Early July-late July

DOMANIL

A Belgian variety which comes into full fruit as the *Cambridge Favourite* season starts to decline. The flavour is good and yields are heavy. Growth is vigorous and leaves are large — but it has lost favour with commercial growers because of virus and fruit softness.

Domanil

Elsanta

Gorella

Grandee

Hapil

ELSANTA

This new Dutch variety is considered by many professional growers to be the replacement for *Cambridge Favourite*. It has the properties they require — high yields, attractive glossy fruit and excellent shelf life. The flavour is outstanding but disease resistance is not.

Type:	Summer fruiting
Fruit size:	Large
Skin colour:	Orange-red
Picking time:	Mid June-mid July

ELVIRA

The modern replacement for *Cambridge Vigour* if you want a June crop. Yields are heavier and the conical fruit is larger. The flavour is good but mildew can still be a problem. This is one they recommend for growing under cloches as it has an open growth habit.

Type:	Summer fruiting
Fruit size:	Large
Skin colour:	Dark red
Picking time:	Early June-late June

GENTO

One of the long-established perpetuals — the flavour is very good and the conical, red-fleshed berries have a tangy flavour. Yields are generally good but it is occasionally unreliable. Still, it does better on chalky soil than other Strawberries.

Type:	Perpetual
Fruit size:	Large
Skin colour:	Bright red
Picking time:	Late summer-autumn

GORELLA

You'll find this one in some lists of recommended varieties. It has been one of Europe's top Strawberries — early cropping, compact habit and strong growth appealed to professional growers. But poor yields, indifferent flavour and mildew have led to its decline.

Type:	Summer fruiting
Fruit size:	Large
Skin colour:	Bright red
Picking time:	Early June-late June

GRANDEE

Enormous fruit when well grown — specimens weighing 3 oz have been picked. Yields are also very high, especially in the second year. One for the show bench, of course, but it's not in many catalogues. The flavour is below average, fruits are often hollow and mildew is a problem.

Type:	Summer fruiting
Fruit size:	Very large
Skin colour:	Dark red
Picking time:	Early June-late June

HAPIL

This Belgian variety has been rapidly accepted by professional growers as a replacement for *Cambridge Favourite* — it does much better than its rival in light soil and dry seasons. Flavour of the conical fruit is very good — yields are high. Well worth a trial.

Type:	Summer fruiting
Fruit size:	Very large
Skin colour:	Orange-red
Picking time:	Mid June-mid July

HARVESTER

There seems to be some disagreement in the catalogues about this one — its value as dessert fruit ranges from 'excellent' to 'poor' depending on the supplier! Still, the crops are certainly heavy and the plants are vigorous. The growth habit is upright and it has many fans.

Type:	Summer fruiting
Fruit size:	Large
Skin colour:	Orange-red
Picking time:	Mid June-mid July

HEDLEY

A new British variety with an upright growth habit. This Strawberry is not grown for the shops as the berries are very soft and the flavour is tangy rather than sweet. Try it if you want a new taste or if you are keen on jam-making — it has no rival as a preserve.

Type:	Summer fruiting
Fruit size:	Large
Skin colour:	Bright red
Picking time:	Early June-late June

Type: Summer fruiting	
Fruit size: Medium	
Skin colour: Bright red	
Picking time: Early June-late June	

HONEOYE

An important early variety with an awful name but a good record. It produces heavy crops for a summer fruiting Strawberry and the glossy fruit is very attractive. The firm, red flesh has a better flavour than *Pantagruella* and its resistance to botrytis is higher.

Honeoye

Type: Summer fruiting	
Fruit size: Medium-large	
Skin colour: Dark red	
Picking time: Early June-late June	

IDIL

A new heavy cropper from Belgium. The flavour is good but not outstanding and the fruits are round or conical. There is some resistance to mildew and verticillium, and the catalogues note that the Strawberries readily part with their plugs. All right, but nothing special.

Type: Perpetual	
Fruit size: Small-medium	
Skin colour: Pale red	
Picking time: Late summer-autumn	

OSTARA

The most popular perpetual in Europe before the entry of *Rapella*. It gives fairly good yields and is dependable. The orange flesh is soft and has an average flavour. Growth is vigorous, but it produces few runners and is susceptible to mildew and verticillium.

Type: Summer fruiting	
Fruit size: Large	
Skin colour: Orange-red	
Picking time: Mid July-mid August	

PANDORA

A new variety which has created interest because it fills the mid July-mid August gap. Yields are very high and the plants are vigorous. It appears to have good disease resistance, but it is unique in requiring a pollination partner such as *Cambridge Favourite*.

Pantagruella

Type: Summer fruiting	
Fruit size: Medium-large	
Skin colour: Orange-red	
Picking time: Late May-mid June	

PANTAGRUELLA

This is the one to grow to beat your neighbours —*Pantagruella* is the first Strawberry to bear fruit. Place cloches over the plants and you can enjoy the fruit in early May. Nothing special apart from earliness — average flavour, disease-prone, frost-prone and poor after the first year.

Type: Perpetual	
Fruit size: Medium	
Skin colour: Orange-red	
Picking time: Late summer-autumn	

RABUNDA

This perpetual still appears in catalogues despite the introduction of outstanding types such as *Aromel* and *Rapella*. The trouble is that everything is 'average' compared to other older perpetuals — average yields, average flavour and average size. Mildew resistance is below average.

Type: Perpetual	
Fruit size: Medium-large	
Skin colour: Bright red	
Picking time: Late summer-autumn	

RAPELLA

A new variety which is expected to challenge *Aromel* for the perpetual crown. It crops more heavily than others in the group and the flavour is good. Fruits ripen earlier than other perpetuals, so all can be picked before the first frosts. Susceptible to mildew — not a good choice for the North.

Rapella

Type: Summer fruiting	
Fruit size: Large	
Skin colour: Bright red	
Picking time: Mid June-mid July	

REDGAUNTLET

Well established — it's been around for over 30 years. Cropping is good but the flavour is disappointing. The disease resistance is quite high, but its main claim to fame is the second crop which appears in September after a hot summer. Interesting, but not a good choice these days.

Redgauntlet

Royal Sovereign

Selva

Tamella

Tenira

ROYAL SOVEREIGN

This is the only pre-War variety in the catalogues, and that's only for sentimental reasons. The flavour was once the standard which others tried to match — it is equalled nowadays by *Elsanta* and *Tenira*. Yields are low and the plants soon fall prey to all sorts of diseases.

Type:	Summer fruiting
Fruit size:	Medium-large
Skin colour:	Orange-red
Picking time:	Early June-late June

SALADIN

This new Scottish variety has produced very heavy yields in trials. The fruit is often ribbed and misshapen and the surface is soft. Growth is erect and leafy, and it is resistant to red core and mildew. The flavour is 'poor', 'average' or 'very good', depending on the catalogue.

Type:	Summer fruiting
Fruit size:	Large
Skin colour:	Orange-red
Picking time:	Early July-late July

SELVA

One of the day neutral varieties which will crop several months after planting at any time of the year if the temperature is kept at 55°F or higher. The fruit is unusually firm and attractive but the flavour is disappointing. Susceptible to mildew.

Type:	Day neutral
Fruit size:	Very large
Skin colour:	Bright red
Picking time:	Late summer-autumn

TAMELLA

A good choice, especially for northern England and Scotland. It crops over a long period and the productive life of the plant is longer than for nearly all other varieties. It also gives the highest yields, but the flavour of the orange flesh is only fair.

Type:	Summer fruiting
Fruit size:	Very large
Skin colour:	Dark red
Picking time:	Mid June-mid July

TANTALLON

A good substitute for *Cambridge Favourite*. It produces heavier crops and the resistance to disease is much higher. Flavour is rather better, but still not top grade. Not many runners are produced. Keep this one well watered, say the growers.

Type:	Summer fruiting
Fruit size:	Medium
Skin colour:	Orange-red
Picking time:	Mid June-mid July

TENIRA

Grow this one if you need to be convinced that a modern variety can taste as good as a pre-War one. Plants are vigorous and disease resistance is better than average, but yields are only moderate. Growth is upright, so ripe fruit is kept off the ground.

Type:	Summer fruiting
Fruit size:	Medium
Skin colour:	Bright red
Picking time:	Early July-late July

TOTEM

Yields are much lower than you would get from *Cambridge Favourite* and the flavour when eaten fresh does not compare with *Bounty, Elsanta* or *Hapil*. The sole reason for choosing this mid-season variety would be for its outstanding freezing properties — it keeps its shape when thawed.

Type:	Summer fruiting
Fruit size:	Medium
Skin colour:	Dark red
Picking time:	Mid June-mid July

TROUBADOR

A useful variety to extend the season — cropping starts about a fortnight after *Cambridge Favourite*. Yields are high and disease resistance is very good, but flavour is only average and the plants suffer in a dry season. The glossy fruit is attractive. Late flowering — an advantage in the North.

Type:	Summer fruiting
Fruit size:	Medium-large
Skin colour:	Dark red
Picking time:	Early July-late July

Planting

A sunny, sheltered site is required — a little shade during the day is acceptable. The area chosen for the strawberry bed must not be in a frost pocket and ideally the land should not have been used for growing Potatoes, Tomatoes, Chrysanthemums nor Strawberries for several years. Good drainage is essential and light soil will ensure early crops. The ground should be slightly acid and a liberal amount of organic matter is required.

Dig at least a month before planting — all weeds must be removed at this stage. Mix in a bucketful of compost or well-rotted manure per sq. yard when preparing the bed. Scatter 2 oz of Growmore per sq. yard over the ground just before planting.

Summer fruiting varieties

Plant bare-rooted plants between July and September. March–April planting is acceptable, but all flowers should be removed during the first season.

Note: Container-grown specimens can be planted at any time of the year when the weather is suitable.

Space between plants: 1½ ft
Space between rows: 2½ ft

Perpetual and day neutral varieties

Plant in July–August or March–April. Remove the first flush of flowers during the first season.

Note: Container-grown specimens can be planted at any time of the year when the weather is suitable.

Space between plants: 1½ ft
Space between rows: 2½ ft

Alpine varieties

Sow seed in autumn — overwinter in an unheated greenhouse. Plant out home-grown or bought-in plants in April or May.

Space between plants: 1 ft
Space between rows: 2 ft

Bare-rooted plants

② Spread out roots evenly

③ Make sure the crown is level with the surrounding soil

④ Replace and firm soil around the roots. Water in thoroughly

① Create a small mound in the planting hole with a trowel

Container-grown plants

② Soak thoroughly in water if the plant is in a peat pot

③ Make sure the top of the soil ball is slightly below the surrounding soil

④ Fill in with planting mixture — see page 7

① Dig hole large enough and deep enough for a 1–2 in. layer of planting mixture around the soil ball

Planting through polythene

Worth trying — cropping is earlier and the fruits are protected from earth and slugs

Plant Strawberries through slits cut into the polythene

Black polythene sheeting — 150 gauge

18 in

6 in.

3 in.

Tuck edges into the soil

Seasonal care

For a May crop grow an early variety such as *Pantagruella, Honeoye* or *Cambridge Vigour* and cover with cloches from late winter onwards. When the flowers appear partially open the cloches during the day to enable pollinating insects to enter.

Cover unprotected plants with newspaper if frost is expected when the flowers are open. Remove the paper during the day.

Newly-planted Strawberries must be watered regularly — so must established plants during dry weather. It is important to keep water off fruits — do this task in the morning so splashes can dry before nightfall.

Strawberries are low-growing plants — yields can be seriously affected by abundant weed growth. Keep weeds under control by hoeing regularly — do not hoe too deeply and keep away from the crowns.

May is the usual time for mulching — see the Feeding and Mulching section overleaf. Make sure that weeds are removed and the soil is moist before putting down a mulch. After mulching it will be necessary to provide bird protection — see page 59.

Most varieties produce runners which bear plantlets along their length. These runners can be removed so that each plant keeps its individuality or you can let the runners grow and root between the plants to form a continuous ('matted') row. Mulching and weeding can be more difficult here and the fruits tend to be smaller than on runner-removed plants, but the total yields are much higher.

Spray as necessary to keep down pests and diseases. After removing the leaves in summer or autumn (see Pruning section overleaf) hoe to remove weeds and excess runners and to loosen the soil between the plants.

Pruning

Pruning takes place neither at planting time nor when the plants are growing. The time for pruning is when the last of the berries have been picked. With summer fruiting varieties cut off all the leaves about 3 in. above the crown. At the same time cut off unwanted runners and rake up together with mulching material, weeds etc and dispose of by composting or burning. Less drastic pruning is required with perpetual and day neutral varieties — remove old leaves only.

Feeding & Mulching

Apply a general fertilizer such as Growmore (2 oz per sq. yard) around the plants in March or April — keep granules off the foliage. After fruiting apply a high-potash feed.

Mulching is essential to prevent the ripening fruit from coming in contact with the soil. The traditional mulching material is barley straw, which is placed along the rows and tucked under the fruit. Alternatively you can use pieces of black polythene sheeting or proprietary strawberry mats. The time to mulch is when the fruit is beginning to swell — place Slug Pellets under the plants before putting the mulch in place.

Picking & Storage

Once maximum size has been reached the fruit ripens very rapidly. This means you must inspect the bed daily — pick Strawberries which have reddened all over. This should be done in the morning and when the fruit is dry. Nip the stalk between thumbnail and forefinger — don't tug the fruit away from the stem. Remove and destroy diseased fruit immediately.

Eat as soon as possible — do not remove plugs (cores) before washing or storing. Strawberries can be kept for a few days in a cool place, but they freeze badly. If you want to freeze them for serving whole rather than as a purée you should choose the variety *Totem* or use small, slightly unripe fruit.

Growing under glass

Strawberries grown in pots in an unheated house will fruit in late April or early May — choose *Elvira* or *Cambridge Favourite*. Put vigorous, well-rooted plantlets into 5 or 6 in. pots in September. Keep them in the open — water regularly and then bury the pots in well-drained ground in November. Transfer the containers to a cold greenhouse in January — hand pollinate when the flowers appear and start to feed weekly with a liquid fertilizer. Ventilate the house when the weather is warm and sunny. Stop feeding when fruits start to redden.

Raising new plants

New Strawberries can be easily raised from runners, but you must make sure that the mother plant is healthy with leaves which are neither crinkled nor mottled. In June or July select 4 or 5 strong runners from each plant and proceed as shown below:

② Secure plantlet to compost with a hairpin

③ Nip off runner beyond the plantlet

① Bury 3½ in. pot filled with compost

④ Keep the compost moist

① After 4–6 weeks the plantlet will have rooted. Sever plantlet from runner and remove hairpin

② About 7 days later remove rooted plantlet from the pot — plant as instructed on page 65

Some perpetual and day neutral varieties do not produce runners. Propagate by division — dig up the plant in early September and divide into a number of separate crowns. Plant each one immediately — the crown of each divided plant should be level with the soil surface after planting.

Strawberries in containers

A problem with many fruit trees, canes and bushes is the need for space and/or free-draining soil. This is a problem for the person with a tiny plot or no garden at all — but Strawberries pose no difficulty. They can be grown in tubs, window boxes, hanging baskets, growing bags etc.

The traditional strawberry pot is a large terracotta jar with cupped holes arranged spirally around its sides. An attractive feature in a cottage garden or some other old-world setting, but perhaps a little out of place on the terrace of a modern house. More fitting here is the plastic tower or the polished wooden tub. The DIY enthusiast can make a strawberry barrel — drill a series of 2 in. diameter holes about 1 ft apart.

There are cultural as well as decorative and space-saving benefits. The fruit is kept away from slugs and picking is made easier. Mulching and hoeing are not required, and bird protection simply involves draping a net over the container. There is an extra task, however — you will have to water regularly.

RASPBERRIES

Raspberries continue to play second fiddle to Strawberries in the gardens of Britain. There are some obvious reasons — the plants are much taller which makes bird protection more difficult. Strong supports are necessary, and so is annual pruning. Still, there's the other side to the coin. Raspberries freeze extremely well, and canes can be expected to remain productive for 8 to 12 years. The cropping period for summer fruiting varieties lasts from 3 to 6 weeks — almost double the Strawberry season. An even more important advantage is the late flowering of Raspberries — frost damage is rarely a problem. No worries here for the northern gardener — Raspberries thrive in cool, damp summers.

The summer fruiting varieties are by far the more popular type. The root ('stool') of each plant produces tall canes — fruit is borne on those canes which developed in the previous year. Picking early varieties begins in early July — mid-season varieties start to crop in mid or late July and late varieties are not ready until late July or early August. To make a start you will need land which does not waterlog in winter — if drainage is poor, create a raised bed. This site should not have grown Raspberries for 7 or more years — if it has then change the soil to a spade's depth. You will need some form of support — a stout fence, a line of strong poles or a custom-made post-and-wire structure. Finally the plants — these must be bought from a reputable supplier and be certified as virus-free.

Autumn fruiting varieties can be used to extend the cropping season from late August to the arrival of the first frosts. These Raspberries fruit on the top of this year's canes, which means that they are pruned differently from the more popular summer fruiting types. Autumn Raspberries have smaller canes and smaller yields — they do best in mild regions.

Raspberries are an easy crop and very rewarding — only Strawberries start to bear fruit more quickly and give a higher yield per sq. yard of bed. Birds and viruses are the major menaces. Deterioration usually starts after about 8 years — matters get steadily worse and after a few more years (or even less) it will be necessary to dig them out and burn the virus-ridden plants.

Consider the newer varieties when replanting — look for aphid resistance. Grow *Malling Admiral* if you have room for only one variety. *Autumn Bliss* should be your first choice amongst autumn fruiting varieties — it's so much better than some of the older ones.

SUMMER FRUITING RASPBERRY

Yellow   Orange-red   Pink   Red   Dark red

By far the more popular group. Yields are higher and plants can be grown in all districts.

Fruit is borne over a 3–6 week period in July and/or August, depending on the variety.

Fruit is borne on canes produced in the previous year.

Support is essential.

Protection against birds is essential.

Removal of fruit from the plug is very easy at picking time.

Average yield — 4½ lb per yard of row.

AUTUMN FRUITING RASPBERRY

Yellow   Red   Dark red

Less popular than summer fruiting varieties. Yields are lower and plants do not thrive in cold districts.

Fruit is borne over an 8–9 week period between late August and the first frosts, depending on the variety.

Fruit is borne on the tips of canes produced this year.

Support is desirable but not essential.

Protection against birds is desirable but is not always essential.

Removal of fruit from the plug is often difficult at picking time.

Average yield — 1½ lb per yard of row.

Varieties A~Z

Autumn Bliss

Delight

Glen Clova

AUTUMN BLISS

A new autumn fruiting Raspberry which has become the recommended choice. It significantly outyields the other varieties and the fruits start to ripen in August. The texture is firm and the flavour is quite good. Sturdy — support is not needed. The site must be sheltered and sunny.

Type:	Autumn fruiting
Fruit size:	Medium-large
Skin colour:	Bright red
Picking time:	Mid August–October

DELIGHT

This is one of the most widely stocked of all Raspberries, but it certainly isn't the best. You won't find larger fruit and the crops may be extremely high, but there is a list of problems. Flavour is below average, fruits tend to bleed and disintegrate, and disease resistance is low.

Type:	Summer fruiting
Fruit size:	Very large
Skin colour:	Dark pink
Picking time:	Early July–late July

FALLGOLD

This is the yellow Raspberry which fruits in autumn. A novelty, but the unique colour is not matched by any other unique properties. The flavour and sweetness are good without being outstanding — so are fruit size and yields. Not generally available at garden centres.

Type:	Autumn fruiting
Fruit size:	Medium-large
Skin colour:	Yellow
Picking time:	Mid September–October

GLEN CLOVA

A very popular variety — yields are high and the fruits herald the start of the Raspberry picking season in many gardens. The berries are firm and rather small, making them ideal for freezing. Not perfect — flavour is only fair and the plant is susceptible to virus. Plant it away from other varieties.

Type:	Summer fruiting
Fruit size:	Small-medium
Skin colour:	Red
Picking time:	Early July–late July

GLEN MOY

A new variety to compete with *Glen Clova*. There are advantages — no spines, larger berries, good aphid resistance, a small autumn crop in warm summers and a better flavour. Gives good yields, but the picking season is quite short. The fruit is conical with a downy skin.

Type:	Summer fruiting
Fruit size:	Medium-large
Skin colour:	Pale red
Picking time:	Early July–late July

GLEN PROSEN

A new variety to compete with *Malling Admiral*. The fruit is round and very firm — the canes are spine-free and easy to control. Flavour is good and there is some resistance to both aphids and virus. A heavy cropping variety, but it needs better soil than most Raspberries.

Type:	Summer fruiting
Fruit size:	Medium
Skin colour:	Bright red
Picking time:	Mid July–mid August

GOLDEN EVEREST

The standard yellow summer fruiting variety. The stock may not be certified — grow them away from red varieties. Flavour is quite sweet but very mild — yields are quite low. An interesting variety which bears some fruit on new wood in autumn. You will have to order from a specialist nursery.

Type:	Summer fruiting
Fruit size:	Small-medium
Skin colour:	Yellow
Picking time:	Early July–late July

HERITAGE

Quite a popular autumn Raspberry, but you can do better these days. Yields are not very high, and picking starts late even for an autumn fruiting variety. The berries are firm, the flavour about average and the canes numerous and vigorous. Needs a warm spot.

Type:	Autumn fruiting
Fruit size:	Small-medium
Skin colour:	Bright red
Picking time:	Mid September–October

Type: Summer fruiting	
Fruit size: Large	
Skin colour: Dark red	
Picking time: Mid July–late August	

JOY

A summer fruiting variety which neatly fills the cropping gap between *Glen Clova* and *Leo*. There are a number of good points — it crops for about 6 weeks, the yields are high and the flavour is very good. There is some aphid resistance. No real problems, but the stems are very spiny.

Joy

Type: Summer fruiting	
Fruit size: Medium-large	
Skin colour: Orange-red	
Picking time: Late July–late August	

LEO

This is the last of the popular summer fruiting Raspberries to bear fruit. The taste is good and quite tangy — texture is firm and growth is vigorous. Stems are both aphid- and botrytis-resistant. The major problem is that the canes are rather sparse and the yields are below average.

Type: Summer fruiting	
Fruit size: Large	
Skin colour: Bright red	
Picking time: Mid July–mid August	

MALLING ADMIRAL

Choose this one if you are restricted to one variety. The spine-free canes are numerous, vigorous and resistant to spur blight, botrytis and some viruses. Flavour is very good, the texture is firm and yields are reasonably high. Protect from strong winds.

Type: Summer fruiting	
Fruit size: Medium	
Skin colour: Dark red	
Picking time: Early July–late July	

MALLING JEWEL

An all-purpose and reliable variety which has been very popular for many years. The flavour is good but yields are not high. Growth is compact — it is a good idea to plant 2 canes at each station. An important virtue is tolerance to virus infection.

Malling Jewel

Type: Summer fruiting	
Fruit size: Small-medium	
Skin colour: Pink	
Picking time: Mid July–mid August	

MALLING ORION

An old variety which is making something of a comeback. The round fruits have a good flavour and firm texture. Growth is vigorous, yields are quite heavy but all these properties are matched by newer varieties which have additional benefits such as aphid resistance.

Malling Orion

Type: Summer fruiting	
Fruit size: Large	
Skin colour: Orange-red	
Picking time: Early July–late July	

MALLING PROMISE

Shares with *Glen Clova* the honour of being the earliest Raspberry in the garden. It also shares the rather insipid taste of the fruit, but yields are very good and it is tolerant of virus infection. It is an easy variety to grow and it does well in poor soil.

Type: Autumn fruiting	
Fruit size: Small-medium	
Skin colour: Dark red	
Picking time: Early September–October	

SEPTEMBER

Still offered by a number of nurseries, but it is a variety with virtually nothing to recommend it. The flavour is only fair, yields are low, growth is rather weak and the fruits tend to crumble. Canes need thinning and the plugs are hard to remove. Give it a miss.

Type: Autumn fruiting	
Fruit size: Medium-large	
Skin colour: Dark red	
Picking time: Early September–October	

ZEVA

Does well in the North, but it has now lost its place to *Autumn Bliss*. *Zeva* produces attractive fruit which has a reasonably good flavour but tends to crumble. The canes are numerous but cropping is only moderate. You should find this one at larger garden centres.

Zeva

Planting

A sheltered spot is required — shoots can be damaged by strong winds. Raspberries grow best in full sun but partial shade is acceptable. The ideal soil is slightly acid, not too heavy and rich in organic matter. The great danger is waterlogging — Raspberries rapidly die if their roots stand in wet, airless earth for long periods. Raise the proposed planting site by adding topsoil to the surface if the subsoil is solid clay.

Dig at least a month before planting — make a trench about 18 in. wide and 9 in. deep. All weeds must be removed at this stage. Add a bucketful of compost or rotted manure every yard and spread it across the bottom of the trench. Fork in and return the soil. Consolidate the surface and scatter 2 oz of Growmore per sq. yard over the ground before planting.

Plant bare-rooted canes in November or December — plant in March if this is not possible.
Note: Container-grown specimens can be planted at any time of the year when the weather is suitable.

Space between plants: 1½ ft
Space between rows: 6 ft

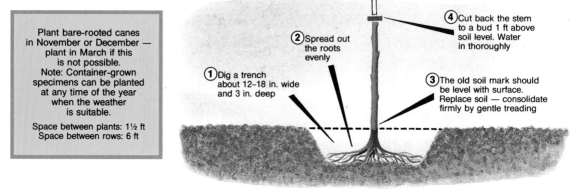

① Dig a trench about 12–18 in. wide and 3 in. deep

② Spread out the roots evenly

④ Cut back the stem to a bud 1 ft above soil level. Water in thoroughly

③ The old soil mark should be level with surface. Replace soil — consolidate firmly by gentle treading

See page 8 for details of planting container-grown specimens. In this case there is no need to cut back the stem after planting.

Support systems

Summer fruiting varieties must be supported. All sorts of systems can be seen in gardens — string or wire stretched between poles, chain-link fences, nylon twine across fruit cage supports, etc. For a very small garden the **single post system** is useful, but harvesting is cumbersome and it is a poor method for more than a few plants. By far the most popular support is the **post-and-wire system** — canes are tied to the wires with soft twine. The **double fence system** allows for more canes to be grown from each root — these canes are not tied to the wires.

Post-and-wire system

Omit the top wire for an autumn fruiting variety

straining bolt

10 ft

6 ft

5½ ft

3½ ft

2½ ft

heavy-gauge (12–14) galvanised wire

The post must be fixed securely. Bury 2 ft deep — support with a stout angled strut

Single post system

3 in. x 3 in. post

Plant 2 Raspberries at the base — allow 12 canes to grow up the post. Secure with twine

6 ft

Bury the post 2 ft deep

Double fence system

galvanised wire

2 ft

1½ ft

5 ft

3 ft

cross-tie of wire or twine

Pruning

Newly-planted Raspberries

The cane will have been cut to 1 ft at planting time — see page 70

In spring cut down the old cane to near ground level when new growth appears

Established summer fruiting varieties

Immediately after picking cut down all the canes which have fruited. Retain the best 6–9 young unfruited canes and tie to wires 3–4 in. apart.

In February cut back tall growth to 6 in. above the top wire

Established autumn fruiting varieties

In February cut down all canes to ground level. Tie new canes to the wires with soft twine as they grow in the spring and summer. There is no need to thin these canes

Seasonal care

Raspberries are a thirsty crop. You must water them regularly during the first season if the weather is dry, and it is especially important to keep the soil moist when the fruit is swelling.

Keep weeds down by hoeing regularly — do not hoe too deeply or you will damage roots growing near the surface, and this will promote suckering.

March is the usual time for mulching — see next column. Suckers should be removed in summer and stems growing away from the row should be pulled out.

With summer fruiting varieties remove any flowers which may appear on the canes in the first summer after planting — this applies to container-grown plants.

Raspberry beetle is a serious pest. Spray when the first fruits start to turn pink — see page 101.

Feeding & Mulching

Apply a general fertilizer such as Growmore (2 oz per sq. yard) along the rows in March. Water in, and then apply a mulch. This should be a layer of well-rotted manure or compost — peat or bark is less effective. The purpose of this mulch is to keep the soil cool and moist in summer and to keep down weeds.

Picking & Storage

Pick when the fruits are fully coloured but still firm. Pull each Raspberry gently away from the stem, leaving the plug and stalk behind. Inspect the crop daily but try to pick fruit only when it is dry — wet fruit soon starts to go mouldy. Eat or freeze as soon as possible — small, slightly unripe fruits are the best ones for freezing.

Raising new plants

Raise new plants from your stock only if the canes look healthy and they were planted as certified stock within the past 2 seasons. Propagation is very simple — merely remove and plant suckers in October or November.

Lift up sucker and use secateurs to cut away from parent root. Plant immediately where the new Raspberry is to grow

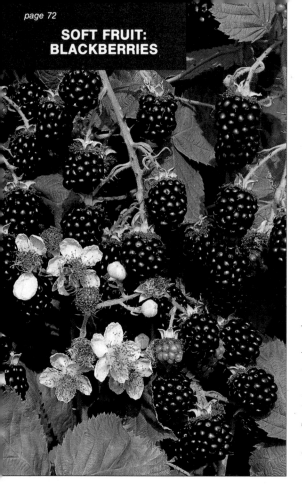

BLACKBERRIES & HYBRID BERRIES

The Blackberry is often regarded as a wild fruit (the Bramble) for picking in late summer from the hedgerows. Not one for the garden — a rampant grower with viciously thorny stems. This generalisation is no longer true — there are reasonably compact hybrids and there are several thornless types.

If you have a large trellis or a tall fence to clothe, then consider a modern Blackberry variety. No soft fruit is less trouble — birds may take a share but protection is not necessary, flowers open between May and July so frost protection is not necessary. The long arching canes will yield 10–25 lb per plant and it will grow against a north-facing wall. Choose certified stock and the plant can remain productive for up to 20 years.

Fruits appear between late July and September, depending on the variety. Grow *Oregon Thornless* or *Loch Ness* if people are likely to brush against the stems — choose *Ashton Cross* for real Blackberry flavour or *Himalaya Giant* for a vandal-proof screen. More and more people are turning to the hybrid berries which have been bred by crossing Blackberries, Raspberries, Dewberries etc. There is a wide range of flavours here, and nearly all are less vigorous than the Blackberry. Loganberries have been around for about a century and are the most popular, but Tayberries are perhaps the best choice.

Blackberries and their hybrids need strong supports for their thick and strong stems and there are several training systems as described on page 76.

Planting

Plant bare-rooted canes in November or December — plant in March if this is not possible.

Note: Container-grown specimens can be planted at any time of the year when the weather is suitable.

Space between plants: 6–15 ft (see Variety section)
Space between rows: 6 ft

Blackberries are not fussy about location — they will tolerate partial shade and also will grow in soils with less than efficient drainage. The canes are hardy but the tips can be damaged by hard frosts on exposed sites. Choose an area which has not grown Raspberries nor Blackberries for a number of years.

Dig at least a month before planting — cultivate a 2 ft x 2 ft area at each planting site. All weeds must be removed at this stage. Remove the top spit of soil and add a 3 in. layer of garden compost at the bottom of the hole. Fork in and return the soil. Consolidate the surface and scatter 2 oz of Growmore over the ground before planting. Plant in the same way as Raspberries — see page 70. Apply a mulch around the new canes in March.

Support systems

There are a number of support systems. Thornless varieties can be grown over arches. All varieties can be grown against a series of strong wires stretched across fences, trellises or walls. The support has to hold last year's canes which will bear fruit in summer or autumn, and also this year's canes for fruiting next year. The best support is the post-and-wire system — see illustration. This enables pruning, tying-in and picking to take place from both sides.

3 in. x 3 in. post

straining bolt

7 ft
6 ft
5 ft
4 ft
3 ft

heavy gauge (10–12) galvanised wire

The post must be fixed securely. Bury 2 ft deep — support with a stout angled strut

Varieties A-Z

ASHTON CROSS

A wiry-stemmed variety which bears very heavy crops. The fruits are carried in large clusters and have a high reputation for freezing, but the feature noted in the catalogues is the 'true' flavour of the wild Blackberry. You can expect to pick for 6–8 weeks.

Spacing:	12 ft
Fruit size:	Medium
Thorns:	Yes
Picking time:	August–September

Ashton Cross

BEDFORD GIANT

Very vigorous — not suitable for small gardens. The round and shiny fruit are borne in large clusters and herald the start of the Blackberry picking season. It is a reliable variety, giving fairly good yields under all sorts of conditions. The flavour is sweet but bland.

Spacing:	15 ft
Fruit size:	Large
Thorns:	Yes
Picking time:	Late July–August

BLACK SATIN

A new one from the U.S — this one bears fruit earlier than any other thornless variety. It is not yet in the popular class but is well worth a trial. Growth is vigorous and the flavour of the fruit is rather sharp. Use it to cover a large arch or a pergola.

Spacing:	12 ft
Fruit size:	Large
Thorns:	No
Picking time:	Late July–August

FANTASIA

A new star of the Blackberry world — discovered on an allotment at Kingston-upon-Thames. Thorny, vigorous and cropping in August and September. Nothing special there — the unique feature is the outstanding size of the fruit. When well grown the berry is the size of a 10p piece.

Spacing:	15 ft
Fruit size:	Very large
Thorns:	Yes
Picking time:	Late August–late September

Fantasia

HIMALAYA GIANT

Choose this one only if you have a large space to cover and you require an impenetrable barrier or a windbreak. Very vigorous and very spiny — yields of 25 lb per plant are not uncommon. The flavour is fair and quite acid — for cooking rather than for eating fresh.

Spacing:	15 ft
Fruit size:	Medium
Thorns:	Yes
Picking time:	Late August–late September

LOCH NESS

Something new in Blackberries. The stout stems are semi-erect, requiring little or no support. Winter hardy with good yields and reasonably-flavoured fruit, this one is bound to become very popular. Train and prune like a summer fruiting Raspberry.

Spacing:	6 ft
Fruit size:	Large
Thorns:	No
Picking time:	Late August–September

Himalaya Giant

MERTON THORNLESS

A fine thornless variety where space is limited — the rather short canes and the complete absence of thorns make maintenance a simple job. The yields are nothing special but the flavour is quite good. The plant is not as popular nor as attractive as *Oregon Thornless*.

Spacing:	8 ft
Fruit size:	Large
Thorns:	No
Picking time:	August–September

OREGON THORNLESS

The popular thornless variety — the fruit has a mild flavour and the canes are easy to train. A decorative plant for a trellis or arch — the leaves are deeply divided and there are bright autumn colours. Other thornless varieties include *Smoothstem* and *Thornfree*.

Spacing:	10 ft
Fruit size:	Medium
Thorns:	No
Picking time:	Late August–late September

Oregon Thornless

Hybrid berries A~Z

Boysenberry

Dewberry

Japanese Wineberry

Loganberry

BOYSENBERRY

The fruit is round or oblong, looking like a large, dark and rather long Raspberry. The flavour, however, is more akin to a wild Blackberry. The prickly canes are borne in profusion — the *Thornless Boysenberry* is less vigorous. A good choice for sandy soils — Boysenberry is remarkably drought-resistant.

Parentage:	Loganberry x Blackberry x Raspberry
Spacing:	8 ft
Fruit size:	Large
Skin colour:	Purple
Picking time:	July–August

DEWBERRY

The few catalogues which list this Blackberry-like plant include it in the hybrid berry section, but it is not a hybrid at all. It is a distinct species — popular in the U.S but finding little favour in Britain. The slender stems can be left to trail over the plot as ground cover — the dull fruit has a good flavour.

Parentage:	Rubus caesius
Spacing:	6 ft
Fruit size:	Small
Skin colour:	Black, covered with grey bloom
Picking time:	July

HILDABERRY

A new hybrid berry raised by an amateur and named for his wife. Not yet popular, but the flowers are 1½–2 in. across and the fruits can be more than 1 in. in diameter. The rounded berries can be eaten fresh or made into jam or jelly. You won't find this one at your garden centre —look through the specialist catalogues.

Parentage:	Boysenberry x Tayberry
Spacing:	8 ft
Fruit size:	Very large
Skin colour:	Red
Picking time:	June–mid July

JAPANESE WINEBERRY

An unusual type in many ways. Firstly, it's not a hybrid — it is a separate Rubus species. It is also extremely decorative — the arching canes are covered with soft, bright red bristles. The small, seed-filled berries are sweet but bland, and they ripen all at once during August. Yields are quite low.

Parentage:	Rubus phoenicolasius
Spacing:	6 ft
Fruit size:	Small
Skin colour:	Orange or red
Picking time:	August

JOHN INNES

Listed as a hybrid, but really a Blackberry bred at the John Innes Institute nearly 70 years ago. It is noted for its extra-large jet black and shiny fruits which have a distinct sweet flavour. Spines are few and crops are heavy, but fruiting is rather too late to recommend it for northern districts.

Parentage:	Blackberry x Blackberry
Spacing:	10 ft
Fruit size:	Very large
Skin colour:	Black
Picking time:	September–October

KING'S ACRE

An old hybrid which is related to the Loganberry but from which it differs in a number of ways. The red fruit turns black when ripe and the flavour is mild and similar to a Blackberry — not sharp like a Loganberry. It is also earlier ripening than the Loganberry. Finally, it is suitable for a small garden.

Parentage:	Raspberry x Blackberry
Spacing:	8 ft
Fruit size:	Medium
Skin colour:	Black
Picking time:	Early July–August

LOGANBERRY

The basic hybrid bred in Canada in the last century was a prickly and moderately vigorous plant. *LY59* is the type you can buy today — still quite thorny and with long fruit which has a sharp taste. Loganberries are excellent for culinary uses but not for eating fresh. A thornless and less vigorous variety (*L654*) is available.

Parentage:	Raspberry x Blackberry
Spacing:	8 ft
Fruit size:	Large
Skin colour:	Dark red
Picking time:	Mid July–August

Parentage:	Unknown
Spacing:	12 ft
Fruit size:	Large
Skin colour:	Black
Picking time:	Mid July–September

MARIONBERRY

Something of a mystery — the Marionberry has long been considered to be a hybrid berry, but is now thought to be a true Blackberry, despite its sharp Loganberry-like flavour. The canes are thorny and very vigorous. The most outstanding feature is the length of the picking season, extending for 8 or 9 weeks.

Marionberry

Parentage:	Includes Loganberry, Young-berry, Marionberry & Boysenberry
Spacing:	15 ft
Fruit size:	Large
Skin colour:	Dark red
Picking time:	Early August–September

SILVANBERRY

A new hybrid from Australia which is claimed to do well in heavy soils and exposed situations. It is also claimed that disease resistance is excellent, but it will have to stand the test of time. Fruits are large and sweet but growth is very vigorous and spreading — not one for a small garden.

Parentage:	Raspberry x Blackberry
Spacing:	15 ft
Fruit size:	Medium
Skin colour:	Dark red
Picking time:	Mid July–late August

SUNBERRY

A recent hybrid from East Malling — its main claim to fame is that the cropping period lasts for many weeks. It is far too vigorous and thorny to become really popular, although the very dark and glossy berries have a reasonably good Loganberry-type flavour. Tayberry or Tummelberry is a better choice.

Tayberry

Parentage:	Raspberry x Blackberry
Spacing:	8 ft
Fruit size:	Large
Skin colour:	Dark purple
Picking time:	Mid July–August

TAYBERRY

Pick this one if you plan to buy only one hybrid berry, and ask for the virus-free Medana strain. Growth isn't rampant but yields are good and the juicy aromatic berries are larger than a Loganberry and also much sweeter. The stems are slightly thorny and they can suffer in winter in exposed northern locations.

Parentage:	Tayberry x Tayberry seedling
Spacing:	8 ft
Fruit size:	Large
Skin colour:	Red
Picking time:	Mid July–August

TUMMELBERRY

A new hybrid berry from the Scottish Crop Research Institute — hardiness has been bred into the Tayberry. Here is one which will stand up to cold winters, but some of the sweetness of the Tayberry has been lost — the flavour is more like a Loganberry. The hairy canes grow upright rather than arching.

Tummelberry

Parentage:	Raspberry x Blackberry
Spacing:	8 ft
Fruit size:	Large
Skin colour:	Dark red
Picking time:	August–September

VEITCHBERRY

One of the older Raspberry/Blackberry crosses. You will still find it in a number of catalogues because the fruit is larger than either parent and the flavour is excellent. Canes are stout and stiff rather than wiry and arching and the fruit is difficult to pull away from the plug. Birds can be a problem.

Parentage:	Loganberry x Dewberry
Spacing:	8 ft
Fruit size:	Large
Skin colour:	Purple
Picking time:	Late July–September

YOUNGBERRY

The fruit looks like a Boysenberry or a rounded Loganberry. This hybrid has never become popular and you will have to search for a supplier. The flavour is very close to a Loganberry and the juicy fruits contain very few seeds. If you want to try this one, choose the new *Thornless Youngberry* variety.

Youngberry

Pruning & Training

The **fan** method of training gives high yields and is often recommended for the less vigorous hybrids. With this system the new canes are trained vertically and then along the top wire. The fruiting canes are tied as a fan to either side of this central column. After fruiting these old canes are removed and the central ones are then spread out to both sides to provide next year's fruiting canes. The fan method is a lot of work — even more troublesome is the **weaving** system which gives top yields. Here the new canes are woven up and down along the bottom 3 wires after the old canes have been removed in autumn. In summer the current wood is trained vertically and along the top wire.

The simplest but not the most productive system is **roping**. This is the procedure recommended for general garden use and is shown below. Wear leather gloves — burn old canes. In February cut back any dead shoot tips.

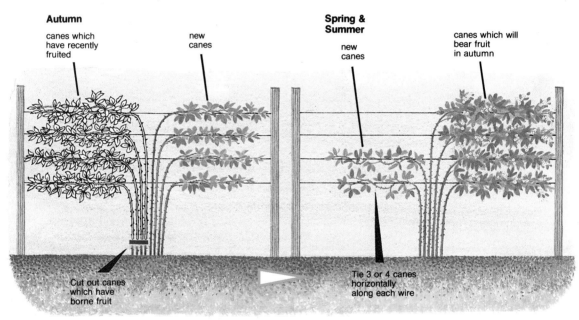

Autumn

canes which have recently fruited

new canes

Cut out canes which have borne fruit

Spring & Summer

new canes

canes which will bear fruit in autumn

Tie 3 or 4 canes horizontally along each wire

Seasonal care

Water in summer if the weather is dry when the fruit has started to develop. Water the ground and not the stems in order to reduce the disease risk.

March is the usual time for mulching — see below. Canes growing away from the row should be pulled out. Keep weeds down by regularly shallow hoeing.

Spray against raspberry beetle if this pest has been serious in previous years — see page 101.

Raising new plants

② Use secateurs to sever 1 ft of the rooted tip from the parent stem. Plant where the new Blackberry is to grow

① In July–September dig a hole and bury the tip of a healthy shoot about 6 in. deep. Hold down with a hairpin — replace soil and tread down

Feeding & Mulching

Apply a general fertilizer such as Growmore at the rate of 2 oz per sq. yard around each plant. Water in, and then apply a mulch. This should be a layer of well-rotted manure or compost — peat or bark is less effective. The purpose of this mulch is to keep the soil cool and moist in summer and to keep down weeds.

Picking & Storage

Pick when the fruits are fully coloured and soft. Pull each Blackberry gently away from the stem — the plug generally comes away with the fruit. Pick when the fruit is dry — wet fruit soon starts to go mouldy. Eat or freeze as soon as possible — use in jams, jellies, pie-making, puddings etc.

BLACKCURRANTS

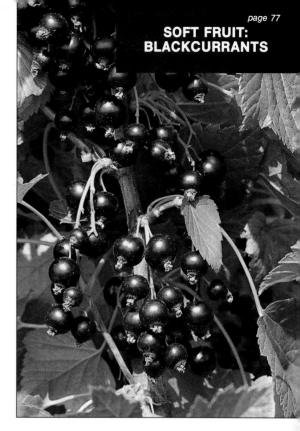

Blackcurrants are grown mainly for use in pies and puddings. They are also excellent for jam and jelly making, but are not popular for serving fresh. They are not difficult to grow, but you must know what to do at planting and pruning time. The reason is that most of the fruit is borne on last year's stems, and that means a regular supply of new growth from below ground level is required each year. To ensure this you must plant deeply with the root/shoot union well below the surface and you must cut out some old wood in winter.

Buy 2 year old certified plants with at least 3 shoots. The bush should eventually reach a height and spread of 5 ft, producing 10–15 lb of fruit each summer and staying productive for 10–15 years. Reversion or big bud mite may reduce this long and active life by a few years, but the real threat until recently was frost. Older varieties bloom in early April, and both flowers and small fruitlets are susceptible to frost damage. Fortunately, plant breeders have introduced a range of late-flowering and partially frost-hardy types — the 'Ben' group and *Malling Jet* are examples. Choose *Ben Sarek* if the garden is small, *Ben Lomond* or *Ben More* as reliable all-rounders or *Malling Jet* for picking in September. Some people claim that the modern varieties have lost the 'real' Blackcurrant flavour, but there never has been a standard taste — *Baldwin* is distinctly sharp and old *Wellington XXX* is sweet.

Varieties A-Z

Bush size: Medium	
Fruit size: Medium	**BALDWIN**
Cropping: Heavy	The most popular choice until *Ben Lomond* came along. An age-old variety — choose the productive Hilltop strain. Growth is quite compact and the tart fruit hangs on the plant for a long time without splitting. The early flowering habit is a problem in northern districts.
Picking time: Late July	

Baldwin

Bush size: Medium	
Fruit size: Large	**BEN LOMOND**
Cropping: Heavy	The first of the 'Ben' varieties which have brought late flowering, some mildew resistance and very heavy yields to Blackcurrants. Growth is upright and reasonably compact — the strigs (flower stalks) are short and the plump berries have an acid flavour.
Picking time: Late July	

Bush size: Medium	
Fruit size: Large	**BEN MORE**
Cropping: Heavy	A recent introduction to challenge *Ben Lomond*. The growth habit is neater and yields are reputed to be heavier. Best feature of all if you live in the North is the lateness of flowering — even later than *Malling Jet*. Resistance to mildew is quite high and the fruit flavour is sharp.
Picking time: Late July	

Ben Nevis

Bush size: Large	
Fruit size: Medium–large	**BEN NEVIS**
Cropping: Heavy	Similar to *Ben Lomond* in many ways — it flowers and fruits at the same time as *Ben Lomond*, the well-flavoured berries are borne on short strigs and there is both mildew and frost resistance. The growth habit is different — it is taller, more vigorous and more upright.
Picking time: Late July	

Ben Sarek

Jostaberry

Tsema

Wellington XXX

BEN SAREK

The main feature here is the dwarf nature of the bush — it grows only 3–4 ft high and should be planted at 4 ft spacings. There are in-bred frost resistance and some mildew resistance, but also one or two drawbacks. Branch support is necessary and so is prompt picking before the fruits fall.

Bush size:	Small
Fruit size:	Large
Cropping:	Heavy
Picking time:	Mid July

BLACK REWARD

A tall and vigorous Dutch variety launched to rival *Baldwin*. This one flowers 1–2 weeks later than the old favourite, which means much higher yields in a summer following a cold spring. Flavour is good, but there is no mildew resistance. Spraying will be necessary.

Bush size:	Large
Fruit size:	Medium
Cropping:	Heavy
Picking time:	Late July

BOSKOOP GIANT

A giant of a plant — recommended spacing is 6 ft. Vigorous and spreading, but the yield is lower than that of a modern Ben variety. The sweet fruit appears early — provided that frost has not affected the cold-susceptible flowers. Not for the North or small gardens.

Bush size:	Large
Fruit size:	Large
Cropping:	Moderate
Picking time:	Early July

JOSTABERRY

Not a Blackcurrant variety — it's a Blackcurrant x Gooseberry hybrid. Grow it like a Blackcurrant, but leave 6 ft between the plants. Resistant to mildew and very prolific. You will tell the difference from an ordinary variety at picking time — the currants are twice the size.

Bush size:	Large
Fruit size:	Very large
Cropping:	Heavy
Picking time:	July

LAXTON GIANT

Another early-fruiting giant like *Boskoop Giant*. Susceptible to spring frosts, but it is still chosen by exhibitors for the remarkable size of its fruit when well-grown. Plant 6 ft apart — very vigorous and spreading. Berries are sweet and can be eaten fresh for dessert.

Bush size:	Large
Fruit size:	Very large
Cropping:	Heavy
Picking time:	Early July

MALLING JET

Something different — a vigorous bush (too large for small gardens) which bears very long strigs of smallish berries in August and early September. Flowering is also very late so frost damage is unlikely. The flavour is acidic but rather bland. Plant 6 ft apart.

Bush size:	Large
Fruit size:	Small–medium
Cropping:	Moderate
Picking time:	Late August

TSEMA

This Dutch variety bears long strigs like *Malling Jet*, but picking time is July instead of August/September. Flavour is only fair, and you will have to support the branches if the crop is a heavy one. There is neither frost nor mildew resistance — not a very good choice.

Bush size:	Large
Fruit size:	Small
Cropping:	Heavy
Picking time:	Early July

WELLINGTON XXX

The *Wellington XXX* fan club says that the fruit has the best flavour of all — sweet and juicy. Growth is vigorous and spreading — crops are usually heavy but late frosts can cause a problem. Launched over 60 years ago, you will still find it in many catalogues.

Bush size:	Large
Fruit size:	Medium–large
Cropping:	Heavy
Picking time:	Mid July

Planting

Blackcurrants will tolerate poor drainage better than other soft fruits, but they do need organic-rich soil and some shelter from the wind. Full sun is preferred but light shade is not a problem. Do not plant on a site prone to late frosts unless you grow a modern frost-resistant variety and are willing to cover the bushes if April nights are unusually cold.

Prepare the planting sites well before the bushes arrive — follow the instructions for Blackberries on page 72.

Plant bare-rooted bushes in November — plant in February-March if this is not possible.
Note: Container-grown specimens can be planted at any time of the year when the weather is suitable.
Space between plants: 5 ft
Space between rows: 5 ft

② The old soil mark should be 2 in. below the surface. Replace soil — consolidate firmly by gentle treading

③ Cut back the stems to a bud 1-2 in. above the surface

① Dig a hole wide enough for roots to be spread out

Pruning

Prune between November and March. Start 2 years after planting, cutting out weak branches. From 3 or 4 years onwards remove some old wood each year, as shown below.

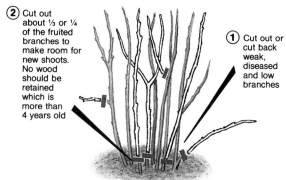

② Cut out about ⅓ or ¼ of the fruited branches to make room for new shoots. No wood should be retained which is more than 4 years old

① Cut out or cut back weak, diseased and low branches

Raising new plants

Take 10 in. cuttings from this season's wood in October — the cuttings should be pencil-thick. Make a sloping cut at the top — a straight cut at the bottom.

① Cut V-shaped trench — place layer of sand at bottom

② Insert cuttings 6 in. apart — 2 buds should show above the surface

③ Replace and consolidate soil. Dig up and plant in the following October — cut back canes to 1-2 in. as noted under 'Planting'

Seasonal care

In spring make sure that the bushes have not been lifted by frost — tread down if this has happened. Another spring job is to provide frost protection, especially for older varieties — drape netting or sacking over the bushes when night frosts threaten at flowering time. Remove the cover during the day.

Keep weeds under control. Hoe with great care — keep the blade near the surface to avoid damaging the shallow rooting system. It is better to keep weeds in check by mulching and hand pulling.

Water regularly and thoroughly during dry weather — keep water off the stems.

Bird protection is necessary. Drape nets over the bushes when the fruits begin to change from green to purple.

Feeding & Mulching

Mulching is important. Place a mulch around the bushes after planting and renew this mulch each April with a 3 in. layer of garden compost or rotted manure.

Blackcurrants do require feeding. Spread about 4 oz of Growmore around each bush in March before mulching, and apply a potassium-rich liquid feed in summer when the fruits are swelling.

Picking & Storage

Fruit is ripe and ready for picking about 7 days after it has turned blue-black. For immediate use you can pick individual currants — the fruits at the top of the strig are the first to ripen. For show purposes or for keeping in the refrigerator it is better to cut the whole strig. Harvest early varieties promptly.

Blackcurrants can be kept in the refrigerator for a week. For longer storage you should freeze, bottle or dry.

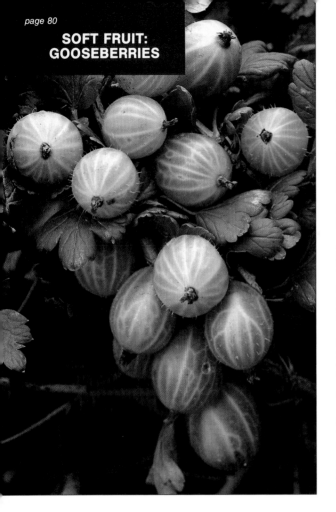

GOOSEBERRIES

The Gooseberry is a long-suffering plant — left unfed and unpruned a bush will continue to give some fruit for many years. Because of this it is sometimes called an 'easy' plant, and that is not true. Pruning in winter and summer is necessary to give an abundant crop which can be readily reached and which is not borne at ground level — and pruning among the vicious thorns is troublesome. Winter protection against birds is important in many areas, and failure to spray against american mildew can result in a totally mouldy crop.

Gooseberries bear a permanent framework of young and mature branches. The usual growth form is a 2–5 ft high bush which is open centred and is borne on a 4–6 in. bare stem ('leg'). Alternatively you can grow the plant as a cordon with 1, 2 or 3 upright 6 ft stems — much less popular are the fan and the half standard.

The bush yields 6–12 lb of berries — you can expect about 2 or 3 lb from a cordon. The plants are not generally troubled by virus and should remain productive for 10–15 years. Choose a 2 or 3 year old bush for planting — cultivation is similar to the Red or White Currant.

Culinary varieties have a sharp taste and are not suitable for eating fresh. Dessert varieties are not usually available in the shops — they are larger, thinner-skinned and sweeter. The best plan is to buy a dessert variety from which you can pick unripe fruit in late May or June for cooking and then pick ripe fruit in July or August for eating fresh.

Planting

The standard rules for siting soft fruit apply. Full sun is preferred — partial shade is tolerated. Protection from strong winds is necessary and frost pockets must be avoided.

Prepare the planting sites well before the bushes arrive — follow the instructions for Blackberries on page 72.

BUSHES

Plant bare-rooted bushes in October–November — plant in February–March if this is not possible.

Note: Container-grown specimens can be planted at any time of the year when the weather is suitable.

Space between plants:
5 ft   (bushes)
1½ ft (single cordons)
2 ft   (double cordons)
3 ft   (triple cordons)
Space between rows:
5 ft

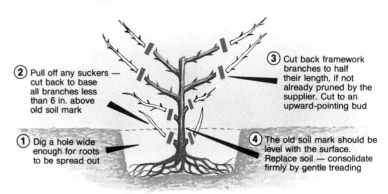

② Pull off any suckers — cut back to base all branches less than 6 in. above old soil mark

③ Cut back framework branches to half their length, if not already pruned by the supplier. Cut to an upward-pointing bud

① Dig a hole wide enough for roots to be spread out

④ The old soil mark should be level with the surface. Replace soil — consolidate firmly by gentle treading

CORDONS

As Red & White Currants — see page 86.

Varieties A-Z

Type:	Dessert
Fruit size:	Small–medium
Bush shape:	Upright
Skin colour:	Dark red
Picking time:	Mid July

BLACK VELVET

A new Gooseberry x Worcesterberry hybrid. The smallish Grape-like fruits have a refreshing flavour — even more important is the complete resistance to american mildew of the bushes. It is an easy-to-grow plant which does well as a cordon — yields are high.

Type:	Culinary
Fruit size:	Large
Bush shape:	Spreading
Skin colour:	Pale green
Picking time:	Mid July

CARELESS

The most popular variety — available everywhere. It is reliable and not fussy about soil type. The smooth berries are crisp — excellent for all cooking purposes. Susceptible to american mildew. Despite its popularity, *Whinham's Industry* or *Invicta* is a better choice.

Careless

Type:	Dessert/Culinary
Fruit size:	Medium
Bush shape:	Upright
Skin colour:	Yellow
Picking time:	Late June

EARLY SULPHUR

An old favourite which is returning to the catalogues — it is one of the first to bear fruit. The primrose yellow fruits are hairy and semi-transparent, and the flavour is good. It is a heavy cropper with a long-established reputation as a top Gooseberry for jam-making.

Type:	Dessert
Fruit size:	Small
Bush shape:	Upright
Skin colour:	Greenish-yellow
Picking time:	Mid July

GOLDEN DROP

A good choice if you are looking for fruit to serve fresh — the small, round berries have thin skins and an excellent flavour. Another virtue where space is limited is the neat and compact growth habit. No resistance to american mildew. Yields are only moderate.

Early Sulphur

Type:	Culinary
Fruit size:	Small–medium
Bush shape:	Upright
Skin colour:	Dark green
Picking time:	Mid July

GREEN GEM

The round smooth fruit is dark with prominent pale veins. There is not much going for this variety these days and it is no longer popular. Yields are not high and it is susceptible to american mildew. The flavour is acceptable but not top rate.

Type:	Dessert/Culinary
Fruit size:	Large
Bush shape:	Spreading
Skin colour:	Pale green
Picking time:	Late July

INVICTA

The new star of the Gooseberry world. It is now widely available and widely praised. The reasons are immunity to american mildew and very high yields. But it is very prickly, growth is vigorous and spreading, and the dessert quality when ripe is not particularly good.

Green Gem

Type:	Dessert/Culinary
Fruit size:	Large
Bush shape:	Upright/spreading
Skin colour:	Greenish-yellow
Picking time:	Mid July

JUBILEE

An improved form of the ever-popular *Careless*. All agree that it is more productive, and some catalogues claim all sorts of extra benefits. Examples are less spreading growth habit, better flavour as a dessert variety when ripe, earlier fruiting and larger-sized berries.

Type:	Culinary
Fruit size:	Medium–large
Bush shape:	Spreading
Skin colour:	Pale green
Picking time:	Early July

KEEPSAKE

The fruit when ripe is almost white and is sometimes eaten fresh for dessert, but *Keepsake*'s main claim to fame is that the small unripe fruit can be picked in late May onwards for tarts, Gooseberry fool etc. The flavour is very good but late frosts can be a problem.

Invicta

Leveller

May Duke

Whinham's Industry

Worcesterberry

LANCASHIRE LAD

This dual-purpose variety has some resistance to american mildew. The oval hairy fruits have an attractive red colour and a moderately good flavour, but it is disappointing where soil or situation is not good. Still, some people swear by it.

Type:	Dessert/Culinary
Fruit size:	Medium–large
Bush shape:	Spreading
Skin colour:	Red
Picking time:	Late July

LANGLEY GAGE

The almost white berries are semi-transparent. They are smooth and oval, and are perhaps the sweetest of all Gooseberries. Unfortunately there are not many suppliers but it is worth looking for. Yields can be high, but tend to be variable.

Type:	Dessert
Fruit size:	Small–medium
Bush shape:	Upright
Skin colour:	Pale yellow
Picking time:	Late July

LEVELLER

Rightly popular, sharing the dessert crown with *Whinham's Industry*. The extra-large fruit is oval and downy — a standard choice for the exhibitor. Not just pretty — the flavour is exceptional. The catalogue will tell you that yields are very high — but only in good soil.

Type:	Dessert/Culinary
Fruit size:	Very large
Bush shape:	Spreading
Skin colour:	Greenish-yellow
Picking time:	Late July

LORD DERBY

Easy to recognise in July or August — a small bush with drooping branches and nearly black fruit. The round berries are smooth with an average to good flavour. Eye-catching — excellent for the show bench. Yields are high for such a compact bush.

Type:	Dessert/Culinary
Fruit size:	Very large
Bush shape:	Arching
Skin colour:	Dark red
Picking time:	Early August

MAY DUKE

An old favourite which is traditionally picked at the green stage in May and June for pies and bottling and then in July at the red stage for stewing or even eating fresh. The fruit is oval and downy with a moderately good flavour — the bush is neat and compact.

Type:	Culinary
Fruit size:	Medium
Bush shape:	Upright
Skin colour:	Dark red
Picking time:	Early July

WHINHAM'S INDUSTRY

A rival to *Leveller* as the best all-rounder. The fruit does not have *Leveller*'s size nor its sweetness, but the growth is upright and the flavour is excellent. The main point is that it does much better than *Leveller* in shade and heavy soil.

Type:	Dessert/Culinary
Fruit size:	Medium–large
Bush shape:	Upright
Skin colour:	Dark red
Picking time:	Late July

WHITESMITH

A popular dual-purpose Gooseberry which is a good choice. The near-white fruit is oval and downy with an exceptional flavour. The bush has a strong constitution, doing well in all sorts of soils. Yields are high. Available in fan and half standard form.

Type:	Dessert/Culinary
Fruit size:	Medium–large
Bush shape:	Spreading
Skin colour:	Yellowish-white
Picking time:	Late July

WORCESTERBERRY

Small purple or black 'Gooseberries' but it is really a Currant species — *Ribes divaricatum*. Very vigorous and thorny — leave 8 ft between the plants. Excellent for jam-making. Cultivate like a Gooseberry — immune to american mildew.

Type:	Culinary
Fruit size:	Small
Bush shape:	Upright
Skin colour:	Purple
Picking time:	Late June

Pruning

BUSHES

Cut to an outward-facing bud for an upright variety or to an inward-facing bud for a spreading variety. Always wear a pair of leather gloves when pruning Gooseberries.

The full method shown below is somewhat time consuming. If growth is not vigorous carry out the winter pruning and omit the summer cutting-back of the side-shoots.

November–March

① Cut back the new growth produced by the leaders this year by a half

② Reduce the side-shoots growing from the leaders to about 2 in.

③ Cut out dead and diseased wood, and any branches crowding the centre

Late June

Cut back all side-shoots produced this year to 4 or 5 leaves from the base

CORDONS

As Red & White Currants — see page 86.

Seasonal care

Winter protection against birds is necessary — finches attack the buds which produce next year's fruit. Netting is suitable, but Gooseberries are best grown in a fruit cage.

Check the plants after a heavy frost — firm down with your feet if the bushes have been lifted. Flowering time is early or mid April — cover at night with netting or sacking if frosts threaten at this time.

Keep weeds down by mulching and by hand pulling. Hoeing can damage surface roots and lead to excess suckering. Pull suckers away from roots during the dormant season.

Water thoroughly and regularly in summer if the weather is dry and the fruit is beginning to swell.

If the crop is heavy start to thin in May or June. Remove some of the berries when they are large enough for cooking — do this in stages until the fruits which are to mature to full ripeness are left 2 in. apart. Cover the ripening fruit with netting.

Feeding & Mulching

Apply a general fertilizer such as Growmore (2 oz per sq. yard) around each bush or cordon in March. Water in, and then apply a mulch of well-rotted manure or compost to keep down the weeds. Use peat or bark if compost is not available.

Picking & Storage

The usual plan is to pick some small green fruit from both culinary and dessert varieties in late May. These are crisp and tart — excellent for crumbles, pies, tarts etc. For dessert varieties which are to be eaten fresh, you will have to wait for the fully ripe stage. The fruit will be fully coloured and rather soft when gently squeezed. Not all will ripen at once — go over the bushes 2 or 3 times. Eat as soon as possible, although ripe Gooseberries can be kept in a refrigerator for a couple of weeks.

Raising new plants

Take 12 in. cuttings from this season's wood in October — the wood should be well-ripened. Make a sloping cut at the top — a straight cut at the bottom.

① Cut V-Shaped trench — place layer of sand at bottom

② Strip off buds along lower part of cutting — leave 4 buds at the top. The lowest bud should be 2 in. above the surface. Space cuttings 6 in. apart

③ Replace and consolidate soil. Dig up and plant in the following October — there should be 6 in. of bare stem as noted under Planting

RED & WHITE CURRANTS

Shops have never been really interested in Red and White Currants, and so many people have never tasted them. Nor are they a feature of pick-your-own farms, which means that you must grow your own to be sure of a midsummer supply of these delicious fruits.

Red Currants are tart — use them for pies, jams, jellies and wine-making. The White Currant is a sport of the red one — the flavour is Grape-like and the fruits are perfectly suitable for serving fresh.

The big surprise is that these two plants are planted, pruned and cared for like Gooseberries and not like Blackcurrants to which they are closely related. The usual form is an open-centred, goblet-shaped bush with a height and spread of about 5–6 ft. Fruit is carried on stubby side-shoots on the main branches — you can expect about 10 lb and the plant should remain productive for about 15 years. The purpose of annual pruning is to ensure an abundance of these fruiting spurs.

Red and White Currants can also be grown as vertical cordons bearing 1, 2 or 3 stems. Stretch wires horizontally across a wall or fence 2 ft and 4 ft above the ground — fix firm canes where the cordons are to be planted. You can expect about 3 lb of fruit from each single cordon.

Buy 2 year old plants from a reputable supplier — look for a stout bush with at least 4 evenly-spaced branches. The choice of varieties is not large — the usual Red Currant choice is *Red Lake* or *Laxton's No.1*, although *Redstart* is expected to be the variety of the future. *White Versailles* is a good all-rounder and is the only White Currant you are likely to find at the garden centre.

Varieties A-Z

Laxton's No.1

Red Lake

JONKHEER VAN TETS
This one starts the Red Currant picking season — the bright fruit is juicy and rated very highly for flavour. Crops are heavy and bushes grow large with untidy and brittle branches. This variety does best when grown as a cordon. Quite widely available.

Type:	Red Currant
Fruit size:	Large
Bush shape:	Upright
Picking time:	Early July

LAXTON'S NO.1
This old favourite shares many features with the modern Dutch variety *Jonkheer van Tets*. It is early, strong growing, good flavoured and heavy yielding. However, it is later flowering, the fruit is smaller and the branches tend to spread with age. Widely available.

Type:	Red Currant
Fruit size:	Medium
Bush shape:	Upright
Picking time:	Mid July

RED LAKE
This reliable variety remains the most popular all-rounder. The fruit is carried on long trusses which are easy to pick, and heavy crops are borne on moderately vigorous bushes. No problems — flavour is good, juice content is high and stocks are sold everywhere.

Type:	Red Currant
Fruit size:	Very large
Bush shape:	Upright
Picking time:	Late July

Type: Red Currant	
Fruit size: Medium	
Bush shape: Upright	
Picking time: August	

REDSTART

The experts predict a great future for this new variety from East Malling Research Station. It is very late, cropping in mid August. The bright fruits are produced in long strigs and yields are reported to be high and consistent. The flavour is distinctly acid.

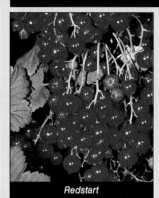

Redstart

Type: Red Currant	
Fruit size: Medium	
Bush shape: Upright/spreading	
Picking time: Early August	

RONDOM

A dark red variety — the acid, rather dry fruits are borne in tight trusses. Crops are heavy and growth is vigorous — recommended for exposed sites where wind can damage other varieties. Growth is upright at first, but mature bushes have a spreading habit.

Type: Red Currant	
Fruit size: Large	
Bush shape: Upright	
Picking time: Early August	

ROVADA

A late flowering and late fruiting Dutch variety which appears in a few catalogues but not at the garden centre. Most of its other features are typical of the average Red Currant, but its cropping capacity appears to be exceptional. Flavour is good.

Stanza

Type: Red Currant	
Fruit size: Small–medium	
Bush shape: Upright	
Picking time: Late July	

STANZA

A new Red Currant with some interesting features. The fruits are quite small and darker than the popular varieties — it also flowers later which means that the chance of frost damage is lessened. Flavour is more acid and the growth habit is more compact.

Type: White Currant	
Fruit size: Large	
Bush shape: Spreading	
Picking time: Late July	

WHITE DUTCH

Long trusses of pale golden fruits are borne in midsummer. Flavour is not as good as *White Grape*, and the growth habit is more spreading and untidy than other White Currant varieties. It scores by producing heavier crops than the others.

Type: White Currant	
Fruit size: Large	
Bush shape: Upright	
Picking time: Mid July	

WHITE GRAPE

Second to *White Versailles* in popularity. It is still not easy to find a supplier — go to a specialist fruit nursery. The sweet flavour of *White Grape* is excellent and unmatched by *White Versailles*, but the yield is lower. Colour is near-white.

White Grape

Type: White Currant	
Fruit size: Large	
Bush shape: Upright	
Picking time: Late July	

WHITE PEARL

A late variety, cropping at the same time as *White Dutch*. Strigs are long and the flavour is good, but there is nothing special about this variety. Once sold as *White Transparent*, but now hardly sold at all. Still, it is a heavy cropper and it has its fans.

White Versailles

Type: White Currant	
Fruit size: Large	
Bush shape: Upright	
Picking time: Early July	

WHITE VERSAILLES

The first White Currant in both popularity and picking time. The trusses are long and heavy — the fruits are pale yellow and pleasantly sweet. It is thoroughly reliable, giving good crops year after year. It is the variety to buy if you plan to grow just one White Currant.

Planting

Choose a sheltered spot in sun or semi-shade. Any reasonable garden soil will do, but poor drainage will cause problems. Avoid a frost pocket.

Prepare the planting sites well before the bushes arrive — follow the instructions for Blackberries on page 72.

BUSHES

As Gooseberries — see page 80.

Plant bare-rooted bushes in October-November — plant in February-March if this is not possible. Note: Container-grown specimens can be planted at any time of the year when the weather is suitable.

Space between plants:
5 ft   (bushes)
1½ ft (single cordons)
3 ft   (double cordons)
4 ft   (triple cordons)
Space between rows:
5 ft

CORDONS

③ Cut back the leader to half its length — tie it with twine to the cane

② Pull out any suckers — cut back to base all branches less than 4 in. above old soil mark

① Dig a hole wide enough for roots to be spread out. Insert bamboo cane — attach cane to wires or fence

④ Trim back all laterals to a bud about 1 in. from the main stem

⑤ The old soil mark should be level with the surface. Replace soil — consolidate firmly by gentle treading

Pruning

BUSHES

As Gooseberries — see page 83.

CORDONS

February
Continue basic procedure carried out at planting time. Prune back the leaders to leave about 6 in. of this year's growth. Cut back all laterals to a bud about 1 in. from the main stem.

When the top of the cane is reached it will be necessary to cut back the leader to just one bud above last year's growth.

Late June
Cut back all side-shoots produced this year to 4 or 5 leaves from the base — see Gooseberry Pruning (page 83). This gets rid of aphids clustered at the shoot tips and also reduces the risk of disease.

As it extends tie the leading shoot to the cane.

SINGLE CORDON   DOUBLE CORDON   TRIPLE CORDON

Seasonal care

Birds in winter are a problem — finches attack the buds. Red and White Currants are best grown in a fruit cage — if this is not possible it will be necessary to cover the plants with netting.

Check the plants after a heavy frost — firm down with your feet if the bushes have been lifted. Flowering time is between late March and the end of April — cover at night with netting or sacking if frosts threaten at this time.

Keep weeds down by mulching or hand pulling. Hoeing can damage the mass of surface roots and lead to excess suckering. Pull suckers away from the roots during the dormant season.

Water thoroughly and regularly in summer if the weather is dry and the fruit is beginning to swell.

Birds find the small and succulent fruit irresistible. It will be necessary to cover the plants with netting when the ripening currants begin to show colour.

Feeding & Mulching

Apply a general fertilizer such as Growmore (2 oz per sq. yard) around each bush or cordon in March. Water in, and then apply a mulch of well-rotted manure, peat or compost.

Picking & Storage

Pick when the fruit is fully coloured and shiny — a dull surface indicates you have waited too long. Not all will ripen at once — go over the bushes 2 or 3 times. Pick the whole cluster to avoid damaging the fruits — do not pick off the currants singly. Use as soon as possible, although Red and White Currants can be kept in the refrigerator for about a week.

Raising new plants

As Gooseberries — see page 83.

HEATHLAND BERRIES

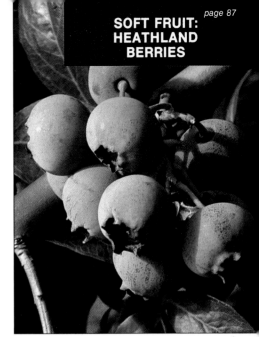

All the heathland berries have one fundamental feature in common — they must have moist and distinctly acid soil. Provided this need is met they are easy to grow — pruning is simple and there is no need to spray with insecticides or fungicides.

North America is the home of the heathland berry — they have never found favour in either shops or gardens in Britain, and only in recent years have they started to appear in specialist nursery catalogues. There are three types. The **Lowbush Blueberry** grows wild in boggy areas and is very rarely cultivated. The **Highbush Blueberry** is the star of the group — very popular in the U.S and now fairly readily available from nurseries in Britain. Try it by all means, but your soil will have to be less than pH 5.5. The **Cranberry** is even more demanding — the soil has to be less than pH 4.5.

The only one worth trying is the Highbush Blueberry. Have a go if your soil grows Rhododendrons and Azaleas *really* well with no sign of leaf yellowing — otherwise you should plant the specimens in stout containers. These will need regular watering with soft water or rainwater — a chore if you live in a hard water area. Still, the result is worthwhile. Dense clusters of pinkish flowers in spring, succulent fruit in midsummer and brilliant red foliage in autumn.

Heathland Berries A~Z

CRANBERRY

Unless your garden is a bog there is only one practical way to grow Cranberries. Dig a hole about 1 yard square and 1 spit deep. Line it with polythene and fill it with a mixture of 3 parts moss peat, 1 part loam, 1 part sharp sand and 1 part sawdust. Add 3 handfuls of Bone Meal to each barrowload. Plant in autumn or spring, leaving 1 ft between plants — water regularly with soft water and pick the red berries when they start to soften.

Cranberry

HIGHBUSH BLUEBERRY

There are several ways of growing the Highbush Blueberry (Blueberry for short) in the garden. The obvious place is the fruit plot. Free-draining soil is necessary — if it is not gritty, acid and rich in organic matter you should fill each planting hole with a mixture of moss peat, coarse sand, soil and a little sawdust.

The bush will eventually have a height and spread of about 5 ft and will bear 6 lb of fruit — dark blue berries about ½ in. across with a grey bloom. Plant 5 ft apart in autumn or spring. Buy 2 or 3 year old container-grown specimens. The site should be reasonably sunny and must be sheltered from strong winds. Frost is not usually a problem.

Prune in winter — cut out damaged or dead branches and a few old stems which have borne fruit. In spring sprinkle a little Dried Blood, Bone Meal or Hoof and Horn around the plants and mulch with peat. Watering regularly with soft water is essential in dry weather.

If your soil is acid it is quite practical to plant Blueberries in a Rhododendron border — the bright autumn tints provide a welcome splash of colour at the end of the season. If, on the other hand, your soil is quite definitely not acid then you will do far better to plant Blueberries in stout containers which should be at least 1½ ft deep. Use an ericaceous compost or make your own by mixing moss peat with a small amount of Sulphate of Ammonia, Sulphate of Potash and Bone Meal.

Birds can be a problem — cover the bush with netting as the fruits begin to ripen. Wait until they are beginning to soften and have been blue for a week before picking individual berries — you will have to go over the bush several times as not all the berries ripen at once. The fruits can be stored in the refrigerator for 2–3 weeks. Use in pies or tarts — best of all, find a recipe for Blueberry muffins.

Several varieties are available — *Bluecrop* is the most popular but there is also the handsome *Jersey*, the fine-flavoured *Herbert* and the early-fruiting *Earliblue*. For maximum yields grow 2 varieties to ensure cross-pollination.

Blueberry

LOWBUSH BLUEBERRY

The Bilberry (other names:- Whortleberry, Blaeberry) is a fruit of the countryside. It grows about 1–2 ft high and is a common sight in high moorland in the North. The fruits appear in autumn — sweet near-black berries with a grey bloom. Eat them fresh or use in pies.

Bilberry

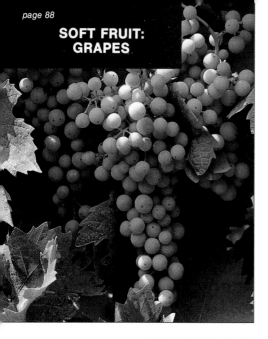

SOFT FRUIT: GRAPES

GRAPES

You will read in all the books that outdoor Grapes were grown extensively in Roman Britain — what isn't said is that their decline was due to a change in the climate rather than a change in our taste for wine. For hundreds of years the British climate was too cold for the Grapevine, but in the 20th century you can expect successful results south of a line stretching from Gloucester to the Wash.

You can of course grow Grapes under glass both inside and outside this area, but you should consider carefully whether you are prepared to devote space and time to this vigorous crop which demands attention nearly all year round.

A mature Grapevine will yield about 15 lb of fruit — enough to make a gallon of wine. It should stay productive for about 40 years, but you can't expect any fruit until 3 years after planting. Training and regular pruning are essential if you are to avoid a plant with masses of foliage and very few bunches of fruit — there are several different systems of training and pruning and none can be truly described as simple. Grapes, then, are for the enthusiast and not the reluctant·gardener.

OUTDOOR GRAPES

Black types
purple, maroon

White types
green, gold or pale pink

Outdoor varieties are generally smaller than the greenhouse ones, and the prominent surface bloom is usually missing.

Outdoor varieties are often grown for·wine-making as there is rarely enough sunshine to develop sweet and juicy flesh. There are, however, several dessert varieties which can be used as table Grapes for eating fresh. A few types are recommended for both outdoor and greenhouse use — *Siegerrebe, Leon Millot, Chasselas* and *Seyval* are examples.

Early varieties are ready for picking in September. You will have to wait until the first half of October for **mid-season** varieties and until the second half of October for the **late** ones. Choose an early variety if you live close to the North-South dividing line.

White types are generally more successful than black ones outdoors.

GREENHOUSE GRAPES

Black types
purple, maroon

White types
green, gold or pale pink

The range of varieties for greenhouse culture is greater and so is the chance of success. Many can be grown in a cold house, but some need a minimum temperature of 55°F in early spring.

The **Sweetwater** group are the easiest to grow, and the ever-popular *Black Hamburgh* belongs here. No heat is needed, and they ripen early — thin-skinned and very sweet. Cut as soon as the recommended stage is reached. The **Muscat** group have the best flavour but they are more trouble, calling for some heat and for hand pollination. They can be left to hang on the vine until they develop a slightly raisin-like taste. The **Vinous** group provide Grapes for Christmas or even later. They hang on the vine for months, but the house must be kept warm throughout late autumn and early winter.

Planting

Grapes need as much sun as possible outdoors — to avoid disappointment choose a wall which faces South, South-East or South-West. Good drainage is vital — don't bother to plant this crop if waterlogging is a problem. All soils but clays and shallow chalks can be used, but the best types are gritty or sandy soils enriched with organic matter.

Dig at least a month before planting — cultivate a 2 ft x 2 ft area at each planting site. All weeds should be removed at this stage. Remove the top spit and add a layer of garden compost at the bottom of the hole. Fork in and return the soil. Consolidate the surface and scatter 2 oz of Growmore over the area before planting.

Plant in October-November or February-March. March is the best time to plant outdoors — cover winter-planted specimens with a 4 in. layer of compost or leaf mould.
Space between plants: 5 ft

1 ft

1 ft

1½ ft

① Stretch support wire 1 ft apart between vine eyes set 9 in. away from the wall (outdoors) or supports (greenhouse)

③ Cut back the main shoot ('rod') to 2 ft. Tie the rod to the cane support

④ Cut back all side-shoots to 1 bud

② Plant the specimen firmly to the old soil mark. Insert a cane before planting. Some people plant greenhouse Grapes outside the house and bring the shoot inside through a hole at the base

Outdoor Varieties A-Z

Brandt

Type:	Dessert
Fruit size:	Small
Skin colour:	Purple
Picking time:	Late

BRANDT

Both fruit and bunches are small, but this hybrid is very popular and easy to find in the catalogues. The heavy crop is sweet and growth is vigorous — useful for covering an unsightly wall. Some mildew resistance. A warm and sunny spot is essential.

Type:	Wine-making
Fruit size:	Small
Skin colour:	Dark purple
Picking time:	Mid-season

CASCADE

Sometimes listed as *Seibel 13.053*. The small Grapes borne in tight clusters produce a dark, acid juice — the red wine quality is described as fair. Resistance to mildew is a definite advantage — so is its vigour if an effective screen is required.

Type:	Dessert/Wine-making
Fruit size:	Medium
Skin colour:	Blue-black
Picking time:	Mid-season

LEON MILLOT

A vigorous French variety, producing near-black Grapes for the table or for turning into a fair quality red wine. Bunches are small — resistance to mildew is good. Can be grown under glass in northern districts. Cropping is both good and reliable.

Madeleine Angevine

Type:	Dessert/Wine-making
Fruit size:	Medium
Skin colour:	Pale green
Picking time:	Mid-season

MADELEINE ANGEVINE

This white variety flowers late but ripens early, which makes it useful for cooler areas. Crops are heavy and it has an unmatched record for reliability. The quality record is much less notable — both fresh fruit and wine flavour are only classed as fair.

Type:	Dessert/Wine-making
Fruit size:	Medium
Skin colour:	Near-white
Picking time:	Early

MADELEINE SYLVANER

A pale white Grape which does much better than nearly all others when conditions are cooler than expected. Wine quality is good — dessert value is fair. It is reliable enough, but it is not a high-yielding variety. Ripens during September.

Seyval

Type:	Dessert/Wine-making
Fruit size:	Small–medium
Skin colour:	Golden
Picking time:	Mid-season

MULLER THURGAU

Our most popular Grape for wine-making — sometimes sold as *Riesling Sylvaner*. The hock-type product has a delicate flavour and fine bouquet. The Grapes are good but not outstanding for eating fresh. Yields are heavy, but not if the weather is poor at pollination time.

Type:	Wine-making
Fruit size:	Medium
Skin colour:	Green
Picking time:	Mid-season

SEYVAL

A popular wine-making Grape, sometimes sold as *Seyval Blanc* or *Seyve Villard*. Easy and reliable — often recommended for chalky soils and colder areas. The wine is described as light and fruity. There is some resistance to mildew.

Siegerrebe

Type:	Dessert/Wine-making
Fruit size:	Medium
Skin colour:	Golden-brown
Picking time:	Early

SIEGERREBE

An excellent dual-purpose Grape which ripens before the cold weather arrives. It gives consistently heavy crops provided the soil is free from chalk, and the white wine it produces is full-bodied and spicy. The flavour as a table Grape is sweet and Muscat-like.

Greenhouse Varieties A-Z

ALICANTE

A good choice for table or show bench — sometimes called *Black Tokay*. The bunches are large but lopsided — thinning is necessary. It sets fruit very freely, crops are heavy and flavour is very good — but it is a Vinous Grape and so heat is required.

Type:	Vinous
Fruit size:	Large
Skin colour:	Black with blue-grey bloom
Picking time:	Late

BLACK HAMBURGH

By far the most popular greenhouse Grape, and quite rightly so. It is the easiest to grow, and the flavour of the round succulent Grapes is good. It sets freely, ripens well without heat and consistently provides large bunches year after year.

Type:	Sweetwater
Fruit size:	Large
Skin colour:	Dark red or purple with blue bloom
Picking time:	Early

BUCKLAND SWEETWATER

A compact vine — worth considering if space is limited. Generally trouble free — it sets freely and yields are good. The round, pale green fruits turn pale golden when ripe and the flavour is sweet but not outstanding. Regular feeding is necessary.

Type:	Sweetwater
Fruit size:	Large
Skin colour:	Amber
Picking time:	Early

CHASSELAS

This variety has been around for centuries, and the various forms appear in the catalogues as *Chasselas d'Or, Royal Muscadine, Chasselas Rosé Royale* etc. Easy, reliable and high yielding like *Black Hamburgh*. Sometimes recommended for outside wall culture.

Type:	Sweetwater
Fruit size:	Medium
Skin colour:	Pink or amber
Picking time:	Early

FOSTER'S SEEDLING

The best of the white Sweetwaters, according to some experts. The bunches are extra-large and the fruit is very juicy. Crops are heavy and flavour is good, but do eat them as soon as possible after picking. Sometimes grown in pots.

Type:	Sweetwater
Fruit size:	Large
Skin colour:	Amber
Picking time:	Early

MADRESFIELD COURT

A very high quality black variety — the oval Grapes are juicy and full of flavour but the skin is tough. The bunches are long and wide and you must pick them as soon as they are ripe as the Grapes tend to split if left on the vine.

Type:	Muscat
Fruit size:	Large
Skin colour:	Near-black with blue-grey bloom
Picking time:	Early

MUSCAT HAMBURGH

The flavour of the fresh fruit is excellent and so is the wine it produces, but it must not be confused with the popular and easy-to-grow *Black Hamburgh*. This one needs heat, and cross-pollination with another variety is recommended.

Type:	Muscat
Fruit size:	Large
Skin colour:	Dark red or purple with blue bloom
Picking time:	Late

MUSCAT OF ALEXANDRIA

This is not a high-yielding variety and you will have to provide some heat either in spring or autumn. But the quality is excellent — large bunches of oval fruit which taste as good or better than any other home-grown Grape. It can be unreliable.

Type:	Muscat
Fruit size:	Large
Skin colour:	Amber with white bloom
Picking time:	Late

Alicante

Black Hamburgh

Chasselas

Foster's Seedling

Pruning & Training

There are several methods — the Cordon system is the usual one for greenhouse culture and the Guyot system is sometimes recommended for outdoor vines. For the sake of simplicity the Cordon system is recommended here for both greenhouse and outdoor cultivation.

1st & 2nd year after planting

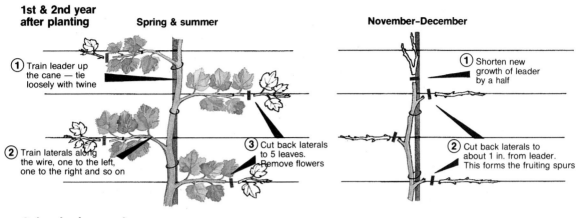

Spring & summer

1 Train leader up the cane — tie loosely with twine

2 Train laterals along the wire, one to the left, one to the right and so on

3 Cut back laterals to 5 leaves. Remove flowers

November–December

1 Shorten new growth of leader by a half

2 Cut back laterals to about 1 in. from leader. This forms the fruiting spurs

3rd and subsequent years after planting

Repeat the basic routine outlined above with the following modifications. When the flowers appear in spring, cut back the fruiting lateral to 2 leaves beyond the truss — cut back sub-laterals to just 1 leaf. Keep only 1 fruiting lateral per spur — rub out all others. For the first few years leave just one bunch per lateral — on a mature vine 2 or 3 bunches can be grown on each lateral.

In November or December prune the leader ('rod') as above. When the top wire is reached prune it back to 1 in. beyond last year's growth — in other words, treat it as a lateral.

Seasonal care under glass

In midwinter remove loose bark from the pruned rod and paint with tar oil winter wash — clean the glass behind the vine. This usually involves undoing the upper ties and letting the rod bend down before retying in the spring.

In early spring apply Growmore (2 oz per sq. yard) around the base of the plant. Water the surface and spread a 2 in. mulch of well-rotted compost around the stem. In March it is time to turn on the heat if available — start gently at first and increase to 55°-60°F after a few weeks. In an unheated house growth begins in April — the ventilators should be closed and damping down can begin.

In May it will be necessary to promote fertilization by shaking the stem at midday or by hand pollination (see page 41).

Watering will be necessary once active growth starts. Thoroughly soak the ground around the base of the stem every 3 weeks — apply a high-potash liquid fertilizer according to the maker's instructions from the time the first fruits form until the Grapes start to colour.

Thinning will be necessary if the set has been heavy. Begin when the berries are pea-sized, using a pair of long-bladed scissors in one hand and a small forked stick in the other. Never touch the fruit with your fingers — remove some of the berries within the bunch and get rid of small berries. Do this on several occasions over 7–10 days so that there is a ½ in. space between the remaining Grapes. A fussy job — but worth it for top quality results. Snip off any diseased fruits during this ripening stage.

Prune the laterals as noted under Pruning during the spring and summer months and apply Coolglass from June until late August. In August reduce ventilation and stop damping down in order to aid ripening. Reduce watering at this stage.

Seasonal care outdoors

In early spring apply Growmore (2 oz per sq. yard) around the base of the plant. Water the surface and spread a 2 in. mulch of well-rotted compost around the stem.

Water thoroughly and regularly during drought conditions — this will not be necessary for established vines in most seasons. Feed dessert Grapes with a high-potash liquid fertilizer from the time the fruits form until they begin to show colour.

Thinning may be necessary for dessert varieties but not for wine-making types. Bird protection will certainly be necessary when the Grapes start to ripen — use netting to protect the bunches. Remove a few leaves as the bunches ripen in order to improve air circulation and to expose the fruit to sunlight.

Picking & Storage

Colour is not a good guide to choosing the right time to pick — Grapes may have to hang on the vine for some time to allow all the sugars to form — this may take a couple of weeks for an early variety or as much as a couple of months for late varieties. Taste is the best guide.

Grapes are cut with a 'handle' — the whole bunch is removed by cutting the branch at about 2 in. on either side of the fruit stalk. Treat very gently. Grapes can be kept for 4–8 weeks by cutting the bunch with a length of branch attached and then putting one end in a jar of water. Store in a cool and dark place.

MELONS

Melon growing once belonged inside heated greenhouses on the large estates of Victorian times, but it can now be practised much more widely. There are splendid modern varieties such as *Sweetheart* and *Ogen* which ripen well in many parts of the U.K and there are now more garden greenhouses than ever before.

Still, you must be careful. Catalogues and books continue to talk about growing Melons in the South without protection, but that is far too risky. There are three acceptable sites — under cloches, inside a cold frame or up the side of a greenhouse. Growing under cloches or inside a cold frame is usually successful in southern counties provided you choose an early variety and the summer is a sunny one. Growing in a cold greenhouse is more reliable — choose an early or mid-season variety. The heated greenhouse is the true home for the Melon in the U.K — if you can maintain a minimum temperature of 65°F then you can grow any of the varieties listed in the catalogues.

Melons are raised from seed at home, except for the mid-season netted variety *Gaylia* which is only sold as plantlets. If you succeed with greenhouse Cucumbers then you should have no trouble with Melons, although you will have to maintain a drier atmosphere. Early Melons ripen in late July to mid August — the mid-season ones are ready in late August and the late varieties ripen at the beginning of September. Classification is notoriously difficult, but the arrangement shown below is accepted by most experts.

WINTER (Casaba) MELON

Large and oval with hard, ribbed skin — yellow or green. The well-known *Honeydew* Melon belongs here.

Flesh is pale green or white. It can be sweet and juicy. It is always crisp but is never fragrant.

A poor choice for cold greenhouse or cold frame cultivation.

NETTED (Musk) MELON

Small, round or oval with smooth skin which bears fine or coarse fibrous netting — yellowish-green or buff.

Flesh is green, orange or pink. It is juicy and sweet and there is a distinct 'melony' aroma and taste.

Choose with care — some need a heated greenhouse. A poor choice for cold frame cultivation.

CANTALOUPE MELON

Round, oval or flattened with rough skin which is grooved but not netted — greyish-green or buff.

Flesh is green, orange or pink. It is juicy and sweet and there is a distinct 'peachy' aroma and taste.

The most popular group — a good choice for cold greenhouse or cold frame cultivation.

Sowing & Planting

Seed sowing

Sow seed in mid or late April — sow a few extra pots in case of failure. Cover pots with glass and keep at a minimum of 65°F. Remove the glass after germination — maintain a minimum night temperature of 60°F. The seedlings are ready for planting out when there are 3–4 true leaves.

② Press in a single seed edgeways

½ in.

① Fill 3 in. pot with Seed- or Multi-compost

Cold frame planting

Prepare the soil in April. Dig ½ bucketful of well-rotted manure or compost into the soil at the centre of the frame. Water if necessary — close the lights. Harden off seedlings and plant out in late May. Close the lights after planting — cover surface for 7–14 days if sun is bright.

① Mound up soil at the centre of the cold frame

② Plant the seedling in the mound — leave 1 in. of the soil ball above the surface

③ Do not firm. Water in — but keep water off the stem

Greenhouse planting

You can plant into manure-enriched border soil or in compost-filled 10 in. pots, but growing bag cultivation has become the most popular method. Put the bags in position at least 1 week before planting. Always plant at the side of the house and create a support system (see page 94) before planting.

① Place growing bag on the floor or staging

② Plant the seedling in the compost — 2 per bag. Leave 1 in of the soil ball above the surface

③ Do not firm. Water in — but keep water off the stem

Varieties A-Z

Type: Netted	
Fruit size: Large	
Skin colour: Yellow	
Flesh colour: Dark orange	
Picking time: Late	

BLENHEIM ORANGE

An old favourite which keeps its place in some popular catalogues. This is one for the greenhouse, preferably a heated one. The flesh is occasionally more red than orange and the flavour is very good. Fruit is ready for picking in late August or early September.

Type: Cantaloupe	
Fruit size: Small	
Skin colour: Grey-green	
Flesh colour: Orange	
Picking time: Mid-season	

CHARANTAIS

You will find these greyish ball-like Melons with their shallow ribs in the supermarket, and the seeds can be found in some catalogues. The flesh is perfumed and richly golden-red but despite its 'delicious' reputation the flavour of home-grown fruit can be disappointing.

Charantais

Type: Netted	
Fruit size: Large	
Skin colour: Orange	
Flesh colour: Pale green	
Picking time: Late	

HERO OF LOCKINGE

A popular variety for growing in a heated house. Easy to recognise — a ball-like or broadly oval Melon with golden, heavily-netted skin and almost white flesh. The flavour is very good with a high reputation for sweetness. An old one but still widely recommended.

Type: Cantaloupe	
Fruit size: Medium	
Skin colour: Yellow or cream	
Flesh colour: Orange	
Picking time: Late	

NO NAME

Oddly named — and oddly described in some of the catalogues. The skin is creamy yellow with a variable amount of green. It is late fruiting and so you should pick another variety for growing in a frame or unheated house. The shape is oval and the flavour is excellent.

No Name

Type: Cantaloupe	
Fruit size: Small	
Skin colour: Yellow and green	
Flesh colour: Pale green	
Picking time: Early	

OGEN

Not quite as early as *Sweetheart*, nor is it as hardy. Still, it should be your choice for a cold frame or unheated house if you don't grow *Sweetheart*. The small, round yellow fruits with green ribs are very popular — the firm flesh is juicy and sweet.

Type: Netted	
Fruit size: Large	
Skin colour: Green	
Flesh colour: Orange-red	
Picking time: Late	

SUPERLATIVE

An attractive Melon — the ball-like fruit is dark green with prominent cream-coloured netting. The flesh is richly coloured and sweet. You can grow this one in an unheated house, but it is not popular and appears in few catalogues.

Superlative

Type: Cantaloupe	
Fruit size: Medium	
Skin colour: Grey-green	
Flesh colour: Orange	
Picking time: Early	

SWEETHEART

Everyone agrees — this *Charantais*-type Melon is the one to grow in an unheated greenhouse or cold frame. It succeeds under cool conditions where all others would fail, and its flesh is both attractive and full of flavour. One drawback only — seeds are expensive.

Type: Netted	
Fruit size: Medium	
Skin colour: Yellow and green	
Flesh colour: Orange-yellow	
Picking time: Mid-season	

TIGER

A brightly-coloured Melon — the bold yellow and green striped skin explains the name of this cold frame and greenhouse variety. It is shaped like a flattened ball and the flesh has a very good flavour when grown under warm conditions. Seed is not easy to find.

Sweetheart

Training & Seasonal care

GREENHOUSE

Before planting it is necessary to create supports for the climbing plants. Stretch wires up to the eaves or to the ridge — the stem will be about 6 ft high. After planting tie a cane to the wires behind each plant.

② Tie a stout cane to the wires behind the plant

⑤ Tie a lateral along each wire. Remove unwanted laterals

③ Tie the main stem loosely to the cane

④ Remove all laterals below the first wire

① Stretch support wires 1 ft apart between vine eyes set 15 in. away from the glass

Remove the growing point when the greenhouse eaves or ridge has been reached. The stem should be about 6 ft high. Pinch out the growing tip of each lateral when 5 leaves have been produced — this induces the production of side-shoots. It is these side-shoots which produce the flowers.

The flowers are of 2 types. The males appear first (thin stalk behind the petals) and then the female flowers open (tiny Melon behind the petals).

Hand pollination is necessary. Wait until 6 female flowers are open — each one on a separate lateral. Remove a mature male flower, fold back the petals and push gently into the heart of each female flower. Do this at midday — one male flower will fertilize 4 females. Thinning the fruit and stopping the side-shoots will be necessary when the Melons are marble-sized — see below:

② Pinch out stem 2 leaves beyond the fruit

① Remove unwanted fruit to leave just one Melon per lateral

You should now have 4–6 developing Melons on each plant — remove any further shoots or flowers which appear.

Throughout the life of the plant careful watering is necessary. The compost should be thoroughly moist but never waterlogged — this can mean watering twice a day when the fruit is swelling but you must keep water off the stems. Reduce watering when the Melons start to ripen.

Regular feeding is also necessary. Begin feeding with a high-potash liquid feed when the fruits are the size of a golf ball and continue every 7–10 days until they start to ripen.

Gentle damping down and misting are desirable at most times, but should not take place during pollination time nor when the fruits start to colour. At this later stage the ventilators should be opened as a dry atmosphere is needed. Another requirement at the ripening stage is physical support — see below:

Net attached to wires to support fruit from tennis-ball size to maturity

COLD FRAME

The appearance of new growth is an indication that the transplant is established — remove the shading material placed over the glass and start to increase ventilation gradually.

It is time to pinch out the growing point once the 5th true leaf has developed — this will induce side-shoots to form. About 3 weeks later select the 4 strongest shoots and train each one to a corner of the frame.

① Train a strong shoot towards the corner of the cold frame

② Remove unwanted shoots

The male and female flowers are borne separately. Once they appear the frame lights should be opened to allow insects to pollinate — replace at night. In wet and cold weather the lights should not be removed and it will be necessary to hand pollinate the flowers as for greenhouse-grown Melons. Thinning the fruit and stopping the shoots will be necessary when the Melons are marble-sized — see below:

② Pinch out stem 2 leaves beyond the fruit

① Remove unwanted fruit to leave just one Melon per shoot

You should now have 4 Melons on the plant — pinch out the tip of each of the 4 main shoots and remove any further shoots or flowers which appear.

Keep the soil moist but never saturated. Water regularly from the thinning stage illustrated above. Keep water off the stems as far as possible and reduce watering when the Melons start to ripen.

Regular feeding is also necessary. Begin feeding with a high-potash liquid feed when the fruits are the size of a golf ball and continue every 7–10 days until they start to ripen.

Careful control of ventilation is necessary. Reduce ventilation in cold weather — increase ventilation in sunny weather and when fruits are ripening. Apply Coolglass to the lights in July and August. Another requirement at the ripening stage is physical support to keep the fruit off the soil which would cause it to rot — see below:

Tile or piece of wood placed under fruit from tennis-ball size to maturity

Harvesting

Do not harvest Melons until they are fully ripe. There are several indications — the end away from the stalk will give slightly if gently pressed and the end towards the stalk will start to develop a circular crack. Netted and cantaloupe types develop a characteristic aroma and the fruit when lifted parts readily from the stalk. Do not keep for more than a few days in the refrigerator.

KIWI FRUITS

Once listed as Chinese Gooseberry or Actinidia, the post-War success of the Kiwi Fruit has been phenomenal. Now you can buy them anywhere, but this is certainly not a plant you can grow anywhere. The shoot tips are susceptible to frost in spring and prolonged sunshine is necessary to ensure proper ripening of the brown and furry fruit. If you live in the South and have a sheltered wall then it may be worth a try — a locality where sweet Grapes grow successfully can usually be used with confidence for Kiwi Fruit.

There is also a space problem — it is a rampant, twining climber which will reach 30 ft or more if left unchecked. Of course this can be turned to your advantage if you have a large unsightly space or a pergola to clothe — the leaves are large and heart-shaped and the cream-coloured flowers are 1½ in. across.

Forget the recommendation to grow it under glass — this plant is far too vigorous for an average-sized greenhouse and it is not worth the trouble involved. Stick to outdoor growing and choose the female variety *Hayward* — undoubtedly the best and most reliable. Follow the rules for planting, pruning and care described for outdoor Grapes on pages 88 and 91. There are a few differences — you will need to include a male plant such as *Tomuri* in each planting hole alongside the female one, and you will have to leave at least 12–15 ft between these joint planting sites.

Hand pollination is recommended — follow the Melon method on page 94. If the location is suitable you can expect about 20 lb of fruit from a mature plant, but you will have to wait for about 7 years before you get a worthwhile crop. The fruit is ready for picking when the brown surface gives slightly when gently pressed — this will usually be in October. Make sure all fruit is harvested before the first frosts arrive. Keep in a cool place for a month before use — Kiwi Fruit can be stored for a further month or two.

CAPE GOOSEBERRIES

Unlike the Kiwi Fruit, this one is rare in the shops as well as in gardens. You might occasionally find it labelled as Cape Gooseberry, Physalis or Chinese Lantern in a supermarket which offers a wide range of exotic foods (see page 116), or you might be offered it coated with sugar as a dessert at an illustrious banquet if you move in such circles. It is not one you are likely to find in the fruit garden, however, although it is listed in many seed catalogues.

It is grown as a half-hardy annual — outdoors in districts with a mild climate and sheltered situation or under glass where the environment is less favourable. Be careful with this greenhouse recommendation — it can be grown in the same way as a Tomato, but it is much too leafy for a small greenhouse.

Outdoor cultivation is quite straightforward if you have been successful in the past with outdoor Tomatoes. You can expect about 1–2 lb of fruit from each plant and the lantern-like fruits provide an ornamental touch. Follow the general rules for Tomato cultivation — sow seed in gentle heat in March and plant the seedlings under cloches in mid May. Leave 2½ ft between the plants and remove cloches when the danger of frost is past. Insert 4 ft stakes next to the young Cape Gooseberries — tie the stems loosely to each support. Nip out the growing points when the plants are about 1 ft high and feed with a high-potash liquid fertilizer once the first fruits have formed. Watch for pests and spray accordingly.

The fruits in the greenhouse can be left on the plants to ripen — a golden shiny ball within a brown and papery husk. Outdoors you will have to pick at the unripe stage if frost threatens — leave the fruit to ripen on the windowsill.

The major pests and diseases

STRAWBERRIES
Greenfly • Birds • Slugs • Virus
Strawberry mildew • Grey mould • Red core

RASPBERRIES
Greenfly • Raspberry beetle • Birds • Raspberry moth
Cane spot • Spur blight • Grey mould • Virus

BLACKBERRIES & HYBRID BERRIES
Greenfly • Raspberry beetle • Birds
Cane spot • Spur blight • Grey mould • Virus

BLACKCURRANTS
Big bud mite • Greenfly • Birds • Spider mite
Leaf spot • American mildew • Grey mould • Reversion

GOOSEBERRIES
Greenfly • Gooseberry sawfly • Magpie moth
Birds • Die-back • American mildew

RED & WHITE CURRANTS
Greenfly • Capsid bug • Caterpillars
Leaf spot • Coral spot

GRAPES
Scale • Spider mite • Shanking
Powdery mildew • Grey mould

MELONS
Spider mite • Powdery mildew
Soft rot • Mosaic virus

Causes of poor yields

● IMPATIENCE Fruiting is light or absent and is often undesirable in the first season after planting. Strawberries and Melons are an exception, but autumn-fruiting Raspberries may not fruit properly for 3 years after planting. With Blackcurrants, Gooseberries, Red Currants and White Currants you will have to wait 4 or 5 years before a full crop is obtained.

● POOR PRUNING & CARELESS PICKING The pruning instructions for Grapes, Blackberries etc may seem very severe as a large amount of growth is removed in winter. But it is necessary if you are to avoid an abundance of leafy growth and a dearth of fruit. Careless picking can also be a problem — do follow the instructions in the appropriate section. Tugging unripe fruit away from the stem can break fruiting spurs and damage stems — the remaining fruit may not ripen.

● BIRDS Perhaps the most serious of all soft fruit problems — even a neglected plant may sometimes produce a good crop, but in nearly every case you can rely on birds to reduce or eliminate the ripening fruit. Netting is the only answer — see page 59.

● FROST A serious problem of soft fruit — see page 100.

● POOR LOCATION OR POOR PLANTING Too much shade, poor soil, waterlogging, cold winds, too little time between digging and planting, dryness at the roots and planting at the wrong depth can all lead to disappointing crops.

● WATER & FOOD SHORTAGE Soft fruit plants are often shallow rooting — regular and thorough watering is usually necessary during dry weather. Shortage of potash is a common cause of poor yields — feed as recommended. Apply a foliar feed such as Fillip if the leaves or stems have been damaged in any way.

● POOR POLLINATION Rain, cold weather, strong winds or very dry air can all lead to defective pollination — see the Blossom Drop section on page 100. Nature needs a helping hand in the case of indoor greenhouse fruit.

● PESTS & DISEASES Pages 97–101 show that there are unfortunately a large number of problems which can beset the leaves, stems and fruits of soft fruit. Viruses are especially important and the effect on the infected plant gets steadily worse as time passes.

● SOIL DISEASES There are a number of soil-borne diseases which can reduce the productiveness of affected plants — in severe attacks the cane or bush may be killed outright. Honey fungus (page 54) is well known, but there are also soft rot of Melons (avoid overwatering), red core of Strawberries (grow a resistant variety) and verticillium wilt of Strawberries (grow a resistant variety).

● OLD AGE Soft fruit has a limited life span in the garden, after which yields are disappointing. The average life expectancy of Strawberries is 3 years, Raspberries 10 years and Gooseberries 10–15 years.

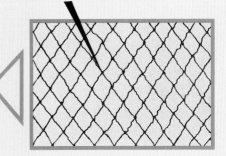

Netting is required to keep birds away from buds and/or fruit. Polypropylene is preferred by many to nylon

Fruit grown under glass needs pollinating by hand. Tap flowers which are bisexual. With plants which bear unisexual flowers (Melons, Kiwi Fruits) transfer pollen to the stigma with a soft brush, cotton wool or by pushing a male flower into the female flower

CLEARWING MOTH

Dead or dying shoots of Currants and Gooseberries may indicate the presence of the ¾ in. white caterpillars of this pest. The moths lay eggs in June on the shoots of the bushes and the caterpillars tunnel into the pith of the shoots. Cut back affected shoots to where the pith is no longer discoloured. Currant clearwing moth is not a widespread pest.

RASPBERRY MOTH

Dead or dying shoots of Raspberries may indicate the presence of the ⅓ in. red caterpillars of this pest. Young caterpillars hide in the soil or stakes during winter and move to the shoots in April, where they bore into and feed inside the pith. A Tar Oil spray in winter will kill the hibernating caterpillars in the soil. Cut out and burn withered shoots.

SOFT FRUIT TROUBLES: Holes in Leaves & Shoots

There is a bewildering array of pests which can produce holes in the foliage of soft fruit. The most common culprits are illustrated on this page — others include the fruit tree tortrix moth (page 51) which spins leaves together and the clay-coloured weevil (page 52) which occasionally attacks cane fruit. Many caterpillars can damage the leaves of soft fruit — not shown here are the winter moth, mottled umber moth and the vapourer moth (page 51). Slugs and snails (page 101) may attack Strawberry leaves.

YELLOWTAIL MOTH

A hairy, colourful caterpillar which can cause a skin rash if handled. It is sometimes found on Raspberry canes, where it can cause partial skeletonization of the foliage if present in sufficient numbers. The yellowtail moth, however, is a solitary feeder and so spraying with Fenitrothion is rarely necessary. Just pick off and destroy the caterpillars.

GOOSEBERRY SAWFLY

1 in. spotted caterpillar

A serious pest of Gooseberries and Currants which can cause complete defoliation in a severe attack. Identification is easy as the caterpillars generally feed round the edge of the leaf. Keep a careful watch for gooseberry sawfly from May onwards and spray with Fenitrothion or Malathion at the first sign of damage. There can be up to 4 broods a year of these destructive caterpillars, so a second spray may be necessary later in the season.

STRAWBERRY TORTRIX MOTH

A serious pest of Strawberries in some areas of Britain. Several leaves are joined together by silken threads. Inside this protective cover the ¼ in. green caterpillars feed. These spun leaves should be picked off and destroyed. If spraying is necessary apply Fenitrothion before flowering and repeat the spray after picking.

CAPSID BUG

Both apple capsid and the common green capsid can cause severe damage. The small green bugs puncture the leaf surface, producing reddish-brown spots. As the leaves expand ragged brown-edged holes are formed, often after the capsid bugs have left the plant. This pest can be a nuisance on all soft fruit, especially Currants and Gooseberries. Capsid bug is not an easy pest to control — spray with Long-last or Fenitrothion when the first flowers are about to open and repeat after the fruit has set.

MAGPIE MOTH

1¼ in. 'looper' caterpillar

This distinctively coloured caterpillar feeds on Gooseberry and Currant bushes in spring and early summer and can cause severe defoliation. Fortunately it is now no longer a common pest and is only likely to be troublesome in small sheltered gardens where bushes are not sprayed. If only a few caterpillars appear hand picking will give satisfactory control. Alternatively spray with Fenitrothion when the first flowers are about to open.

RED-LEGGED WEEVIL

In parts of Britain this distinctive wingless weevil can be a serious pest of Raspberries and Strawberries. The weevils are rarely seen — they feed at night and drop to the ground when disturbed. Control is difficult — regular cultivation around the plants will help.

SOFT FRUIT TROUBLES: Leaf & Shoot Problems

Soft fruit can suffer from a wide range of leaf and shoot problems, as these two pages illustrate. Not shown here are the clay-coloured weevil (page 52), coral spot (page 54), crown gall (page 54) and cluster cup rust (page 101) on Gooseberry leaves. Honey fungus (page 54) can affect Gooseberries, Raspberries, Loganberries, Strawberries, Currants and Vines.

APHID

Many aphids attack soft fruit and their effect can be serious. In some cases there is severe leaf distortion, but the main danger is due to the viruses they carry. Currants are affected by the **currant blister aphid**, producing coloured blisters. Both **lettuce aphid** and **gooseberry aphid** cause severe leaf-curling on Gooseberries. Two aphids attack Raspberries — the **rubus aphid** and the stem-coating **raspberry aphid**. Strawberries can be attacked by other species — the **shallot aphid** which can cripple the plant, and the **strawberry aphid**. In all cases spray with Long-last or Fenitrothion as soon as the pests are noticed.

Blister aphid   Leaf-curling aphid   Stem-coating aphid

SPIDER MITE

Several mites attack soft fruit. The general symptoms are pale or bronze-coloured leaves and the presence of minute 'spiders' on the undersurface. The **red spider mite** infests Blackcurrants and Strawberries in hot summers. On Gooseberries the **bryobia mite** is a common pest, and defoliation is likely to occur in a severe attack. For both these mites spray with Long-last just after flowering if the weather is warm and settled. The **strawberry mite** is much more serious and much more difficult to control. Young leaves turn brown, older leaves are crinkled. Plants are stunted and the crown may die. Lift and burn infested plants.

Bryobia mite   Red spider mite   Strawberry mite

BLACKCURRANT EELWORM

The microscopic pests live on the young leaves and flowers within the bud. The infested buds shrivel and fail to open, so the branches remain bare in spring. There is no satisfactory method of controlling this pest, but luckily it is uncommon. Attacks are worst after a wet autumn. Cut off and burn bare branches.

STRAWBERRY EELWORM

Several types of eelworm attack Strawberries and identification is difficult. Leaf stalks may be abnormally long and turn red ('red plant disease') or leaf and flower stalks may be abnormally short and thickened. In all cases there is no cure — dig up and burn badly infested plants and do not replant for at least 5 years.

GALL MIDGE

A serious pest of Blackcurrants, the small maggots feeding on the young leaves at the shoot tips. The young foliage becomes twisted, puckered and discoloured. Shoot growth may be checked. This is a difficult pest to control by spraying — apply Long-last as soon as damage is first noticed.

CANE MIDGE

The tiny pink maggots of the raspberry cane midge feed under the outer layer ('rind') of young canes. Direct injury is slight, but the damaged tissue is susceptible to attack by serious diseases which may kill the canes. Spray with Fenitrothion if growth splits appear on the stems — repeat the spray 2 weeks later.

DIE-BACK

The dying back of odd branches of Gooseberries is a frequent complaint — the cause is the grey mould fungus (page 101). A whole branch in full leaf suddenly dies; the foliage turns yellow and then withers and falls. Grey mould may be seen in the stem cracks. Remove affected branches promptly — paint cuts with Arbrex.

POWDERY MILDEW

Outdoor and greenhouse Grapes and Melons are attacked by this disease. White powdery patches appear on the leaves. On Grapes this covering is often sparse so that browning may be more noticeable than the white mould. Burn diseased leaves. Apply carbendazim when disease is first seen — repeat at 14 day intervals.

CANE SPOT

Raspberries and Logan-berries can be seriously affected. In early summer small purple spots appear on the canes. These enlarge to form shallow white pits with a purple border. The cane may be killed. Cut out badly diseased canes in autumn. Next spring spray with Supercarb at 14 day intervals from bud burst until the blossom appears.

BROWN SCALE

Several types of scale may be found on the stems of soft fruit. The tiny shell-like creatures do not move and are usually a sign of neglect. The commonest is the brown scale, which attacks Currants, Gooseberries and Raspberries. Spray with Tar Oil winter wash in December. Alternatively spray with Malathion in March or September.

AMERICAN MILDEW

American mildew is a crippling disease of Gooseberries. White powdery patches appear on the young leaves and shoots; later the fruit is affected (page 101). The mould changes from white to brown. This disease is encouraged by overcrowding — grow Gooseberries on an open site and prune regularly. Cut off diseased branches in September. If the bushes have been badly attacked this summer, apply Supercarb next year when the first flowers open and repeat the spray twice at 14 day intervals. Blackcurrants are occasionally affected — spray with Supercarb when the first spots of mould are seen.

REVERSION

HEALTHY   REVERTED

cleft   no cleft

This virus disease causes a change in leaf shape. The basal cleft disappears, the main lobe has less than 5 main veins and 10 serrations. The flower buds are red rather than grey. The virus is spread by the big bud mite (page 100) and reverted plants steadily degenerate. Destroy badly diseased plants — grow new bushes of certified stock on a fresh site.

STRAWBERRY MILDEW

This is the most common disease of Straw-berries. It is easy to recognise — dark patches appear on the upper surface of the leaves, the infected foliage curling upwards to expose greyish mould patches on the undersurface. Fruit may also be affected (page 101). Spray with Supercarb at 14 day intervals from the beginning of flowering until the fruit starts to colour. Cut off and burn leaves after harvesting.

LEAF SCORCH

Leaves of all types of soft fruit may develop brown edges which are sometimes torn and curled. Growth is stunted and the fruit is small. The cause is potash deficiency — water with Bio Tomato Food or Flower Maker immediately and apply a dressing of Growmore in the spring.

BLACKCURRANT RUST

Yellow patches appear on the underside of Blackcurrant leaves in early summer. Towards the end of the summer the leaves turn brown and fall. If rust is a recurrent problem, spray with Dithane immediately after harvest.

LEAF SPOT

Leaf spot is the most serious disease of Blackcurrants. Gooseberries may also be attacked. Brown spots appear on the leaves and early defoliation takes place. The bushes are weakened and next year's crop will be reduced. Leaf spot is worst in a wet season — spraying is a worthwhile precaution. Apply Dithane or Supercarb at the first sign of leaf spotting and repeat at 14 day intervals if weather remains damp. Pick off diseased leaves — rake up and burn all fallen leaves. Strawberry leaves sometimes develop red spots; spraying is rarely necessary.

VIRUS

Virus diseases are a major problem of Raspberries and Strawberries. Aphids and other insects are the carriers, and once the plants are infected there is nothing you can do to save them. **Mosaic** is a serious disorder of Raspberries. Strawberries are affected by several viruses — **crinkle** occurs in late spring, **yellow edge** in autumn and **arabis mosaic** in either spring or autumn. Remove and burn diseased plants.

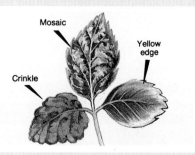

Mosaic

Yellow edge

Crinkle

SOFT FRUIT TROUBLES: Bud & Blossom Problems

BLOSSOM DROP

If the plants are healthy and not suffering from drought then there are two possible causes of lack of fruit set. Either frost occurred when the bushes were in flower or pollination was defective due to wet and cold weather or very dry air at blossom time.

BIG BUD MITE

Healthy bud

Big bud

This gall mite is by far the most serious pest of Blackcurrants. Red Currants and Gooseberries are occasionally attacked. In late spring or early summer these microscopic mites are carried by wind or other insects to the bushes. By July they have entered the buds, which swell and become less pointed. These 'big buds' eventually wither. Inspect the bushes carefully in winter. Pick off enlarged buds; dig out and burn badly infested plants.

RASPBERRY BEETLE

⅙ in. brown beetle

The adult beetles are damaging to blossoms of Raspberries, Loganberries and Blackberries. If beetles are seen on the flower trusses, spray with Fenitrothion late in the evening.

SPUR BLIGHT

Purplish patches appear around the buds on Raspberry and Loganberry canes in early autumn. These patches turn silvery and the buds are killed. Reduce overcrowding by removing unwanted canes. Cut out and burn diseased canes as soon as the purple patches start to appear. To prevent attacks spray with Supercarb at 14 day intervals from bud burst until the blossom appears.

STRAWBERRY BLOSSOM WEEVIL

Both Strawberries and Raspberries can be attacked by this pest. The flower stalk is partially severed after eggs have been laid inside the flower bud, the unopened flower then withers and may fall. Blossom weevil damage is sometimes confused with a strawberry rhynchites attack; blossom weevil is easily recognised by its greyish-black body. The damage is rarely serious — if spraying is necessary use Malathion late in the evening.

FROST: STRAWBERRIES

Open Strawberry blooms are extremely sensitive to frost. The effect is unmistakable — the petals remain apparently unharmed but the central core turns black. Nothing can be done at this stage — the flowers wither and fall. The time to take action is before the frost occurs — cover the plants with cloches or newspaper if frost is forecast at blossom time.

FROST: CANE FRUIT

Some or all of the buds on fruit canes may fail to open in the spring. If the area around the withered bud is discoloured, the cause is raspberry spur blight. If the surrounding bark appears normal then the most likely reason for bud failure is frost. This damage usually occurs when there has been an early mild spell which causes the sap to rise, followed by a frost as the buds were about to burst.

STRAWBERRY RHYNCHITES

Both Strawberries and Raspberries can be attacked by this pest. In May and June the stalks of blossom trusses are punctured, the unopened buds wither and occasionally fall. Rhynchites damage is sometimes confused with a blossom weevil attack; strawberry rhynchites is easily recognised by its greenish metallic body. The damage is rarely serious — if spraying is necessary use Malathion late in the evening.

BIRDS

Birds are a menace to all types of soft fruit when the berries or currants are ripening. At the bud stage Gooseberries are most at risk; in many gardens some or all of the dormant buds are stripped off by bullfinches during the winter months. The only really satisfactory answer is netting. Make sure the base of the net is well secured. If netting is not practical, wind cotton thread through the branches and delay pruning until the buds are breaking in the spring.

Soft fruit is sweet and succulent, so birds are a major menace. Slugs, snails and black beetles devour fruit which is close to the ground and in a wet summer grey mould can destroy a crop. Dropping of small fruitlets occurs occasionally; in Blackcurrants it is known as 'running off' and is due to frost damage or poor pollination. In Raspberries this trouble is often due to damaged fruiting spurs.

SUN SCALD & SHANKING

Sunken patches on Grapes. In shanking the fruit stalks shrivel and there is overall shrinkage of the fruit — the cause is over-cropping or under-watering. Scald occurs in hot weather — stalks do not shrivel and shrinkage is at the top of the fruit. Apply Coolglass and ventilate in sunny weather. Remove damaged fruit.

VINE POWDERY MILDEW

This disease is common on both outdoor and greenhouse Grapes. The fruit is covered with a white powdery mould, and cracking may take place. Prune the vines thoroughly in autumn, following the instructions on page 91. Burn all infected leaves and wood. Apply Supercarb when the first flowers open. Repeat twice at 14 day intervals.

AMERICAN MILDEW

This form of powdery mildew begins as a white coating on Gooseberries and Currants, but later it becomes a brown felt over the surface. Bushes should be pruned regularly and infected shoots removed in September. Apply Supercarb when the first flowers open. Repeat twice at 14 day intervals.

CLUSTER CUP RUST

Minute yellow-edged pits ('cluster cups') appear on the large orange patches covering infected fruit. This easily-recognisable disease occurs only where sedges are growing nearby. If this rust disease has been a problem in the past, spray with Dithane shortly before flowering. Treatment is rarely necessary.

SLUGS, SNAILS & BEETLES

Large holes eaten in Strawberries may be due to slugs and snails (look for slime trails) or strawberry ground beetles. Attacks are worst in enclosed gardens. Slugs, snails and beetles are controlled by methiocarb, the active ingredient of Slug Gard. Scatter pellets thinly around the plants. Remove garden rubbish.

STRAWBERRY SEED BEETLE

These beetles are about ½ in. long, greyish, and very active. They bite at the seeds and the attached flesh so that the fruit is disfigured. Keep down weeds, clear away dead leaves and remove garden rubbish. Sprinkle Slug Gard around the plants. Rather similar damage can be caused by birds.

BIRDS & SQUIRRELS

Animals are usually the cause when fruit is entirely devoured. Birds, such as blackbirds, will eat Strawberries, and squirrels are rapidly becoming the major pest of this crop in many areas. Deterrents are of limited use and the only answer is netting. Ensure the base of the net is well-secured.

STRAWBERRY MILDEW

This powdery mildew is a serious foliage disease of Strawberries, which can attack the berries. Diseased fruit are dull-coloured and sometimes shrivelled. In a severe outbreak they are unfit for use. Apply Supercarb when the first flowers open. Repeat twice at 14 day intervals.

RASPBERRY BEETLE

Raspberry beetle is the most serious pest of Raspberries, Loganberries and Blackberries as the ¼ in. white grubs can soon ruin the crop. The time to spray Raspberries is when the first fruits start to turn pink — Loganberries when the petals have fallen. Use Liquid Derris or Malathion — or Fenitrothion if you can wait 7 days before picking.

GREY MOULD (Botrytis)

This fluffy mould is destructive to Raspberries, Strawberries, Grapes and Currants in a wet summer. Remove diseased fruits and mouldy plant material immediately, but the only answer in a humid season is to spray before the disease appears. Apply Supercarb when the first flowers open. Repeat twice at 14 day intervals.

CHAPTER 4
SHOP-BOUGHT FRUIT

The average gardener with a large vegetable plot and a large freezer can satisfy most of the family's needs for greens and root vegetables throughout the year. The situation is different with fruit — here home-grown produce does have a role to play but it can only provide a minor part of the family's annual consumption.

A minor part, but an important one. On page 3 the special role of growing fruit was highlighted — the ability to eat fruit fresh from the bush or cane, the chance to grow top-flavour varieties which commercial growers ignore and the opportunity to grow some unusual types such as hybrid berries which are in the catalogues but not in the shops.

However, for several reasons we must still turn to the shop and supermarket for most of our year-round fruit needs. Firstly, some of our basic fruits will not grow in Britain — Grapefruits, Oranges, Pineapples, Lemons, Tangerines and Bananas are notable examples. Several other types *can* be grown over here with care but in practice very little is actually grown at home. Examples here are Peaches, Nectarines, Melons and Grapes. But even with our most popular home-grown favourites which do flourish in our climate there is a problem — Apples, Pears and Strawberries cannot be successfully frozen for year-round use in the same way as Broad Beans and Brussels Sprouts. Finally we must face the fact that it is simply not true to claim that *all* fruits taste better when grown at home and eaten straight from the plant. It is indeed so for fruit which is completely at home in Britain, such as the Raspberry and many Apple varieties, but it is not true for fruit which needs warm sun on its back. Examples here are Melons, Kiwi Fruits, Grapes and imported Apples such as *Golden Delicious, Granny Smith* and *Sturmer Pippin.*

So shopping for fruit has to be a regular task all year round, and it is a necessary one. Modern research has shown that fruit is vital for good health. Buy fresh and sound produce — no mouldy spots, no leaking punnets, no squashed soft fruit. Wash it well, peel where necessary and don't worry about scare stories.

Shopping wisely involves learning a few rules. First of all, look at the label. This will be stuck on each individual pre-pack or on each individual fruit, or it will appear as a display card next to fruit which is sold loose. For all popular fruit it is now a legal requirement for this label or display card to tell you the type, the country of origin and the Class of the produce. Class I means that the physical quality is good and there are no important defects. Class II indicates that the quality is reasonable but is deficient in one or two respects — the shape or colour may be less than good or there may be small blemishes or marks present. If quality deteriorates the label should be changed from Class I to Class II or the fruit should be taken off the shelves. In addition, the variety must be shown on the label or display card for Class I Apples, Apricots, Grapes, Oranges, Peaches, Pears and Plums. Remember that the Class is not an indication of eating quality — a Class I Melon can be unripe and tasteless. Telling when fruit is in peak condition is not always easy — look up the notes in this section for the individual fruit.

Buy for a few days only and the general rule is to eat as soon as possible. Storage life decreases as temperature increases, so do keep fruit cool. The supermarket has become the main source of supply — the range is large and quality is generally high. But pre-packed fruit is nearly always more expensive, and sometimes much more expensive, than fruit sold loose. Obviously, there is still a place for the greengrocer and the market stall.

At the opposite end of the scale from the neatly-packed tray of four Apples is the fruit from a pick-your-own (PYO) farm. The popularity of this way of obtaining fruit has increased rapidly during the past decade. In season your local paper will give you the address of some (but not all) growers who offer this service. The produce is usually about half the shop price and you do know it is really fresh.

Strawberries are the favourite PYO fruit — about a quarter of the commercial crop is sold in this way. Blackcurrants and Raspberries are also popular — Gooseberries, Apples, Plums, Pears and Cherries much less so. Half way between the supermarket and the PYO grower is the farm shop. Theoretically all the produce has come from the fields but this is not always so.

Listed on the following pages are scores of different types of fruit — some well-known and others distinctly unusual. There are no rules, but it is a wise plan to satisfy the family's basic requirements with everyday types and to try just a few of the oddities which are described here and are beginning to appear in the shops.

APPLE

The full season for English Apples extends from the first supplies of *Millers Seedling* in August to the last of the *Bramley's Seedlings* in April or May. During this period we can enjoy home-grown dessert varieties such as *Worcester Pearmain, Spartan, Discovery, Laxton's Superb, Tydeman's Early* and the ever-popular *Cox's Orange Pippin.* Alongside *Bramley's*, the popular culinary varieties are *Grenadier, Lord Derby, Newton Wonder* and the recently-introduced *Crispin.*

Our U.K supplies are extended with imports from New Zealand, France, U.S etc. As a result we can buy *Granny Smith, Sturmer, Starking, Gala, Jonathan* and *McIntosh.* And of course the *Golden* and *Red Delicious*, which people either love or hate.

The Apples you buy will be labelled with a guide to quality. Class 1 means that the flesh is in good condition and the skin is unblemished. Class 2 indicates that a few blemishes are present on the skin. Keep shop-bought Apples in a cool place — bring into a warm room a few hours before serving.

Apples turn brown when cut — prevent this by placing in water containing lemon or other acidic juice. Alternatively coat with lemon juice before serving.

Cox's Orange Pippin
Britain's most popular eating Apple — acidity and sweetness finely balanced

Granny Smith
Crisp and sharp, available nearly all year round for dessert or cooking

Red Delicious
Attractive and firm — keeps well in the kitchen. Suitable for baking

APRICOT

You will find them in the shops from May to August and in winter. Apricots look like small Peaches — round with yellow or orange skins. Pick the ones with the least wrinkled and darkest skin — if necessary ripen by leaving in a warm room for a day or two. Before peeling plunge into boiling water for 30 seconds. There are lots of uses for Apricots apart from eating fresh — stewed, poached for serving with chicken, duck or lamb, used for filling pies or turned into wine or jam.

ASIAN PEAR

You will not find this one in the cookery books but it is beginning to appear in the larger supermarkets from November to April. It doesn't look like a Pear — it has the appearance of an Apple with a pale yellow skin. The flesh is crisp and distinctly aromatic, and the refreshing taste is quite unique — nothing like an Apple or Pear. Eat it fresh — don't waste its unusual flavour in a fruit salad. Lightly poach in red wine if you must cook them.

BANANA

The ordinary Dessert Banana is far too well known to require detailed description. Available all year round, the fruit is curved, 6–12 in. long and is ready for eating when the yellow skin is flecked with brown. Always store Bananas at room temperature — they rapidly blacken in a refrigerator.

The other large group of Bananas are the Plantains, also known as Cooking or Jamaican Bananas. These are larger and duller-skinned than the ordinary ones and have an insipid flavour as the sugar content is low. The Plantain is much used in West Indian and African cooking and you will find this fruit in shops catering for these ethnic groups. Other types of Banana are hard to find. There are Lady's Fingers (bright yellow, small, very sweet and thin-skinned) and the Red Banana (dull red skin and pink flesh.)

Bananas provide a snack *par excellence* and also are a basic ingredient for fruit salad. Place in lemon or other acidic juice after peeling and slicing to prevent browning.

There are numerous other ways of using Bananas. They can be boiled, baked, flambéed or fried in sweet batter as fritters.

Lady's Finger Banana

Dessert Banana

Red Banana

Plantain

BABACO

Search for this one between October and March — it is worth looking for. It is large, looking like a fluted marrow and weighing up to 2 lb. Babaco was discovered in Ecuador in the 1920s and has been developed commercially by New Zealand farmers. The fruit is green when unripe and bright yellow when ripe and ready for eating. The centre is hollow with practically no seeds — the skin is edible. Slice and eat like Star Fruit (see page 119).

BER

Here is a truly unusual one which has not been taken up by the supermarkets. You will have to go to an Asian shop during winter if you want to try this fruit. It is eaten fresh, the white flesh around the stone is crisp and refreshing. It has long been known in the tropics — alternative names are Indian Plum and Chinese Apple. It has been used for hundreds of years as a tonic and cure for chest complaints — another alternative name is Jujube.

BERRIES

There is no precise definition for this group — included here are all the berry-type fruits which are not standard greengrocer items, such as Raspberries, Strawberries and Gooseberries.

The basic clustered-berry type is the **Blackberry**, which can be shop-bought or picked from hedgerows in early autumn. Use immediately or deep-freeze — do not store in the refrigerator. The **Dewberry** is similar to the Blackberry in general form, but it is grey, smaller and more delicately flavoured — use fresh or cook with Apples for tarts, jam etc. The **Cloudberry** looks like a small orange Blackberry — popular in Scandinavia. A cross between the Blackberry and Raspberry has produced the **Loganberry** which is larger and more acidic than Raspberry. The closely-related **Tayberry** has a more delicate flavour.

Several single-berry types are beginning to appear in the shops. **Blueberry** is a great favourite in the U.S — round, blue-black fruits with sweet flesh. Eat with sugar and cream or bake in pies. Our own U.K-grown **Bilberry** (Whortleberry) looks like a small Blueberry and is used for jam and tarts. The red **Cranberry** is very tart — cook slowly with sugar until the berries burst.

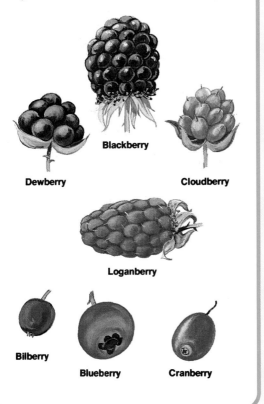

Blackberry

Dewberry

Cloudberry

Loganberry

Bilberry

Blueberry

Cranberry

CHERRY

The Cherry season is all too short — you can buy them from April to August but home-grown produce is only available in June and July (Sweet Cherries) or July and August (Acid Cherries).

The Sweet Cherry group basically splits into two sections, but with so many varieties about these days the dividing line is no longer clear. There are the 'Bigarreau' ones like *Napoleon* — firm and fleshy, and the 'Guignes' such as *Early Rivers* which are soft, sweet and full of juice.

Sweet Cherry varieties you are likely to see in the shops include *Frogmore Early, Merton Heart* and *White Heart*, although unlike Apples the name of the variety is rarely quoted.

The Acid Cherry group is dominated by the dark red *Morello* and the bright red 'Amarelle' varieties. This fruit is used for cooking, baking and jam-making. The Duke (Royale) Cherries are intermediate between the two main types, and are used for both cooking or eating fresh.

When buying make sure that the stalks are attached and the fruit are unsplit — splitting is a sign that the Cherries are past their best. Use immediately, although sound fruit should keep for up to 2 days in the refrigerator.

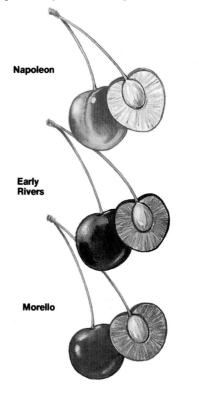

Napoleon

Early Rivers

Morello

CITRON

It looks like an unusually large Lemon, but unlike all other citrus fruits the Citron is used for its thick peel rather than its flesh or juice. This peel is candied for use in cake and biscuit making and decoration. The strips of peel are simmered in boiling water for a few minutes and then washed in cold water. Repeat this process several times. The next stage is to simmer the peel in a sugar syrup for about 3 hours. Dry in a warm place and store in an air-tight jar.

CURRANT (Fresh)

The fresh Currants are small, round berries with tart flesh and a soft skin. The season is short (July-August) and supplies are limited. Fruit in good condition can be frozen or kept in the refrigerator for 1–2 weeks. **Blackcurrants** are sold stripped from their stalks and are always cooked — pies, puddings, jam etc. **Red Currants** are sold with stalks attached — they are served fresh as dessert or used in sauces, jam or jelly. **White Currants** are less acid than the red type — serve fresh.

Blackcurrant

Red Currant

White Currant

CUSTARD APPLE

Custard Apples are fruits of the *Anona* tree — related to the Pineapple and Breadfruit. You may find one or more types in larger supermarkets in late autumn or winter, but you would have to go to the West Indies to find it in all the shops. The white or creamy flesh is soft like custard and the shape is sometimes Apple-like — hence the common name. All contain numerous black seeds.

Sugar Apple (Sweetsop) is a yellowish-green, round or oval fruit made up of large and fleshy scales. The sweet flesh has a Banana-like flavour — when ripe the scales burst open. **Cherimoya** is larger, round or Pear-shaped and smoother-skinned. Inside the pale green skin the aromatic creamy flesh has a Pineapple flavour. **Soursop** is the giant of the group — up to 1 ft long and weighing 10 lb. The thin skin has rows of spines and the flavour is more acidic and refreshing than the others. **Bullock's Heart** is heart-shaped with a rather insipid taste and **Atemoya** is a U.S-bred hybrid.

Buy when the skin is slightly soft to the touch. Keep in the refrigerator and cut in half as a dessert. Eat the pulp with a spoon — the seeds are inedible. Alternatively remove seeds and serve the mashed pulp in a bowl.

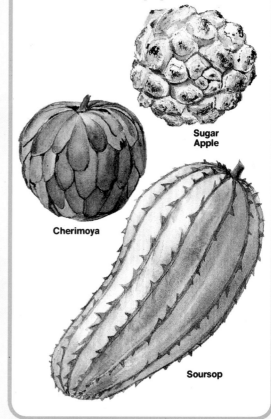

Sugar Apple

Cherimoya

Soursop

DATE

Dates can be bought fresh or dried and are available all year round. The most popular form is dried and packed as a compressed block with a stalk in a long box. The fruit should be plump, smooth-skinned and free from sugar crystals. To remove skin, cut off one end and squeeze the other — the skinned Date will pop out. Remove the stone by cutting the Date lengthwise — serve alone or fill with cream cheese or marzipan. Dates are also used in baking.

DURIAN

You might find this strange fruit in canned form but not in the fresh state, and that is a good thing. The soft flesh within the spiky rind is soft and delicious, but the smell of the fruit is half way between raw sewage and bad eggs. Surprisingly these large oval fruits (5–10 lb) are popular in the markets of Malaysia and Indonesia and are obviously an acquired taste. If offered one, keep in a polythene bag before serving.

FEIJOA

The skin has the texture and colour of an Avocado, but the soft flesh and the seeds in a gelatinous pulp indicate that it is closely related to the Guava. The Feijoa or Pineapple Guava is popular in some parts of the U.S but not in Britain, although New Zealand has started to export them to Britain. Buy when the skin is slightly soft to the touch — eat immediately. Cut in half and scoop out with a spoon. Do not eat the skin.

FIG

Fresh ('green') Figs are available in summer and autumn. The skin colour may be white, green, purple or black and inside the juicy pulp contains a mass of edible seeds. Buy when soft to the touch but not shrivelled — cut off the stalk, do not peel and cut in half before serving. Eat as soon as possible after purchase. Dried Figs are more popular than fresh ones — these can be eaten raw, stewed or used in baking. Canned Figs are available.

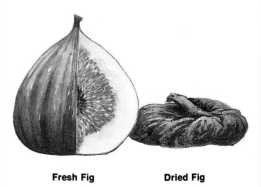

Fresh Fig   **Dried Fig**

GOOSEBERRY

Smooth or hairy ... green, yellow or red — the Gooseberry is too well known to need much description. If you want to eat the fruit fresh then buy a dessert variety such as the dark red *Whinham's Industry* — the ripe berries are large and sweet but tend to have little flavour when cooked. For jam, jelly, pie filling, crumble, wine-making or stewing, choose a culinary variety with a distinctly acid flavour — by far the best-known example is *Careless*. Culinary varieties are much more popular than dessert ones.

GRAPE (DRIED)

A wide variety of Grapes are dried in the sun or by artificial means to produce basic ingredients for cake- and pie-making. There are 3 basic types. The **Currant** is a dried small and seedless black Grape, originally from Corinth. The **Raisin** is larger, and is either eaten raw as a snack or used in baking. White and black Grapes are used — seedless Raisins are available but the seed-bearing *Muscatel* is considered the best. The largest and sweetest of the dried Grapes is the **Sultana** — the best are thin-skinned and pale-coloured.

Currant　　**Raisin**　　**Sultana**

GRAPE

Nearly all dessert (or table) Grapes are imported. They are grown in many parts of the world, so supplies are available in the shops all year round. The basic division is into 'white' and 'black' Grapes. The 'white' ones actually range from pale yellow to mid green, and popular varieties include *Muscat, Almeria* and *Italia*. The small *Californian Seedless* is widely available for people who wish to avoid the trouble of removing the pips.

'Black' Grapes range in skin colour from deep pink to near black, although the flesh colour is the same or slightly pinker than the inside of 'white' ones. *Alphonse* is widely sold — so is *Alicante* and *Royal. Black Hamburgh* is reputed to be the best and *Red Flame* is a seedless variety.

Choose with care. Buy an intact bunch and reject if some of the fruits are shrivelled, split or brown around the stalk. Grapes cannot be stored — buy immediately before use although you can keep unwashed fruit in the refrigerator for 1–2 days. Wash just before serving and dry gently — serve alone or with cheese or in fruit salad. Grapes are peeled before use in cooked dishes — dip briefly in boiling water and pull back the skin with your fingers.

Muscat

Almeria

Californian Seedless

Black Hamburgh

Mini-bunch Corinth

Royal

Red Flame

GRAPEFRUIT

The largest and one of the most popular citrus fruits — an essential start to the day for many people. The usual 'white' types have pale yellow, juicy flesh with a few large pips and a thick skin. Pink Grapefruit is much sweeter — better for eating fresh but less suitable for squeezing. The pinks have rose-coloured flesh but the surface may be yellow, pink or pale green. Look for shiny and heavy fruit which gives slightly when pressed. Grapefruit will keep for a few weeks in a cool place.

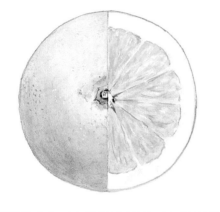

GREENGAGE

A type of Plum, but usually labelled separately on the shelves. This fruit was introduced into Britain 250 years ago by Sir William Gage, and the traditional type can still be seen. Small, green, round and firm, it has an aroma and flavour which is generally considered to be better than the ordinary Plum. One of the features of the Gage is the translucent nature of the flesh. Greengages are usually eaten fresh as dessert, but they are excellent for bottling and jam-making.

GUAVA

You will find these fruits on the shelves in autumn and winter — as small as an egg or Apple-sized, oval or round, yellow or green, rough- or smooth-skinned. The refreshingly tart flesh surrounds a soft pulp containing numerous seeds. The **Lemon Guava** has near-white flesh and the **Strawberry Guava** has pink flesh. The strong musky smell is not particularly pleasant — store away from other foods. Cut in half and eat with a spoon — with a large fruit remove the pulp and eat the flesh.

JACKFRUIT

The Jack(or Jak)fruit is the largest fruit which is grown commercially, sometimes reaching 80 lb or more. However, the ones sent to the U.K weigh only about 3–4 lb — they are oval with a greenish skin which is hard, thick and warty. The aroma is strong when the fruit is ripe — the succulent flesh is eaten fresh and the flavour may be delicious or insipid — you can't tell from the outside. Large seeds are embedded in the flesh — these can be roasted and served like Chestnuts.

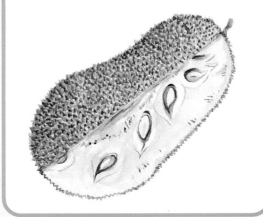

KIWANO

Another novelty from the enterprising New Zealand growers — a brand name for the Horned Melon. The outer case is bright orange and spiky — within is sweet green pulp with lots of seeds. Eat the pulp with a spoon straight from the shell — the taste is claimed to be a blend of Banana, Lime and Passion Fruit. The empty shells can be used as containers for fruit salad. Thin slices can be used for garnishing as an alternative to Kiwi Fruit. Not yet popular, but look for it in the shops between October and March.

KIWI FRUIT

Once an expensive novelty — now a standard shop-bought fruit which is available everywhere. It was called Chinese Gooseberry — the change of name helped to make it popular in the U.S. The brown furry fruit is Plum-sized — the bright green flesh under the thin skin bears tiny black seeds in an attractive pattern. When ripe the surface gives slightly when gently squeezed. Kiwi Fruit is excellent in fruit salad and also as a garnish — uncut fruit will keep for several days in a cool place.

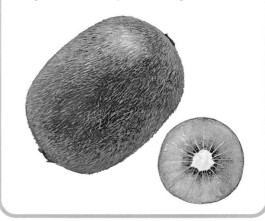

KUMQUAT

A tiny, Orange-like fruit which is usually oval in shape — a round version is sometimes available. All you have to do is to wash the fruit and eat it whole — cut it in half if you want to. The skin is sweet and the flesh is refreshingly tart. Another use is to garnish fruit salads and cakes with thin slices — best of all is to preserve the fruits in brandy. Store fresh fruit in the refrigerator for up to a week. Surprisingly, Kumquats do not belong to the Citrus family.

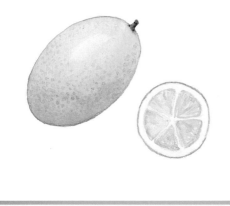

LEMON

One of the most versatile fruits of all — the basic souring agent for the British cook. Lemonade, pies, garnishing, marmalade, salad dressing, sauces, desserts — the uses are truly extensive. Choose fruit which is hard and glossy. Lemons which are rather small and heavy are usually juicier than large, knobbly ones. Lemons will keep for several weeks in a fridge — wrapped in polythene they will keep for a couple of months in a cool place. Cut Lemons, however, should be used as soon as possible.

LIME

Once preferred to Lemons in Britain, the Lime is making a comeback. It contains more citric acid than the Lemon, so reduce the amount you would normally add when using as a Lemon substitute. The shape of the two fruits is similar but Lime has a thinner skin, which changes from green to yellow with age. The flesh, however, always remains pale green. Caribbean Limes are larger and brighter-coloured than Indian ones — both types will stay fresh for many weeks in the refrigerator.

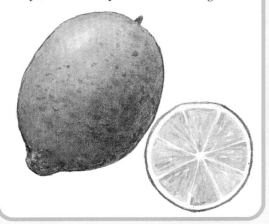

LIMETTA

Many of the fruits in this section are everyday items — others are not yet widely known but have appeared in recent years on supermarket shelves. The Limetta (Sweet Lemon) is one of the few real rarities which have been included. The fruit is rounder than an ordinary Lemon and the taste is quite different — the juice is tangy, not strongly acidic, so that it can be squeezed like Grapefruit to provide a refreshing drink.

LONGAN

These oriental fruits occasionally appear in the shops when the Lychee season is over. The two are very closely related but there are some distinct differences. The skin of the Longan is much less knobbly and the flesh is more aromatic, more translucent and the flavour is less acidic and more Grape-like. Do not buy fruit if the skin is shrivelled — prepare and use Longans in just the same way as Lychees (see page 112).

LOQUAT

The Loquat or Japanese Medlar has the size and the shape of an elongated small Plum and the skin colour and texture of an Apricot. The juicy flesh, which is tart rather than sweet, surrounds 2 or 3 large stones. To serve, wash and remove the stones. The skin can be peeled away if desired. You will find them in the shops in spring and summer — pick ones with firm and unblemished skins. Recommended for poaching — remove skin after cooking.

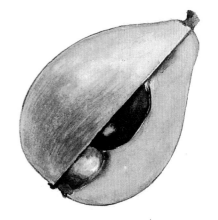

LYCHEE

Try fresh Lychees if you only know this fruit from the canned version served in Chinese restaurants. The tough, knobbly skin is easily peeled away to reveal the juicy white flesh, within which is a large brown stone. Serve cold — eat the flesh, discard the stone. When buying, pick out Lychees with skin which has a distinctly pink flush to the background brown colour, and there should be no sign of shrivelling. Store in a polythene bag in the refrigerator.

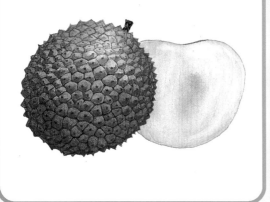

MANGO

A commonplace sight nowadays in the supermarket — not long ago it was a rarity. Size, shape and skin colour are extremely variable — there are green, yellow, orange, red and purple varieties. With the popular types green usually indicates that the fruit is not yet ripe. The flesh is always bright orange with a central large stone. Prepare by slicing the flesh away on either side of the stone. Serve on its own, with ice cream or in fruit salad.

MANGOSTEEN

A round fruit, the size of an Apple or Orange, with a thick and leathery skin. This purplish-brown fruit has the calyx firmly attached at the top. The outer coating is broken open by hand — inside you will find a ring of fleshy segments. These segments are white, juicy and fragrant, with a flavour which is rather similar to Lychees. Each segment contains a couple of seeds.

MEDLAR

An odd and exotic-looking fruit, but it is a native of Europe and not the Tropics. The Medlar is russet brown and the size of a small Apple, and the seeds are visible through the gaping cup below the calyx. Even odder is the preparation for serving. The fruits are picked in November and then allowed to decay ('blet') for several weeks. The flesh turns brown, soft and sweet — it is scooped out with a spoon.

MELON

Shop names often differ from seed catalogue ones — see pages 92–93. One of the most delicious of all fruits, served as wedges, cubed with Parma Ham before the meal, or combined with other fruits when dinner is over. A whole *Ogen* full of flavour, a small slice of Water Melon full of juice — the range of tastes is large. Unfortunately, Melons can be disappointing — the problem is the wrong variety or the wrong stage of ripeness. The Winter Melons (*Honeydew* and *Lavan*) tend to be the main culprits — the thick skin and lack of aroma make it impossible for the shopper to test ripeness, and even when ripe the taste is often insipid.

Things are better with the other varieties. Hold the fruit up to your nose and smell for the aroma of ripeness — this is no problem with *Charantais, Ogen* or *Cantaloupe*. Next, gently press the end of the Melon — it should give slightly. A ripe Melon can be kept for several days in the refrigerator — wrap in polythene to prevent the aroma from affecting other foods.

The standard method of serving is to cut the fruit in half, remove the seeds and slice into wedges. Melon is best chilled and may be served with ginger. Variations include Melon balls, individual Ogen Melons filled with fruit or ice cream, and puréed Melon as an ingredient for a summer drink.

Honeydew
Oval, like a rugby football. Skin thick and ribbed — cream, yellow or green. Flesh is usually pale green — may be pink. Flavour sweet but often insipid. Available all year

Lavan
Similar in general properties to *Honeydew*, but it is more rounded. The quality is higher — the pale yellow flesh is juicier and the flavour is sweeter

Galia
Small and broadly oval. Skin is brownish-yellow when ripe and prominently netted with buff-coloured threads. Flesh is pale yellow and sweet. Becoming very popular

Ogen
Small and round — you need one per person. Skin is thin — yellow with distinct green stripes. Flesh is pale green or cream — sweet, juicy and fragrant

Cantaloupe
Round and slightly flattened. Skin is usually dull yellow and grooved — scaly and bumpy but not netted. One of the best — flesh is orange, very sweet and fragrant

Charantais
Small and round. Skin is very pale green — there is a darker green stripe in each groove. One of the best — flesh is orange, sweet and very fragrant

Rock Melon
Small and oval. Skin is beige and rough — the rougher the skin, the sweeter the fruit. Shallow ribs are present and the flesh is orange-yellow. Becoming popular

Water Melon
Round or oval — usually very large. Skin is smooth and shiny green — plain, mottled or striped. Black pips embedded in red flesh. Juicy but insipid

ORANGE

Oranges are an essential part of the shopping list for many people. Sweet Oranges are by far the most important, and several types are available. *Jaffa* Oranges are large, thick-skinned, almost seedless and very juicy. They are very popular and so is the smooth-skinned *Navel* with its characteristic dimple at one end. The *Valencia* is thin-skinned, perfectly round and small. It is sweet, virtually seedless and very juicy. Another small Orange is the *Blood* Orange — reddish, sweet flesh with red-flecked skin.

Bitter Oranges are darker than the Sweet varieties and contain lots of seeds. *Seville* is the only variety you are likely to find in the shops — it's the one to choose if you plan to make marmalade. Sales of this variety are small — it is far too bitter for eating fresh.

Several hybrids of Oranges and Tangerines are occasionally offered for sale — *Dancy, Ortanique* and so on. These are described in the Tangerine section on page 121.

Look for tight skins, freedom from blemishes and a distinct Orange aroma when buying fruit. Oranges can be kept for about a week in a cool store.

Jaffa

Navel

Valencia

Blood

NECTARINE

Nectarine is a smooth-skinned type of Peach — a mutant and not a cross between a Peach and Plum as sometimes claimed. Reds, oranges and yellows occur on the smooth and edible skin, but the flesh is nearly always orange. Buy Nectarines which have no trace of greenness on the skin — eat on the day of purchase. Few are home-grown — Italy and the U.S are the main source for the U.K. They should always be juicy and rich in flavour, but shop-bought Nectarines are sometimes disappointing.

PASSION FRUIT

The Passion Fruit or Purple Granadilla is about the same size and shape as a Plum, but the purple skin is leathery and wrinkled. The flesh is yellowish-orange with a distinct aroma and flavour. Cut the fruit in half and scoop out the tangy flesh and the crunchy seeds. A popular alternative use is to strain the flesh and incorporate the juice in fruit punches or cocktails. The Sweet Granadilla (larger, orange and smooth) is sometimes available.

PAW PAW

Shaped like a large Pear, Paw Paw (or Papaya) can weigh up to 2 lb. The smooth skin turns from green to yellow or pale orange when ripe — the surface is usually slightly speckled with green. The thick layer of Melon-like flesh under the skin is pinkish-orange and the central cavity is filled with black seeds. Prepare as if it was a Melon. Cut in half, remove the seeds and slice into wedges. Sprinkle with Lemon or Lime juice. A few people are allergic to Paw Paw juice.

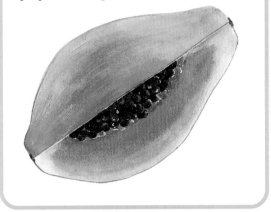

PEACH

A popular downy-skinned fruit with white or yellow flesh — white Peaches are considered sweeter. Ripe Peaches are cream, yellow or orange with a pink or red flush. Choose fruit which is still quite firm but with no trace of greenness on the skin. Peaches can be kept in the refrigerator for several days. There are 2 basic types. The soft-fleshed freestones part easily from the central kernel — the firmer clingstones are good for poaching. Put in boiling water for 15–30 seconds prior to peeling.

PEAR

As with Apples there are both dessert and culinary varieties, but virtually all the Pears offered for sale are dessert types used for eating fresh when ripe and for cooking whilst still rather hard.

Pears deteriorate very quickly when ripe. The best plan is to buy fruit which is still firm and to eat it at this 'nutty' stage or to leave it for 2–3 days to ripen in a warm place. A Pear is ripe when the flesh gives when pressed gently at the stalk end. Eat within a day or two, or store in the refrigerator for a few days.

Home-grown Pears are freely available between October and February — imported fruit is in the shops almost all year round. The most popular ones are *Conference, Doyenné du Comice* and *Williams' Bon Chrétien* — see pages 28–30 for details. Others include *Beurré Hardy* (flesh pale pink when ripe), *Packham's Triumph* (stores better than most Pears), and *Beurré d'Amanlis* (long, greenish-yellow fruit).

Pears are, of course, a superb dessert fruit for eating fresh — alone or in fruit salad. In addition they have many uses in the kitchen for bottling, tart-making, poaching, jam production etc. *Conference* is perhaps the best all-round eating/cooking/bottling variety, but *Williams'* and *Comice* are preferred for freezing.

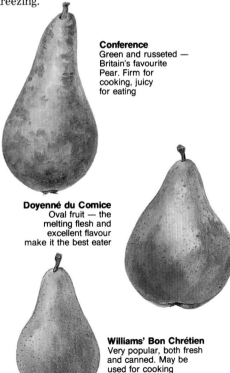

Conference
Green and russeted —
Britain's favourite
Pear. Firm for
cooking, juicy
for eating

Doyenné du Comice
Oval fruit — the
melting flesh and
excellent flavour
make it the best eater

Williams' Bon Chrétien
Very popular, both fresh
and canned. May be
used for cooking
or eating fresh

PERSIMMON

Persimmon (or Kaki Fruit) looks like a large orange-red Tomato with a prominent greenish calyx at the top. The flesh of unripe fruit is unpleasant and bitter when eaten — make sure Persimmon is ripe before serving. Place the fruit inside a bag and keep in a warm place until the tough skin is translucent and the surface gives when gently pressed. Cut off the top and scoop out the sweet, jelly-like flesh with a spoon. Discard the large seeds.

PHYSALIS

An orange-coloured round fruit about the size of a Cherry. It is surrounded by a papery husk and is known as Cape Gooseberry, Physalis or Chinese Lantern. The smooth skin is usually removed before serving — the flesh contains numerous pips and the flavour is sweet but rather sharp. It is sometimes eaten fresh but Physalis is more usually turned into jam, preserves or candied fruit. It is also used in stews and sauces. Available between August and January.

PINEAPPLE

Once a food which only the very wealthy could afford — now this juicy sweet-acidic fruit is available to everyone. Pineapple must be ripe when you buy it — it will not ripen in your home. Smell it — there should be a strong Pineapple aroma. The leaves should be stiff and fresh-looking — on a ripe fruit a central leaf when gently tugged will pull away quite easily. The easiest way to serve is to cut it into slices — then cut into pieces, remove outer rind and then the inner core.

PITANGA

The Pitanga or Surinam Cherry is truly a rarity, although one of its close relatives, the Clove, was a mainstay of the spice trade for hundreds of years. The fruits are red and are borne in clusters like Cherries, but the similarity stops there. The surface of each fruit is deeply ridged and the flesh contains several pips. Pitanga is grown in New Zealand and Israel — the two enterprising pioneers of exotic fruit. It can be eaten fresh, but is more often used in preserves.

PLUM

Numerous varieties are sold under the 'Plum' label — round, oval and egg-shaped — pale yellow to black — honey-sweet to Lemon-sour. The Greengage, Bullace, Damson, Mirabelle and Cherry Plum (see page 32) are usually labelled separately.

Choose Plums which are quite firm and have a distinct bloom on the surface. Culinary Plums are for bottling and jam-making — several varieties are available. The yellow *Pershore Egg* is popular, and so is *Rivers' Early Prolific, Czar, Marjorie's Seedling, Quetsche* and *Burbanks* (known as *Giant Prune* in Britain).

The dessert Plums are juicier, sweeter and often larger. The round, red *Santa Rosa* and the round, violet *Kirke's Blue* have a rich, sweet flavour — *Victoria* and *Japanese Plum* are rather bland. *Victoria* is widely used as a dual-purpose Plum, for cooking when firm and for eating fresh when ripe.

Plum varieties, like Peaches, are either clingstones or freestones, depending on the ease with which the flesh can be pulled away from the kernel. The skin is rather tough, and should be removed before serving. Several special types of Plum are dried in California, S. Africa, Australia etc to produce Prunes. *French Imperial* is reputedly the best.

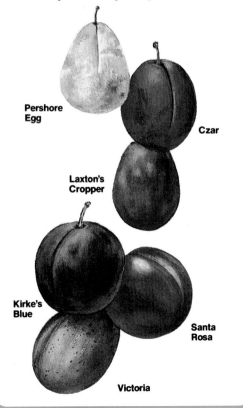

Pershore Egg

Czar

Laxton's Cropper

Kirke's Blue

Santa Rosa

Victoria

POMEGRANATE

Some of the exotic fruit described in this chapter were unknown in Britain before the War. The Pomegranate is different — it has declined in popularity. The Orange-sized fruit has a leathery skin which should be red-tinged and shiny. Neither the skin nor the inner pith are edible — the juice is packed in sacs around each seed. Cut off the top — eat with a spoon, sucking the juicy flesh from each sac and spitting out the seed.

POMELO

The Pomelo or Shaddock looks like a large, misshapen Grapefruit with a yellow or yellowish-green skin. A recent arrival to our shops — surprisingly it is the parent of the Grapefruit and not a new variety. Remove the thick peel and strip away the bitter thin skin around each segment. These sections are served as an alternative to Grapefruit — the texture is coarser but the flavour is less bitter. The peel is recommended for candying.

PRICKLY PEAR

Prickly Pear, Cactus Fruit, Indian Fig — all alternative names for the fruit of the *Opuntia* cactus. Oval, about 3 in. long, the skin is cream, orange or pink. Take care — the surface has small groups of tiny barbed spines. Never handle this fruit — cut in half and peel with a knife and fork before scooping out the flesh. This sweet pulp bears masses of hard but edible seeds. Ripe fruit can be kept for 2 weeks in the refrigerator.

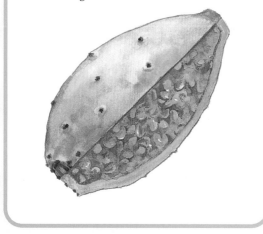

QUINCE

Quince is too hard and bitter to be eaten fresh. When peeled, cored and cooked the pale cream flesh softens and turns pink. This fruit can be stewed with meat or boiled with sugar to produce an excellent jam or jelly. Quince is round or oval, the golden-yellow skin containing highly aromatic flesh. At the centre there are numerous brown pips in an Apple-like arrangement. Available between October and April — store Quince well away from other foods.

RASPBERRY

Raspberries are an extremely popular soft fruit for use in summer and autumn. Many are grown in the garden — others are bought from the supermarket or picked on the farm. Look for stain-free punnets when buying Raspberries. Use as soon as possible — although Raspberries can be successfully frozen, they should not be kept in the refrigerator for more than a day.

There are two basic types. The summer fruiting Raspberries are large and red with July and August as the main season. *Lloyd George* was the popular variety, reputed to have the best flavour. Now there are a number of Malling varieties, such as *Malling Exploit* and *Malling Promise.*

The autumn fruiting varieties are available from mid September until the first frosts of autumn. Generally they are darker red, smaller but juicier. Well-known ones include *September* and *Heritage.*

You may find a number of novelties in the shops. There are the yellow-fruited *Golden Everest* and *Byrnes Apricot,* and black-fruited types are beginning to appear.

Do not wash Raspberries unless it is really necessary — the flavour is impaired. Wipe gently before serving with cream, ice cream or on their own. Raspberries are used in a wide variety of desserts, including Summer Pudding. For jam-making use fruit which hasn't quite ripened.

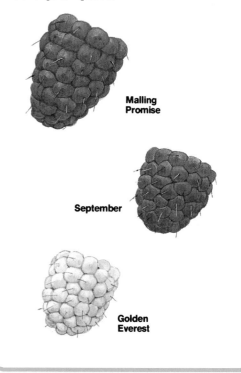

Malling Promise

September

Golden Everest

RAMBUTAN

A close relative of the Lychee, but you wouldn't think so from its appearance on the shelf. The Plum-sized fruit is covered with a mass of curved spines, giving it a fearsome appearance. These soft spines are green at first, but turn rich ruby red when the fruit is ripe. Break this spiny case open and the translucent succulent flesh within immediately reveals its close link to the better-known Lychee. Use in the same way — remove the flesh away from the central shiny stone.

SAPODILLA

The Sapodilla or Naseberry has the appearance of a stalked new Potato. The skin is brown and rather rough — an unappetising cover for a delectable fruit. Within, the flesh is soft, granular and fragrant. This pale brown pulp has a taste like Banana-flavoured brown sugar — obviously a fruit worth looking for. Store until it is ripe — the skin should be yielding and should show no green when scratched. Chill, peel and cut in half to remove the dangerous hooked pips.

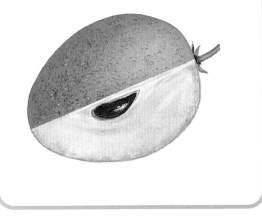

SHARON FRUIT

The Persimmon (page 116) never became popular in Britain. It has been overtaken by a variety bred by the Israelis — named the Sharon Fruit. Rather more orange than red, this variety is seedless and can be eaten whilst it is still quite firm. The skin is edible, so it's just a matter of wash, slice and eat. The flavour is a blend of Melon and Peach — rather sweeter than the parent Persimmon. Available between November and January.

STAR FRUIT

In recent years the Star Fruit, Star Apple or Carambola has appeared on the shelves of larger supermarkets and as a garnish on desserts and fruit salads served in restaurants. The waxy fruit, approximately 4 in. long, is distinctly fluted. When the yellow translucent skin and crunchy flesh is sliced, 5-pointed stars are obtained. Remove the pips and serve fresh. Sometimes sweet, sometimes distinctly tart — it is difficult to predict.

STRAWBERRY

Strawberries and cream are regarded as part of the traditional English summer scene, but the large fruits we know today were the result of a chance cross in the U.S during the 19th century. Before that only the tiny wild varieties, such as the Alpine Strawberry, were cultivated commercially in Europe. Although small, these Strawberries are extremely fragrant and full of flavour.

There is a wide variety of shapes and sizes amongst modern cultivated varieties. *Royal Sovereign*, bred 100 years ago, is conical. *Gorella*, the most widely grown variety in Europe, is irregularly-shaped. *Grandee*, the largest Strawberry of all, is almost round.

The season for English Strawberries lasts from the end of May until early August — this is the time when the 'June Bearers' yield their fruit. Examples include *Cambridge Vigour, Gorella, Pandora, Pantagruella* and *Bogota*. Less important are the 'Everbearers' (*Ostara, Rapella* etc) which produce fruit in late summer and early autumn. *Redgauntlet* can fruit as a June Bearer and again as an Everbearer.

Look for plump fruit with green tops which are not wilted. The punnets should not be stained. Use them on the day of purchase and wash only if it is necessary.

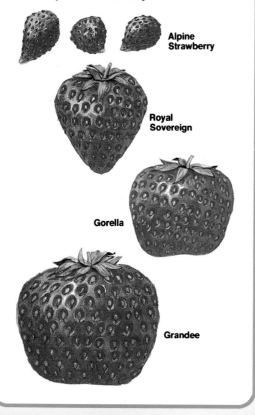

Alpine Strawberry

Royal Sovereign

Gorella

Grandee

STRAWBERRY TOMATO

The Strawberry Tomato or Ground Cherry is closely related to the Cape Gooseberry described on page 116. This species of Physalis, however, produces a berry which is smaller and sweeter with a husk which is thinner and smaller. It is used in the same way as the fruit on page 116 but it is much more difficult to find in the shops. The Strawberry Tomato is more popular in the U.S than in Britain — it is used in sauces and preserves.

SWEETIE

Another Israeli-bred novelty to be found in larger supermarkets between October and March. It looks like an unripe Grapefruit, but the skin remains completely or partly green even when ripe. It is seedless and free from acidity. The promoters recommend a novel way of serving Sweetie. Cut off the top and bottom, and then cut the fruit into 8 segments. Each segment is held by the thick peel and the sweet flesh eaten. Of course you can eat it in the traditional Grapefruit way.

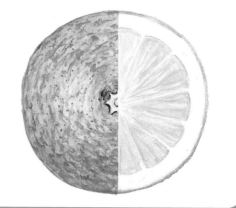

TANGERINE

Tangerines (or Mandarins — the terms are interchangeable) are types of Orange with loose peel which can be easily pulled away. There are several varieties and hybrids, and there is much confusion over the naming.

The basic *Tangerine* is small and sweet with bright orange skin and numerous pips. The smallest variety is the *Wilkins* with yellowish-orange skin and lots of pips. The *Satsuma* is larger and more popular — originally from Japan but now grown in Spain for the European market. The flesh is sweet and almost seedless — the skin is loose. Similar but bigger is the *Clementine* — sweet, almost seedless with rather firm, deep orange skin.

There are several Tangerine x Sweet Orange hybrids. *Dancy* is an American one with a rather tart flavour — *Topaz* has a richer, sweeter taste. *Temple* is easily recognised by its red skin and is usually sold as an Orange. The largest Tangerine x Sweet Orange cross is the *Ortanique*, which looks like a flattened Orange.

The *Tangelos* are Tangerine x Grapefruit hybrids. The *Minneola* has deep orange skin, very few seeds and a sharp flavour. The *Ugli* fruit is widely available and is more Grapefruit-like — see next column for details.

Tangerines are at their best at Christmas time and are nearly always eaten fresh. However, they do make excellent marmalade and are attractive for garnishing cakes and desserts.

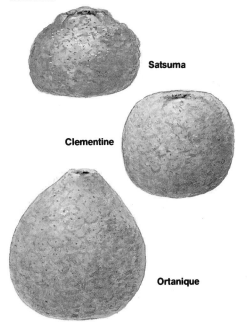

Satsuma

Clementine

Ortanique

TAMARILLO

The Tamarillo (other names Tree Tomato, Java Plum) is always included in the fruit section, but it is close to a Tomato in appearance, taste and use. It is large (about 5 in. long) and oval — the orange-red skin is tough and inedible. When ripe the flesh gives when gently pressed. Cut in half and scoop out the flesh with a spoon — the flavour is sweet and acidic. Excellent when baked, stewed or grilled as a vegetable. Peel before use.

UGLI

An ugly fruit, hence the name. This Tangerine x Grapefruit hybrid exhibits characteristics from both parents. It is the size of a Grapefruit and the pinkish-yellow flesh is more tart than a Tangerine. The greenish-orange wrinkled peel, however, is distinctly Tangerine-like — it is loose and easily pulled away to reveal the segments. The skin around these segments should be removed before serving. Buy fruit which feels quite firm and is free from bruises. Store in a cool place.

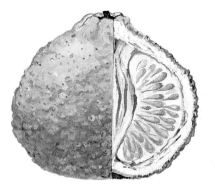

CHAPTER 5

GLOSSARY

A

ACID SOIL A soil which contains no free lime and has a pH of less than 6.5.

ADULT FOLIAGE Leaves on a mature branch which differ in shape and size from the *juvenile foliage*.

ADVENTITIOUS BUD A growth bud which appears abnormally on the stem, compared to a normal *axillary bud*.

ALKALINE SOIL A soil which has a pH of more than 7.3. Other terms are chalky soil and limy soil.

ALTERNATE Leaves or buds which arise first on one side of the stem and then on the other. Compare *opposite*.

ANNUAL A plant that grows from seed, flowers and dies all within one season.

ANTHER The part of the flower which produces pollen. It is the upper section of the *stamen*.

APEX The tip of a stem or other plant organ.

APICAL BUD A growth bud at the tip of a stem.

ARMED Bearing strong thorns.

AWL-SHAPED A narrow leaf which tapers to a stiff point.

AXIL The angle between the upper surface of the leaf stalk and the stem that carries it.

AXILLARY BUD A growth bud which appears in the angle between a leaf and the stem.

B

BARE-ROOTED A plant dug up at the nursery and sold with no soil around its roots.

BARK-RINGING The removal of a strip of bark around a tree so as to reduce vigour and increase fruitfulness. Compare *root pruning*.

BASAL CLUSTER A group of leaves forming a complete or partly complete ring at the base of a shoot.

BEDDING PLANT A plant which is bedded out in quantity and has only a limited life outdoors.

BERRY A pulpy fruit bearing several or many seeds.

BIENNIAL A plant which grows from seed, producing stems and leaves in the first season and flowering in the next.

BIENNIAL BEARER A tree which regularly bears a good crop of blossom or fruit every other year with little or no crop in the intervening years.

BISEXUAL A flower bearing both male and female reproductive organs — compare *dioecious* and *monoecious*.

BLEEDING The abundant loss of sap from severed plant tissues.

BLOOM Two meanings — either a fine powdery coating or a flower.

BOLE An alternative name for the trunk of a tree.

BRANCHED HEAD The collection of branches at the head of a tree in which there is no *central leader*.

BREAKING The development of shoots as a result of removing wood above an *axillary bud*.

BREAKING BUD A bud which has started to open.

BREASTWOOD Shoots which grow forward from a *supported tree*.

BUD A flower bud is the unopened bloom. A growth bud or *eye* is a condensed shoot.

BUDDING A form of *grafting* where a single bud rather than a shoot is used as the *scion*.

BUSH A tree pruned to give 2–2½ ft of clear stem.

C

CALCAREOUS Chalky or limy soil.

CALCIFUGE A plant which will not thrive in *alkaline soil*.

CALLUS The scar tissue which forms over a pruning cut or at the base of a cutting.

CALYX The whorl of *sepals* which protect the unopened flower bud.

CAMBIUM A thin layer of living cells between the bark and the wood.

CANE A long and slender shoot arising from the *crown* of the plant.

CANKER A diseased and discoloured area on the stem.

CENTRAL LEADER The main vertical leader at the centre of the tree — the *trunk*.

CHELATE An organic chemical which can supply nutrients to a plant in a soil which would normally lock up the plant-feeding element or elements in question.

CHLOROSIS An abnormal yellowing or blanching of the leaves due to lack of chlorophyll.

CLINGSTONE A type of *stone fruit* in which the flesh is tightly attached to the stone. Compare *freestone*.

CLONE A group of identical plants produced by *vegetative reproduction* from a single parent plant.

COMPATIBLE The *scion* (or bud) and the *rootstock* are able to unite successfully after grafting.

COMPOST Two meanings — either decomposed vegetable or animal matter for incorporation in the soil or a potting/cutting mixture made from peat ('soilless compost') or sterilized soil ('loam compost') plus other materials such as sand, lime and fertilizer.

COMPOUND A type of leaf which is composed of several leaflets.

CORDON A supported type of tree trained vertically or obliquely and with a main stem or stems pruned to produce *spurs*.

COROLLA The whorl of petals within the *calyx* of the flower.

CROSS The offspring arising from cross-pollination.

CROTCH The angle between large branches or between a branch and the trunk.

CROWN The bottom part of a *herbaceous* plant from which the roots grow downwards and the shoots arise.

CULINARY FRUIT Fruit which is cooked or processed by jam-making etc rather than being eaten fresh. Compare *dessert fruit*.

CULTIVAR Short for 'cultivated variety' — it is a variety which originated in cultivation and not in the wild. Strictly speaking, all modern varieties are cultivars, but the more familiar term *'variety'* is used in this book.

CURRENT YEAR'S GROWTH Shoot development which has been made this season. Also known as *this year's growth* — the wood produced is called *first year* or *new wood*.

CUTTING A piece of stem cut from a plant and used for propagation.

D

DEBLOSSOMING The removal of flowers or flower trusses to avoid overcrowding in mature plants or to direct the vigour into vegetative growth in young plants.

DECIDUOUS A plant which loses its leaves at the end of the growing season.

DEHORNING The cutting back of stout branches to a point at which another branch arises.

DESHOOTING The removal of unwanted shoots while they are still small and soft.

DESSERT FRUIT Fruit which is suitable for eating in the fresh uncooked state. Compare *culinary fruit*.

DIOECIOUS A plant which bears either male or female flowers. Compare *monoecious*.

DISBUDDING The removal of surplus buds before they have started to develop.

DORMANT PERIOD The time when the plant has naturally stopped growing due to low temperature and short day-length.

DOUBLE WORKING The grafting of a variety on to a compatible *rootstock*, which in turn is grafted on to the desired rootstock. This system is used when the variety and the rootstock are *incompatible*.

DOWNY Covered with soft hairs.

DWARF BUSH A tree pruned to give 1½–2 ft of clear stem.

DWARF PYRAMID A tree pruned to form a broadly conical shape with a *central leader* about 7 ft high.

E

ESPALIER A supported type of tree trained to form a vertical main stem with pairs of branches stretched horizontally to form a series of tiers.

EXTENSION GROWTH A shoot which has arisen from an *apical bud*.

EYE A dormant growth bud.

F

FAN A supported type of tree trained to form a series of main branches spreading like the spokes of a wheel or the ribs of a fan.

FEATHERED MAIDEN A one year old tree bearing lateral shoots. Compare *maiden whip*.

FERTILIZATION The application of pollen to the *stigma* to induce the production of seed. An essential step in hybridisation.

FILAMENT The supporting column of the *anther*. It is the lower part of the *stamen*.

FIRST YEAR WOOD See *current year's growth*.

FLUSH A crop of flowers or fruit, which may or may not be followed by other flushes.

FOLIAR FEED A fertilizer capable of being sprayed on and absorbed by the leaves.

FRAMEWORK The basic woody skeleton of the main branches of the tree or bush.

FREE-STANDING TREE A tree grown in the open without any horizontal supports. Compare *supported tree*.

FREESTONE A type of *stone fruit* in which the flesh is free from or loosely attached to the stone. Compare *clingstone*.

FROST POCKET An area where cold air is trapped during winter and in which tender plants are in much greater danger.

FRUIT The seed together with the structure which bears or contains it.

FRUIT BUD Large rounded bud which produces blossom and then fruit.

FUNGICIDE A chemical used to control diseases caused by fungi.

FUNGUS A primitive form of plant life which is the most common cause of infectious disease — mildew and rust are examples.

G

GENUS A group of closely-related plants containing one or more species.

GERMINATION The emergence of the root and shoot from the seed.

GRAFTING The process of joining a shoot or bud of one plant (the *scion*) on to the stem and root system (the *rootstock*) of another.

GROWTH BUD Small flat bud which gives rise to a shoot.

H

HALF-HARDY A plant which will not survive if the temperature falls below 0°C.

HALF STANDARD A tree pruned to give 4–4½ ft of clear stem.

HARDENING-OFF The process of gradually acclimatising a plant raised under warm conditions to the environment it will have to withstand outdoors.

HARDY A plant which will survive outdoors over winter without protection.

HEADING BACK Pruning the *central leader* of a *maiden*.

HEELING-IN The temporary planting of a new tree or shrub pending suitable weather conditions for permanent planting.

HERBACEOUS A plant which does not form permanent woody stems.

HUMUS Term popularly (but not correctly) applied to partly decomposed organic matter in the soil. Actually humus is the jelly-like end-product which coats the soil particles.

HYBRID Plants with parents which are genetically distinct. The parent plants may be different *cultivars, varieties* or *species*.

I

INCOMPATIBLE The *scion* (or bud) and the *rootstock* are not able to unite successfully after grafting. *Double working* is required.

INORGANIC A chemical or fertilizer which is not obtained from a source which is or has been alive.

INSECTICIDE A chemical used to control insect pests.

INTERNODE The part of the stem between one *node* and another.

J

JOINT See *node*.

JUVENILE FOLIAGE Young leaves which differ in shape and size from the *adult foliage*.

L

LATERAL A side-shoot borne by a *leader*.

LEADER A main branch. The leading shoot determines the general direction of growth of the tree.

LEAFLET One of the parts of a compound leaf.

M

MAIDEN A one year old tree or shrub.

MAIDEN WHIP A one year old tree with no lateral shoots. Compare *feathered maiden*.

MONOECIOUS A plant which bears both male and female flowers. Compare *dioecious*.

MULCH A layer of bulky organic material placed around the stems.

MUTATION A sudden change in the genetic make-up of a plant, leading to a new feature. This new feature can be inherited.

N

NATIVE A *species* which grows wild in this country and was not introduced by man.

NEUTRAL Neither acid nor alkaline — pH 6.5-7.3.

NEW WOOD See *current year's growth*.

NODE The point on the stem at which a leaf or bud is attached.

NUT A one-seeded hard fruit which does not split when ripe.

O

OFFSET Young plant which arises naturally near to or at the base of the parent plant and is easily separated.

OLD WOOD Stem growth which was produced before the current season.

OPPOSITE Leaves or buds which are borne in pairs along the stem. Compare *alternate*.

ORGANIC A chemical or fertilizer which is obtained from a source which is or has been alive.

OVULE The part of the female organ of the flower which turns into a seed after fertilization.

P

PEAT Plant matter in an arrested state of decay obtained from bogs or heathland.

PERENNIAL A plant that is capable of living for at least 3 years.

PETAL One of the divisions of the *corolla* — generally the showy part of the flower.

pH A measure of acidity and alkalinity. Below pH 6.5 is acid, above pH 7.3 is alkaline.

PINCHING OUT The removal between finger and thumb of the growing tip of the stem.

POLLEN The yellow dust produced by the *anthers*. It is the male element which fertilizes the *ovule*.

POLLINATION The application of *pollen* to the *stigma* of the flower.

POME FRUIT A hardy tree which bears fleshy fruit with several small seeds in the central cavity.

PRICKING OUT The first planting out of a seedling or rooted cutting into another container or outdoor bed.

PRIMARY BRANCHES The first branches to develop on the main stem or trunk.

PROPAGATION The multiplication of plants.

PRUNING The removal of parts of the plant in order to improve its shape and/or performance.

PYRAMID A tree pruned to form a broadly conical shape with a *central leader* over 7 ft high.

R

REGULATORY PRUNING The removal of weak, diseased and overcrowded branches.

RENEWAL PRUNING The removal of wood to ensure a steady supply of new shoots.

REVERSION Two meanings — either a *sport* which goes back to the colour or growth habit of its parent or a cultivated variety which is outgrown by suckers arising from the rootstock.

ROD The main stem of a Grape vine.

ROOT PRUNING The removal of part of the root system so as to reduce vigour and increase fruitfulness. Compare *bark-ringing*.

ROOTSTOCK See *grafting*.

RUNNER A shoot which grows along the soil surface, rooting at intervals.

RUSSET A brown roughening or scurfing on the surface of some fruits, especially Apples and Pears.

S

SCION See *grafting*.

SECONDARY BRANCHES The branches which develop on a *primary branch*.

SELF-FERTILE A flower which can be successfully pollinated by its own pollen or from pollen produced by other flowers on the tree or bush.

SEPAL One of the divisions of the *calyx*.

SNAG A short stump left after careless pruning.

SPECIES Plants which are genetically similar and which reproduce exactly when self-fertilized.

SPINDLEBUSH A form of *pyramid* tree in which the side branches are permanently tied down.

SPIT The depth of the spade blade — usually about 9 inches.

SPORT A plant which shows a marked and inheritable change from its parent — a *mutation*.

SPUR A short and slow-growing branch which bears fruit buds.

SPUR BEARER A tree which bears all or most of its fruit on *spurs*.

STAMEN The male organ of a flower, consisting of the *anther* and *filament*.

STANDARD A tree pruned to give 6–7 ft of clear stem.

STIGMA The part of the female organ of the flower which catches the *pollen*.

STONE FRUIT A hardy tree which bears fleshy fruit with a large hard seed at the centre.

STOPPING See *pinching out*.

STRIG Fruit cluster of Red Currant, White Currant or Blackcurrant.

STRIKE The successful outcome of taking cuttings — cuttings 'strike' whereas grafts 'take'.

SUB-LATERAL A side-shoot on a *lateral*.

SUCKER A shoot growing from the rootstock.

SUPPORTED TREE A tree which is grown against a fence, framework of wire or a wall. Compare *free-standing tree*.

SYNONYM An alternative plant name.

SYSTEMIC A pesticide which goes inside the plant and travels in the sap stream.

T

TAKE The successful outcome of budding — grafts 'take' whereas cuttings '*strike*'.

TERMINAL BUD A bud at the end of a one year old shoot.

THIS YEAR'S GROWTH See *current year's growth*.

TILTH The crumbly structure of surface soil.

TIP BEARER A tree which bears most of its fruit at the tips of one year old shoots.

TIPPING Removal of the growing point by means of secateurs rather than *pinching out*.

TRANSPLANTING Movement of a plant from one site to another.

TRUNK The woody *central leader* of a tree.

TRUSS A cluster of fruit or flowers.

U

UNION The junction after grafting of the *scion* and *rootstock*. Also the name of the raised scar where this junction has taken place.

UNISEXUAL A flower of one sex only — see *monoecious* and *dioecious*.

V

VARIETY Strictly speaking, a naturally occurring variation of a species (see *cultivar*).

VEGETATIVE GROWTH The development of stems and leaves as opposed to blossom and fruit development.

VEGETATIVE REPRODUCTION Division, cuttings, grafting and layering as distinct from sexual reproduction by seeds.

VIRUS An organism which is too small to be seen through a microscope and which is capable of causing serious malformation of a plant.

W

WATER SHOOT A vigorous soft shoot which is unbranched and unfruitful.

CHAPTER 6

FRUIT INDEX